THE BIRTHPLACE OF OFF BROADWAY

100 YEARS OF CHERRY LANE THEATRE

CONTENTS

Preface by David Henry Hwang 7
Introduction by Mary Geerlof 9

1 WHERE OFF BROADWAY WAS BORN 12
A Barn Can Be a Theater 21
A Radical New Artist Colony 26
Saturday Night (1924) by Robert R. Presnell 30
Stigma (1927) by Donald Duff and Dorothy Manley 32
The Vegetable (1929) by F. Scott Fitzgerald 36

2 THE SHOW MUST GO ON 40
The Bigot (1930) by Slater LaMaster 50
The Bishop Misbehaves (1937) by Frederick Jackson 54

3 WARTIME IN THE WINGS 58
The Savoy Opera Guild 76
Tony Curtis, Golden Boy 80
Henry IV (1947) by Luigi Pirandello 82

4 A SAFE HAVEN ON COMMERCE STREET 86
The Living Theatre 95
James Dean Doodles 102
A Curious Evening with Gypsy Rose Lee 106
Endgame (1958) by Samuel Beckett 110

5 A NEW GENERATION TAKES THE STAGE 114
Albarwild 125
The American Dream (1962) by Edward Albee 134
Dutchman (1964) by LeRoi Jones 138
To Be Young, Gifted and Black (1969) adapted by Robert Nemiroff 142

6 KEEPING THE HOUSE LIGHTS ON 146
Godspell (1971) by John-Michael Tebelak and Stephen Schwartz 154
Sexual Perversity in Chicago (1976) by David Mamet 158
The Passion of Dracula (1977) by Bob Hall and David Richmond 162

7 ALL ROADS LEAD TO CHERRY LANE 166
True West (1982) by Sam Shepard 178
Nunsense (1985) by Dan Goggin 182
The Sum of Us (1990) by David Stevens 186

8 NEW MENTORS NEW VOICES 190
Angelina Fiordellisi on Building the Cherry Lane Theatre Company . . . 199
Mentor Project 203
Stephen Adly Guirgis and Nathan Yungerberg on Mentorship 209
Saint Lucy's Eyes (2001) by Bridgette Wimberly 212
Hoodoo Love (2007) by Katori Hall 216
First Love (2018) by Charles Mee 220

Epilogue by Jesse Eisenberg 223
Cherry Lane Theatre Production History 225

CHERRY LANE THEATRE

Preface

By David Henry Hwang

I DISCOVERED MY VOICE as a playwright at the age of twenty, during a summer when I studied with two legendary playwrights, Sam Shepard and María Irene Fornés. Both were fierce believers in a writer's unique, idiosyncratic, and unrestrained voice. They taught me to create from my subconscious, without worrying about rules or conventional dramaturgy or even comprehending where my voice was taking me. Fundamentally, they believed playwrights need the freedom to be themselves.

Three years later, in 1992, when I moved to New York to become a playwright myself, I went to Sam Shepard's *True West*. Walking through the winding streets of Greenwich Village, I came across a theater that stood on its own, surrounded by residences, like an outpost that had sprung up fully formed: Cherry Lane Theatre. There, I watched a young Gary Sinise and John Malkovich tear into the ferocity and hilarity of Sam's play. I felt the emotion, the heat, the anarchy, the rage, the absurdity—and most of all the freedom he so embraced.

Appropriately, I discovered Sam's play at a theater that embodied the principles he and Irene had taught me. For longer than any other theater in New York City, Cherry Lane has existed to give life and power to the writer. For a hundred years, it has provided a home to one revolution after another—off Broadway, absurdism, performance art, experimental musicals, Black theater—introducing new writers who would go on to define the culture. Cherry Lane was even operated for a time by one of America's greatest playwrights, Edward Albee. It also felt right to me that in 2010, Cherry Lane was part of a festival of works by my other great teacher, María Irene Fornés.

Starting in 1996, when Angelina Fiordellisi breathed new life into Cherry Lane, my artistic life came full circle. Among other exciting initiatives, Angelina founded the Mentor Project, which gave talented young playwrights the extraordinary opportunity to see their works fully produced, and paired them with a more experienced dramatist to mentor them throughout the process. By then a well-known writer myself, I became a mentor, working over the years with Lina Patel, Ruth McKee, Julia Cho, and David Wiener. The Mentor Project built on Cherry Lane's legacy by introducing dramatists Rajiv Joseph, Katori Hall, Anne Washburn, Sheila Callaghan, Jen Silverman, Jiehae Park, Jocelyn Bioh, Christopher Shinn, David Adjmi, Bathsheba Doran, Winter Miller, and so many more. I had the opportunity to pay back what I had received at the theater, which has always granted writers space to unleash their true voices.

At its hundred-year mark, Cherry Lane has turned a page and begun its next chapter. It is now owned and operated by A24, a company renowned for giving artists the freedom to bring their visions to life. This partnership promises to continue the theater's legacy, offering a stage for bold, groundbreaking, and transformative voices, those that change the direction of culture and blaze a path forward. From the past through the present and into the future, Cherry Lane Theatre remains the place where writers rule.

OPPOSITE
A photograph of the Cherry Lane by Berenice Abbott. The photographer, who was known for documenting a changing New York, was a neighbor on Commerce Street for nearly thirty years. 1948.

Introduction

By Mary Geerlof

SERENDIPITY BROUGHT ME to Cherry Lane Theatre. In 2002 I walked in as a theater-loving NYU student, and walked out as an assistant. Little did I know it was the first of many hats I would wear at Cherry Lane. Since then, I've done every job at the theater—directing, producing, development, community engagement, house and theater management—as well as jobs that weren't really mine, like working the box office and handling the facilities. Through it all, Cherry Lane allowed me to grow and make a home within its walls—the building itself feels like a dear friend. It's a place where artistic risk has its rewards, where the exploration of ideas is celebrated, and where theater magic happens.

My time at Cherry Lane has been enriched by the beloved people I've met, their spirit of collaboration and the community we've fostered together. I remember many late nights, sitting on stage with my colleagues, enjoying their company, and relishing in the buzz of a successful live performance. I loved knowing that this was the place I wanted to be.

I have vivid memories of sitting with Amiri Baraka in the lobby during the 2007 revival of *Dutchman*, waiting for his show to end. He remarked how even though culture had changed since *Dutchman* premiered at Cherry Lane in the 1960s, the actual making of theater remained the same. Theater artists still waited in the lobby for the show to come down, wondering if the audience liked it, anticipating the moment of silence followed by beats of applause. I was so struck by Amiri's generosity of spirit in including me, a young theater manager at the time, in this long history of stagecraft.

Another constant is the positive, "can-do" attitude of the many stage, facilities, and production managers, who have wrung possibility out of impossible situations. Early one morning in 2022, Nina Tendy, our facilities manager, and I got a call that a pipe burst above the stage and the entire set was soaked. It was twelve hours before opening and we had miles of pink carpets and mattresses that had to be removed or replaced, but at no point did anyone think we couldn't get the show up and running. By the time the audience members were seated, no one could tell that mere hours before the theater was a water-logged calamity. Together, I felt like we really could do anything.

Even in the pandemic, my co-producer Seri Lawrence and I continued to work at Cherry Lane during the fifteen-month shutdown. From opposite sides of the stage or the lobby, we worked and talked to one another. And although we'd been colleagues for many years, that time together, alone in this big theater, gave us a safe place to connect.

For over one hundred years, people have come to Cherry Lane to share their stories with audiences. The brick wall behind the stage, which has remained naked and unchanged for the past century, has borne witness to the full range of human emotion, every player's struggles and triumphs since 1923. I think of the innumerable artists who got their start on our stage and Amiri's words about how culture changes, but the theater-making experience is constant. Did those artists feel that same electric mix of excitement and fear on opening night? The brick wall stretches up to the office above the canopy, where the many managers and producers over the years worked tirelessly to push the theater

OPPOSITE
Interior as seen from the Cherry Lane stage. Circa 1956.

forward, strategizing how to sell tickets in hard times, or worrying about if the fire department might shut down a show.

Even back when the building was a box factory in pre-Cherry Lane times, there was a history of using the space for entertainment—the energy of live performance is baked into the foundation. This collective history makes our theater a sacred space, a sentiment that my mentor and Cherry Lane's previous owner Angelina Fiordellisi imparted on me.

For the next hundred years, I hope that when people come to Cherry Lane—whether it's as an artist, staffer, or audience member—they feel the theater joy, that distinct feeling that art can happen here. The art itself doesn't have to be perfect or even beautiful, but we can share in the experience of the play. What I've learned within these four walls is that the art of theater making is to explore unafraid, and have some fun doing it.

—Mary Geerlof, managing director, Cherry Lane Theatre

ABOVE
Gas station at Commerce and Seventh Avenue. Circa 1958–62.

Where Off Broadway Was Born

NEW YORK CITY, 1923—Then, as now, Broadway was the undisputed epicenter of theater in the city, if not the country. Starting at the turn of the century, more than three dozen new theaters were constructed around Times Square, forming the hub around which the entire theatrical ecosystem spun. These ornate, gilded palaces, many of which are still in use today, were grand in every sense of the word: large in size, with an average capacity of over one thousand, and home to hundreds of productions each season. So how exactly did a group of downtown, bohemian artists establish a tiny theater in an abandoned box factory forty blocks south of 42nd Street that would go on to outshine the bright lights of Broadway?

With World War I over and the Nineteenth Amendment ratified (giving women the right to vote), the 1920s roared in with a wave of optimism and economic freedom that washed over the country. This was the decade that saw the construction of the Chrysler Building, the opening of Yankee Stadium, and the height of the Harlem Renaissance—an explosion of art and commerce that secured New York City's place as the cultural capital of the country. It proved to be an opportune moment for a group of hopeful young theater artists to stake their claim against the Broadway establishment.

It's not surprising that the centralized nature of "big theater" didn't easily lend itself to innovation or risk-taking. The Shubert family, who owned and operated the vast majority of Broadway theaters, was far more concerned with profit than in taking chances on new plays or untested playwrights. At a time when audiences had many popular entertainment options—not just on Broadway but in the movies produced by a burgeoning film industry, as well as endless vaudeville variety acts—the odds were not on the side of a bunch of theater upstarts looking to chart a different direction.

Yet that is precisely what the Little Theatre Movement accomplished during this era. Across the country, small groups of artists banded together to found companies interested in bold experimentation and art for art's sake. These small stages, often no bigger than a hundred seats, launched a generation of American playwrights such as Eugene O'Neill and Susan Glaspell, and forged a fresh pathway in American theater that privileged the playwright over profits.

One of the first and most significant of these groups, the Provincetown Players, which famed poet, playwright, and sometime actor Edna St. Vincent Millay joined in 1917, opened their own small theater in Greenwich

PAGE 13
Publicity photo of the Lenox Hill Players in John Ford's *'Tis Pity She's a Whore* at Cherry Lane. 1926.

OPPOSITE
A photograph of Commerce Street from Bedford Street taken by Brown Brothers, a partnership between Arthur and Charles Brown, now the nation's oldest stock photo agency. 1925.

BELOW
Founders of Cherry Lane Theatre (*from left to right*) William S. Rainey, Evelyn Vaughn, and Reginald Travers.

Village in 1918. A few years later, a trio of artists—Evelyn Vaughn, William S. Rainey, and Reginald Travers—founded Cherry Lane Theatre a few blocks away on Commerce Street. With the artists occupying a series of row houses behind the theater (where Millay would become their neighbor in an "artists' village"), Cherry Lane was "the main attraction, the real center of the Little Theatre community" coalescing in the West Village.

Cherry Lane was a space for platforming independent artistic voices, developing nontraditional storytelling, and fostering a community that explored, supported, and promoted ambitious work by American playwrights. This experimentation allowed artists to wear many hats—an actor may also be painting sets, a playwright may direct or act in their own works—which in turn afforded them more creative flexibility than they would find at any theater uptown. Early productions, such as *The Vegetable*, written by F. Scott Fitzgerald and directed by a young Lee Strasberg (1929), *Stigma* by Dorothy Manley and Donald Duff (1927), and *The Garbage Man* by John Dos Passos (1926), used the stage for critiques of politics and social mobility.

Cherry Lane became the home of many of the twentieth century's most groundbreaking productions and important dramatic voices working outside the mainstream. It was *the* off Broadway destination for scores of artists—a full three decades before off Broadway was even an official theatrical designation. To this day it stands as New York's longest continually running off-Broadway theater, where it has nurtured generations of playwrights, directors, actors, and designers, and provided fertile ground for many of the most significant and exciting theatrical voices.

RIGHT
A map of Greenwich Village drawn by Robert Edwards, from the *Quill*, a magazine popular with the Village community. 1925.

BELOW
Pen-and-ink architectural drawing of Cherry Lane Playhouse, Grove St. Theatre, and Provincetown Playhouse by Anthony F. Dumas, a prolific artist who documented the theaters of New York City. 1926.

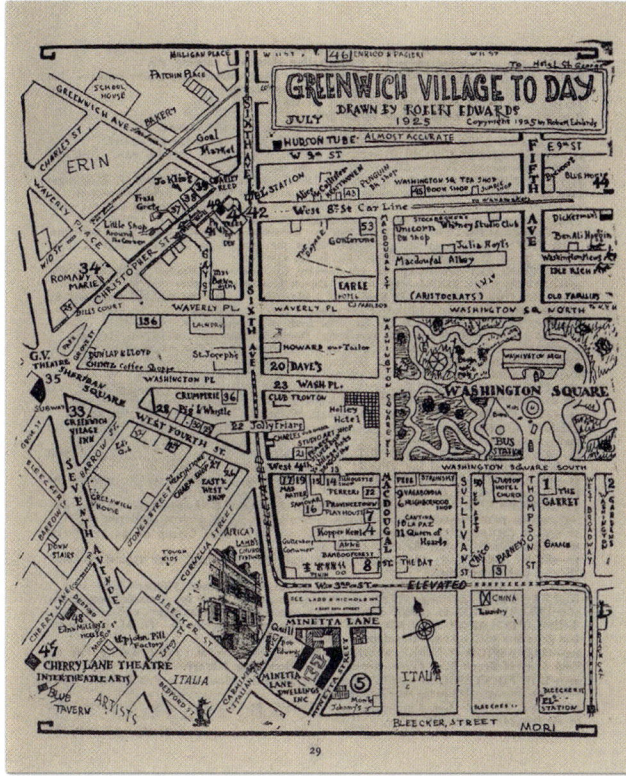

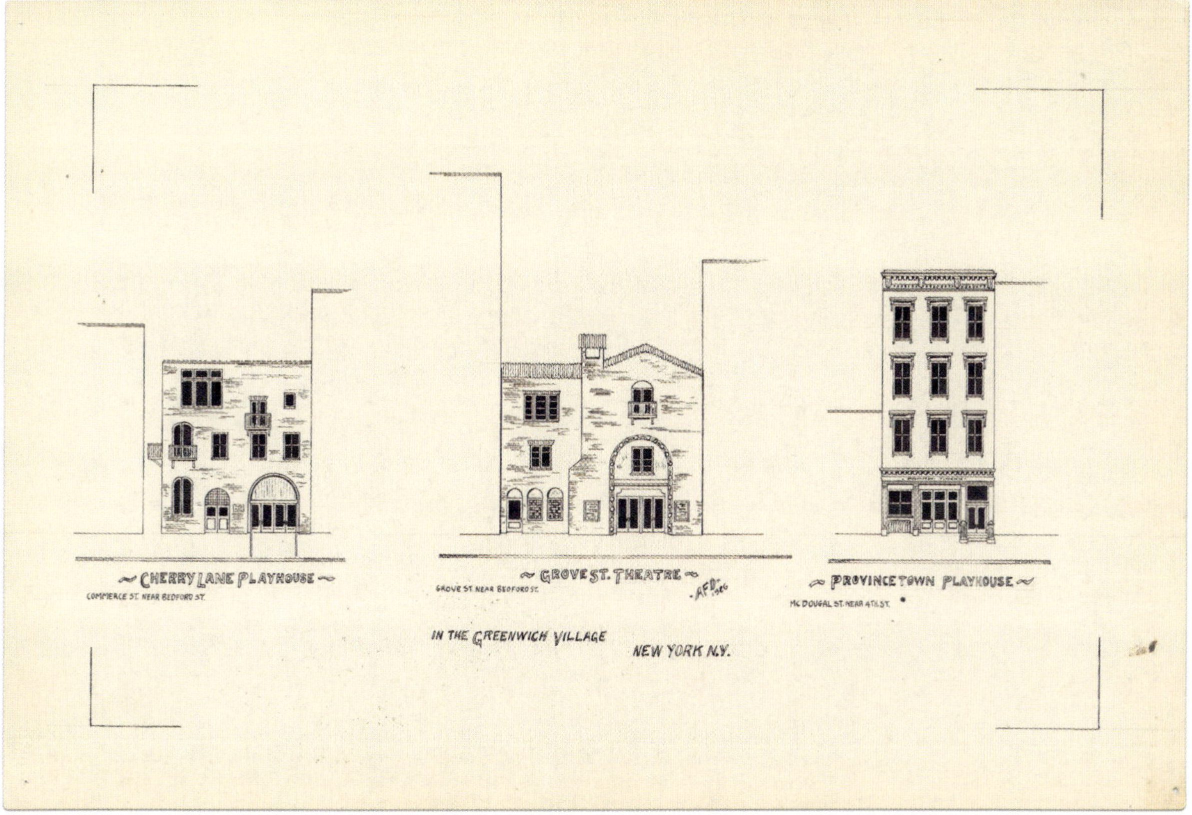

WHERE OFF BROADWAY WAS BORN

RIGHT
The New York Times announces Cherry Lane and "a new community art center" in Greenwich Village. November 18, 1923.

BELOW
Publicity photo of the Lenox Hill Players in John Ford's *'Tis Pity She's a Whore* at Cherry Lane. 1926.

ARTISTS FORM NEW CENTRE IN GREENWICH VILLAGE

Remodel Old Box Factory, Stable and Other Landmarks on the Community Plan—Three-Story Nest Only Nine Feet in Width for Poetess—Theatre to Seat 255

GREENWICH Village has a new community art center. It is in Bedford and Commerce Streets, where the noise of motor traffic on Seventh Avenue never penetrates and yet so near Sheridan Square as to make it possible to reach, within a few minutes, the busy theatrical and art centres from Times Square to Fifty-seventh Street.

Edna St. Vincent Millay, to whom the Pulitzer poetry prize was awarded last May, has joined the group in its sequestered nook in the old Village. Her house, which is the smallest one there, doubtless is the tiniest three-story residence on Manhattan Island. It seems destined also to be the coziest home of its size when the remodeling is entirely finished and then equipped to the taste both of a poetess and a newlywed, for it was only last July that Miss Millay was married to F. Eugene Boissevain at Croton-on-the-Hudson. The new home is but nine feet wide and, therefore, is considered worthy of only half a number, being known as 75½ Bedford Street.

Next door, at 77 Bedford Street, on the corner of Commerce Street, is a fairly large house for that section of the Village, having a frontage of nearly twenty-five feet on Bedford Street. It is an old timer, dating back to the early part of the last century, for Commerce Street was on the city map soon after 1800. It also is characteristic of many ancient houses in old city centres in that the side facing the more fashionable Bedford Street is of substantial red brick while the more humble Commerce Street side presents a plain wooden exterior. This economical method of building was employed, it will be remembered, in the erection of the City Hall, the front being of white marble while the rear, which it was said at the time would be seen by few persons, was of ordinary brown stone.

By DIANA BOURBON

JUST how big ought the "ideal theatre"—if there is such a place—to be? Or rather just how small can it be?

Down at 40 Commerce Street, in Greenwich Village, is the Cherry Lane Playhouse which has been described as the smallest theatre in New York. It isn't that. Both the Provincetown and the Triangle are smaller. But to most people an auditorium with a capacity of 250, and a stage measuring twenty feet by thirty over all will seem small enough. Perhaps we may call it the smallest non-freak theatre in New York—for its aims, though including originality both in plays and presentation and favoring the choice of productions which would not readily find a market in the ordinary commercial theatre, are emphatically not "art-for-the-arty, with a border in the Greek key pattern." On the contrary, it is hoped that the Cherry Lane Playhouse may unearth plays that will afterward obtain success on Broadway. Incidentally its promoters have all been connected with the most successful of the professional (as opposed to the amateur), Little Theatres in California. The Cherry Lane, in other words, while its aims will be artistic, is to be conducted on a commonsense plan. Its idea is to be a sort of Theatre Guild on a much smaller scale.

However that may be, the conversion of the former box factory on Commerce Street raises questions today on both "the Little Theatre—and the ideal theatre." And a number of people-who-ought-to-know have been asked to settle it.

The small playhouse wins by a considerable majority — our own George M. Cohan alone holding out in favor of the auditorium with a capacity of over 1,000. Even Max Reinhardt inclines to the Little Theatre for serious dramatic work—though he declines to commit himself irrevocably to anything. Theresa Helburn, with all the others of the Theatre Guild behind her, Pirandello, of course, the promoters of Cherry Lane, Jacques Copeau of the most famous artistic theatre in Paris—the Vieux Colombier, and various London managements are uncompromisingly "little." Though they vary considerably as to what they characterize by that adjective, and hardly two of them choose to support the same cause for the same reason.

The Cherry Lane Theatre—40 Commerce Street, Greenwich Village.

ABOVE
An illustration of the facade of Cherry Lane Theatre for *The New York Times Magazine*, included as part of "Great Minds on Little Theatres" by Diana Bourbon. February 10, 1924.

CHERRY LANE THEATRE

A Barn Can Be a Theater

By Tom Miller

THE STORY OF the building that Cherry Lane Theatre has called home for over a century is the story of Lower Manhattan. In the late 1600s, European settlers transformed the timber forests of much of what is now the West Village into agricultural land. Before 38 Commerce Street was a theater, it was a brewery, and later a tobacco warehouse and box factory.

On November 24, 1827, Alexander McLachlan, a well-to-do Greenwich Village resident, pressed a local brewer named Bacon for payment on a loan. Unable to pay, Bacon put up his "stock of beer, malt and hops, together with the brewing utensils, hogsheads, barrels and kegs in the brewery," as well as "two horses, two drays and the harness of same, a pleasure waggon [sic] and harness," as a guarantee to McLachlan against the $1,523 debt (around $47,000 in 2025).

Bacon could get it all back if he paid the mortgage within six months. In the meantime, McLachlan, according to the courts, was "frequently in the brewery, but never interfering in the business, or intimating that he had any control over the property." Bacon hid his financial troubles from his business partner and creditors—until he ultimately defaulted on the loan, and McLachlan suddenly found himself the owner of a brewery. Rather than sell the business, he embraced the role of brewer (perhaps due to those frequent visits). In 1836 he leased land from the Gomez family, which owned much of the surrounding property, and constructed a new brick brewery on Commerce Street, just west of Bedford Street.

McLachlan's choice of site is a bit surprising. At the time, similar businesses were cropping up closer to the riverfront, where Hudson Street currently runs. The neighborhood of Commerce and Bedford Streets was quiet, residential, and still sparsely developed. Even though it was nestled among family homes, McLachlan's architect made no attempt to pretend this was anything but a utilitarian structure. The three-story brewery featured a double-door truck bay where horse-drawn wagons came and went with loads of heavy barrels. But it wasn't all work—McLachlan's employees liked to let loose after a long day. After hours, people stayed late into the night to have a brew and enjoy poetry, music, and dance in a pre-vaudeville format of showcasing the talent of the workers in the room.

Sometime in the late 1850s McLachlan moved his business to 99 Greenwich Avenue, and the Commerce Street building became a tobacco warehouse operated by established tobacco merchant T. R. McDermott. A decade later, in 1873, the building became the storage warehouse of Jas. Michales & Son, a firm that touted its modern improvements for storing valuable household items. A typical advertisement published in *The New York Herald* on April 28, 1874, read:

> Storage Warehouse—For furniture, pianos, baggage, &c., in separate rooms, and low rates; separate department for pianos, mirrors, paintings, &c.; we invite the attention of parties who intend to store their furniture to our accommodations for the storing of goods, style of rooms, light, ventilation, &c.; all goods taken up and down on elevators; the warehouses are guarded day and night by private watchmen.

OPPOSITE
A view of Commerce Street from Barrow Street, photographed by Brown Brothers. On the back of the photograph it is noted that "this tree was planted about 1835." 1904.

OPPOSITE
"I have now acquired an interest in ten houses and a theatre!" *The Brooklyn Citizen* profiles "Evelyn Vaughan" [sic] and the genesis of Cherry Lane. November 18, 1923.

BELOW
A Michales & Son classified ad offering warehousing for "furniture, pianos, baggage . . . at low rates," from *The New York Herald*. 1874.

Michales & Son appears to have gone out of business in 1878. A stock liquidation ad in *The New York Herald* offered: "Nine upright showcases, with stands, for sale cheap to pay charges."

When the storage warehouse became a box factory around 1891, workers continued the former tradition of staying late to use the space for entertainment. By the end of World War I, Greenwich Village was the center of Manhattan's art, music, and literary community. By the mid-1920s, intimate off-Broadway theaters appeared along the tree-lined streets, including the Greenwich Village Theatre (1917), the Provincetown Playhouse (1918), and the short-lived Grove Street Theatre (1925).

In 1923 Alexander McLachlan's brewery building underwent a conversion to a theater. A group of theater artists led by Evelyn Vaughn, William S. Rainey, and Reginald Travers commissioned famed scenic designer Cleon Throckmorton to convert the box factory into Cherry Lane Theatre, complete with a top-floor artist studio, as was common throughout the neighborhood at the time. In December, the tiny auditorium with its 233 seats officially opened to the public.

Today, the theater still retains the patina of its previous lives: The stage-left wall of the theater bears the outlines of the arch where horse-drawn wagons once entered and exited the building on their way to the Hudson River. The undercross, which actors have used since the founding of the theater, is possible because a stream used to run under the building. (When the undercross floor was removed for renovations in the 1950s, live baby turtles were found in the damp mud below.) Upstage, the brick wall that has become synonymous with Cherry Lane is the original from Alexander McLachlan's brewery. These architectural histories remind us of the audacity of Cherry Lane's founders to imagine that a theater could be anywhere—as Evelyn Vaughn lovingly quipped, even "a barn can be a theater."

ACTRESS IS GOOD LAND DEALER, BUT SHE STICKS TO HER LITTLE THEATRE IDEA

By HORTENSE SAUNDERS

The latest Lady Lochinvar to go East, instead of West, and make herself successful in New York is Evelyn Vaughan. She left San Francisco to become a Broadway star.

She has turned out to be a successful dealer in real estate, and has built up one of the most unique residential districts of Gotham.

"Of course," she confides to me, "I really knew less about real estate than a teething baby when I arrived. And I had only money enough for current living expenses. But now I have acquired an interest in ten houses and a theatre!"

It began this way. Miss Vaughan had theatrical successes enough in California to warrant her coming to New York and experiment with the drama. She wanted her own theatre, where she could have a hand in producing the type of plays she believes the average theatregoer wants to see. And she wanted to act in her own plays.

"But Broadway couldn't see it in my way," she goes on. "They weren't at all interested in renting a theatre to an aspiring actress who had only theories to offer.

"I could have made them listen to reason—reason that spoke in terms of $2,000 a week for rent and a gross gate receipt of $6,000, or that would have built me a theatre for $100,000. But just to let space to some unknown woman who wanted to do slightly different things—that was not to be thought of."

But Miss Vaughan kept thinking. If she couldn't have a theatre on Broadway, why not have one somewhere else? One day a friend, showing her through the picturesque slums of Greenwich Village, pointed out a group of rookeries on Commerce street that formed an elbow around a miscellaneous assortment of backyards.

She spotted a real old-fashioned barn in the midst of them. Then she knew she had found her theatre. So in a short time she had formed a real estate corporation, had leased the ten houses and the barn, and was engaged in transforming them into the most modern studios and living apartments.

The backyards were thrown together into a community garden. The fronts were rebuilt and restored, and soon a bit of Old World loveliness blossomed right out in the slums.

Some of New York's most celebrated artists and musicians took out leases as quickly as they could be made out.

"But, best of all," Miss Vaughan exclaims, "the Cherry Lane Theatre came into existence out of the barn—and the Cherry Lane players will open for their first Manhattan engagement early in December.

"And it has all happened in six months!"

EVELYN VAUGHAN

ABOVE
A land survey by Elbert Roosevelt. Identified as "Herring farm along Skinner Road," lots in the area were primarily used for agricultural purposes. 1795.

OPPOSITE
A photo of the Corell family, who lived at 33 Commerce, by Percy Loomis Sperr. From the early 1920s through the 1940s Sperr was contracted by the New York Public Library to document the city's street life, and he produced over thirty thousand photographs over two decades.

WHERE OFF BROADWAY WAS BORN

A Radical New Artist Colony

IN 1923, silent screen actors and Hollywood transplants Spaulding Hall and Cyrus Brown purchased and leased a block of ten homes around the intersection of Commerce and Bedford Streets in Greenwich Village, with a vision to transform the buildings into a "community housing plan in which are incorporated some novel ideas," as reported in *The New York Times*. Aside from generally improving the neighborhood, those "novel ideas" included developing a mix of studios and apartments for artists, poets, and playwrights to live and work together. At the center of it all was "an amusement house, to be known as Cherry Lane Theatre, which will be managed by William Rainey and Reginald Travers."

Cooperative living was quite radical at the time, and the relationship between the artist colony and the theater received a significant amount of interest. In the *Sun*'s profile of the colony in May 1924, a reporter glowingly described a property with "letter boxes in the garden wall, a flagstone court, a fountain made from a horses' drinking trough." The homes and theater were largely situated around a shared green space that could be publicly accessed through a side entrance to the theater and through a community restaurant run by Mary St. Gaudens. The shared courtyard stood as "one of the most picturesque spots in New York . . . Even genius must be fed!"

Despite the interest in co-op living, the reporter underscored, "It is the theater that is the main attraction—the real center of the community." The heart of Cherry Lane remains intact today: a space for artists to explore the convergence of life, community, and creativity.

Early members of the Cherry Lane artist colony included:

Erik Barry *
John Barrymore, actor
Cyrus Brown, actor
Gladys Brown *
Morgan Farley, actor
Arthur Davison Ficke, poet and playwright
Cary Grant, actor
Spaulding Hall, actor
Marguerite Kurlius *
Edna St. Vincent Millay, poet and playwright

Olga Merwald *
Alice O'Neill, costume designer
Willy Pogany, illustrator
Tom Powers, actor
William S. Rainey, actor and theater producer
John Smeraldi, muralist
Reginald Travers, director
Evelyn Vaughn, actor and producer
Henry Winston *

OPPOSITE
From left to right, top to bottom: Evelyn Vaughn, Willy Pogany, Morgan Farley, Reginald Travers, Edna St. Vincent Millay, Arthur Davison Ficke, Cary Grant, Tom Powers, and John Barrymore.

* Occupation unknown

OPPOSITE
A view of the inner courtyard at 30–32 Commerce Street. Photograph by Brown Brothers. 1925.

RIGHT
Edna St. Vincent Millay, framed by the rear entrance to her home in a photograph by Alexander Alland for the book *Portrait of New York* by Felix Riesenberg and Alland. "This is reputed to be the smallest dwelling (9.6 feet in width) in New York City." 1938–39.

Saturday Night
1924

WRITTEN BY
Robert R. Presnell

DIRECTED BY
Reginald Travers

WITH
Herbert Ashton Jr.
Marie Chambers
Lyle C. Clement
Fay Courtenay
Juliette Day
Vincent Duffy
George Haller
Ida Fitzhugh
William Friend
Luis Frohoff
Della Trout
Lester Vail

WRITTEN BY ROBERT R. PRESNELL (SR.), then an aspiring playwright and foreign correspondent for *The Chicago Tribune*, *Saturday Night* is the story of a "lonely shopgirl [played by Juliette Day] who got caught in the swirl . . . and primitive appeal" of jazz music, per an opening-night review in *The New York Daily News*. The production was the first subscription bill at Cherry Lane Theatre, encouraging audience members to purchase a season pass to support the long-term financial success of the playhouse. When the show opened to the public on February 9, 1924, Cherry Lane was still the newest theater in Greenwich Village, and the novelty of the Little Theatre Movement was underscored in the review: "The purpose of the organization is said to be to cultivate a taste for literature, music and art."

Beyond its initial staging at Cherry Lane, *Saturday Night* is largely forgotten, with little information around the publication of the play script or the show's performance history. Presnell went on to become a screenwriter and producer in Hollywood, receiving a Best Story Oscar nomination (a category that existed until 1956) for *Meet John Doe* (1941), before rising to the rank of lieutenant colonel and becoming the chief photographic officer for combat films in the Southwest Pacific, making war propaganda films for the US Army during World War II.

RIGHT
A photo from the *Daily News*' announcement of Juliette Day in *Saturday Night* at Cherry Lane, "Greenwich Village's newest and most intimate theatre," February 3, 1924.

VILLAGE THEATRE IS OPENED WITH 'SATURDAY NIGHT'

The primitive appeal of jazz music from its embryonic tom tom state in the African jungles to the present gilded age and the adventures of a lonely shopgirl who got caught in its swirl are the dominant tones in "Saturday Night," the first subscription bill at the Cherry Lane playhouse, 40 Commerce street, the newest theatre in Greenwich Village.

Juliette Day

A smart audience which filled the intimate little playhouse to capacity attended the opening Saturday evening. Juliette Day, who played the principal role, that of the shopgirl, was given an ovation.

In the supporting cast are William Friend, Ida Fitzhugh, Lyle C. Clement, Luis Frohoff, Marie Chambers, Herbert Ashton Jr., Della Trout, George Haller, Fay Courtenay, Lester Vail and Vincent Duffy.

One of the principal executives of the Cherry Lane players is Evelyn Vaughn, who in private life is Mrs. Bert Lytell, wife of the picture star. The purpose of the organization is said to be to cultivate a taste for literature, music and art. Several subscription bills will be given.

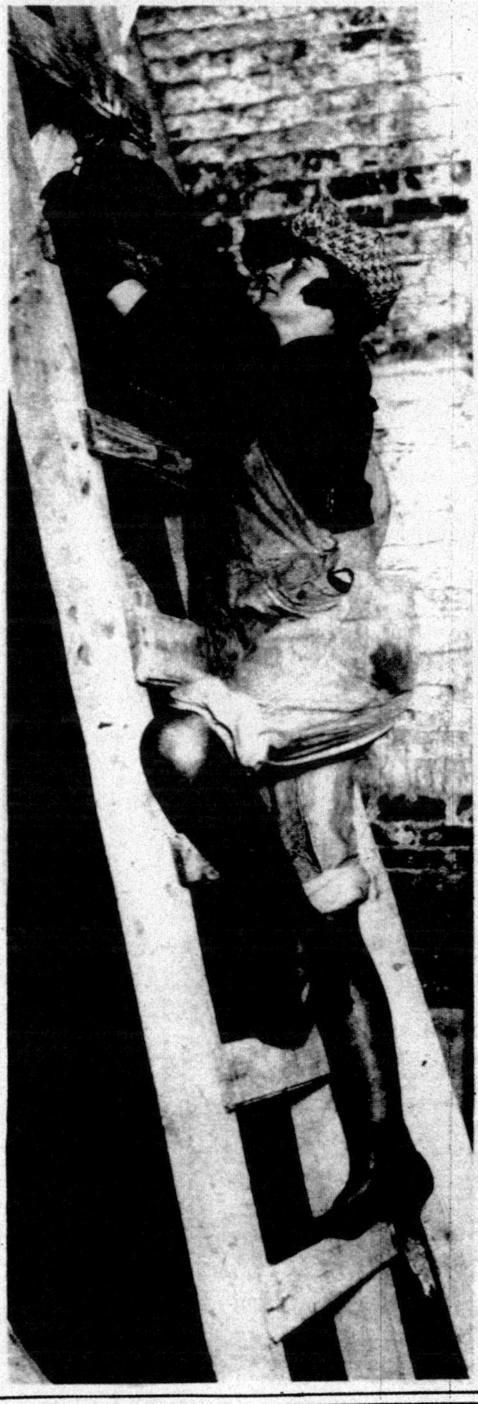

HELPS TO BUILD HER OWN THEATER

—Miss Juliette Day, who is to star in "Saturday Night", is helping to build her own theater, which is to be known as the "Cherry Lane Playhouse", in Greenwich Village. The Theater will be completed and ready for the premier performance early in February. *(International)*

ABOVE LEFT
A *Daily News* review of the opening night of *Saturday Night*, "the first subscription bill at the Cherry Lane playhouse, . . . the newest theatre in Greenwich Village." February 11, 1924.

ABOVE RIGHT
Juliette Day is photographed for the *Buffalo Courier* "helping to build her own theater." February 3, 1924.

Stigma
1927

WRITTEN BY
Donald Duff
Dorothy Manley

PRODUCED BY
Donald Duff
Edmond Rickett

WITH
Donald Duff
Edmond Rickett
Joanna Roos
Doralyne Spence

SET IN THE LIVING ROOM of a professor and his wife in a small university town in the Virginias, *Stigma* sets up a love triangle between the professor's young wife, Elaine Carleton; college student Pierre Maynard, Elaine's object of affection; and Mina, the maid, with whom Pierre is having an affair. Depicting an interracial relationship like that of Pierre, a white man, and Mina, a "colored" woman, was quite controversial at a time when Jim Crow laws codified racial segregation and dozens of states prohibited interracial marriage. Staging the play was not without risk: It was reported by *The New York Age*, in a review from February 19, 1927, that "on Friday evening there were two telephone calls alleging to be from representatives of the Ku Klux Klan, threatening visits of the hooded gang in case the performance was continued. They were given a cordial invitation to come on down, but failed to materialize."

The play received lukewarm reviews, including Theophilus Lewis's note in *The Messenger*, the "World's Greatest Negro Monthly," that the play's "numerous and egregious flaws not only show that they were only wholly unfamiliar with Negro life but also cause one to wonder if they didn't write the play before they had even seen the photograph of a genuine Negro." *Stigma* was one of a number of "miscegenation plays" being staged at the time, including the Provincetown Players' production of Eugene O'Neill's *All God's Chillun Got Wings*, starring a young Paul Robeson, which opened in May 1924.

ABOVE
Doralyne Spence (*left*) and Donald Duff (*right*) appear in a photograph accompanying a theater review from Countee Cullen for the monthly academic magazine *Opportunity: A Journal of Negro Life*. March 1927.

BELOW
Stigma received lukewarm reviews from publications ranging from the *Daily News* (*left*), *The New York Age* (*right*), *The New York Times* (*opposite page left*), and *The Messenger* (*opposite page right*).

BLACK AND WHITE LOVE PORTRAYED AT CHERRY LANE

Another of the dramas belonging to the miscegenation group is on view at the little Cherry Lane theatre in darkest Greenwich Village.

This one is called "Stigma," and is the work of Dorothy Manley and Donald Duff, the latter of whom is also producer and leading player of the piece.

The setting is in an aged professor's living

Joanna Roos

room in a small university town in the Virginias. The professor has a young wife by the name of Elaine, a self-confessed graduate of an insane asylum, who is in love with an equally young Rhodes scholar. The student has been making love on the sly to the mulatto maid of the household—hence the miscegenation stuff.

Joanna Roos, Doralyne Spence, Edmond Rickett and Mr. Duff compose the entire cast.

Brave Playwright Is Daring Ostracism By Miscegenation Drama

By LUCIEN H. WHITE

Cherry Lane Theatre, 40 Commerce street, down in the heart of Greenwich Village, has housed, for the past week, a dramatic offering in three acts that strikingly indicates development of the ability on part of some of the modern white playwrights to look the socalled race problem square in the eye, and give courageous expression to critical opinions that recognize the southern white man's fundamental weakness—an ultra-defined "double standard" of judgment in all matters as between the white man and Negro.

"Stigma" is the title given the play being shown on Cherry Lane boards, and it was written by Dorothy Manley and her husband, Donald Ruff. Mr. Ruff also interprets the central male character, "Pierre Maynard," who believes that miscegenation will result in the development of a race stronger and more potential than either whites or blacks, eventually to control the government. It is being produced by Edmond Rickett, who plays the part of "Porfessor John Carleton," an elderly college professor, in whose home, in a small university town in Virginia, the scene of the drama is laid.

The only other characters in the play are "Elaine Carleton," the professor's wife, enacted by Joanna Roos, and "Mina", the Carleton's housemaid, in which role has been cast Doralyne Spence of Brooklyn, the only colored member of the cast.

Briefly, the plot reveals that "Maynard," in his advocacy of miscegenation as a solution, has become enamored of both "Mrs. Carlton" and "Mina", and when he discusses his theory with the professor and "Mrs. Carleton," the latter gives forcible utterance to her aversion to such a solution, although she admits that the southern white woman has long quietly acquiesced in the maintenance of illicit relations between white men and colored women. And she declares that if she discovered such on part of one she loved it would alienate her affections and relations.

THE PLAY
By J. BROOKS ATKINSON.

Disturbance in Cherry Lane.

STIGMA, a play in three acts, by Dorothy Manley and Donald Duff. Produced by Donald Duff and Edmond Rickett. At the Cherry Lane Playhouse.
Elaine Carleton .... Joanna Roos
Mina .... Doralyne Spence
Professor John Carleton ..... Edmond Rickett
Pierre Maynard .... Donald Duff

In the last act of "Stigma," visible and audible at the Cherry Lane Playhouse last evening, Donald Duff, one of the authors and producers, and the chief actor, was compelled to suffer a little. Playing the part of an advanced thinker whose rational gymnastics had given pain to every other character in the drama, he, too, shook with heartrending sobs; in short, he suffered. To most of the people in the thinly scattered audience this appeared, on the whole, to be a fair distribution of justice; and it brought the audience and the actors into that transcendent mood of sympathy, that union of purging emotion, that synthesis of mutual feeling toward which the idealistic stage is struggling. For the time being pain appeared to be evenly divided on both sides of the footlights. If, by a shift of plot, the author-actor had gone off in high spirits and the audience had thus borne the evening's anguish unassisted, one might have been petulant about this sophomoric play of miscegnation.

As a matter of fact, it is difficult to be petulant about the successive dramatic disturbances in the Cherry Lane Playhouse, lost among the evening shadows of Commerce Street. For those who are disciplined to the cramped pace of Times Square theatregoers, the unpeopled back streets and alleys adjacent to the Cherry Lane are fine for walking after dinner. If, by allowing too much time for threading that maze of streets accurately, you arrive long before the appointed hour, you can enjoy yourself in exploration. You can poke timidly into exotic courts hidden mysteriously behind rows of old brick houses. On Hudson Street you can admire the simple proportions of a church built more than a century ago and still combating the malevolent influence of the theatre. There is an unpretentious dignity about that neighborhood on a Winter night; it is refreshing. The streets have individual names. Under the circumstances the play is not depressingly important.

THE MESSENGER
The Theater
The Souls of Black Folks
By THEOPHILUS LEWIS
REFLECTIONS OF AN ALLEGED DRAMATIC CRITIC

It is devoutly to be hoped that Dorothy Manley and Donald Duff, having observed the canonization of Massa Paul, will reflect on the significance of the event and govern themselves accordingly the next time they try their luck with an inter-racial drama. "In Abraham's Bosom" is a play with a message for the thoughtful playwright, and if Miss Manley and Mr. Duff ponder its lesson well and avoid some of the faults of "Stigma," their last play, there is no reason in the world why their next inter-racial drama should not be a corker that will not only win the acclaim of the critics but fetch the authors plenty of bucks as well. "Stigma," of course was hopeless, and the reason was because the authors wrote the play without first giving sufficient study to Negro psychology. Its numerous and egregious flaws not only show that they were only wholly unfamiliar with Negro life but also cause one to wonder if they didn't write the play before they had even seen the photograph of a genuine Negro. For it is only by presuming lack of experience on the part of the authors that one can account for the strange and naive notions of Negro behavior disclosed in the course of the action.

My interest in "Stigma" was limited to Miss Doralyne Spence's acting. The play called for four characters, three white and one colored, all of equal importance. The colored character was a strong, placid Negro woman mated illegally with a brilliant but mercurial white student. Miss Spence interpreted the part in a facile and persuasive manner that left practically no room for improvement. Only two or three minor details of her performance were open to correction. The most noticeable flaw in her work was when, not more than twice, she addressed her lines to the audience instead of the character she was talking to, but for all I know the director had instructed her to do that.

Far too often for comfort the work of colored dramatic actors forces a reviewer to discuss the potential rather than the actual merit of a performance. Miss Spence's acting in "Stigma" was an exception. It was the most competent performance by a colored actress I have seen since Dora Cole played "Hattie" in "All God's Chillun."

The Vegetable
1929

WRITTEN BY
F. Scott Fitzgerald

DIRECTED BY
Lee Strasberg

PRODUCED BY
The Lenox Hill Players

WITH
Martin K. Altman
Herman Bandes
David Kerman
Louis John Latzer
Mitchell Padraic Marcus
Harry Jay Marks
Eve Saxen
Fanny Shack
Jerome Seplow
Harold Smith

THE ONLY PLAY BY NOVELIST F. Scott Fitzgerald, *The Vegetable, or From President to Postman* is a satire of ambition and the American dream based on the author's short story of the same name. The play follows a middle-class railroad clerk, Jerry Frost, his wife, Charlotte, and a cast of acquaintances as they bicker about the nuisances of daily life, unrealized ambitions, and, in an absurdist twist, Jerry's turn as the president of the United States. Setting the tone for the play, Fitzgerald launches with this quote on the title page of the script, attributed to an unnamed "current magazine:"

> *"Any man who doesn't want to get on in the world, to make a million dollars, and maybe even park his toothbrush in the White House, hasn't got as much to him as a good dog has—he's nothing more or less than a vegetable." —From a Current Magazine*

After a single preview at Nixon's Apollo Theatre in Atlantic City in 1923, and against the better advice from Fitzgerald himself, the play was revived by Lee Strasberg and the Lenox Hill Players at Cherry Lane Theatre in 1929. Fitzgerald warned in a letter to Mitchell Padraic Marcus, who played Snooks in the Cherry Lane production, "It simply doesn't play. 2 professional & perhaps 8 amateur companies have said 'Sure—we can do it' (& failed every time), but it [the play] is psychologicly [sic] wrong."

After opening on April 10 and running for thirteen performances at Cherry Lane, the show closed. The play was panned by Brooks Atkinson in his weekly theater column for *The New York Times*: "Although the ungainly antics of the Lenox Hill Players leave a mere playwright at a sore disadvantage, it seems likely that no production of F. Scott Fitzgerald's 'The Vegetable,' which was belabored at the Cherry Lane last evening, could do very much with this play." Both F. Scott Fitzgerald and Lee Strasberg swore that they would never direct or write for theater again. The theater's loss was the literary world's gain: F. Scott Fitzgerald returned to writing novels, publishing *Tender Is the Night* (1934), his final work after *The Great Gatsby* (1925). Lee Strasberg, the "father of method acting in America," went on to cofound the Group Theatre in 1931 and led the Actors Studio beginning in 1951.

RIGHT
Cover art for F. Scott Fitzgerald's book *The Vegetable* (1923). Artwork by cartoonist John Held Jr.

RIGHT TOP
F. Scott Fitzgerald's handwritten "changes and addenda to 'The Vegetable.'"

RIGHT BOTTOM
Typescript of *The Vegetable* with handwritten notes from the Vagabond Players' production at Nixon's Apollo Theatre. The play was such a flop that it ended after a single preview.

---

①

Changes and Addenda to "The Vegetable"

(Numbers refer to pages of the printed book)

Act I

P. 11   Insert after the words "so he went away":

The bell rings again. Jerry answers it with alacrity and in steps a weary, night-bound postman who says "Good Evening" and hands Jerry a lone, uninteresting letter, probably an advertisement. Jerry looks at the postman with

---

The Battle of Buzzard Island.
ACT II
SCENE III

SCENE: On the Buzzard Islands, at the seat of war. We're looking at a cross-section of the opposing trenches —

and the sentry on the side of Justice can, after some inspection, be recognized as one DADA, late the Secretary of the Treasury. Things must be at a desperate pass indeed when a white beard is on duty in the front line. Those creatures with the bodies of men but the heads and beaks of horrible birds are BUZZARDS! Even with death around the corner they can be seen smoking and playing cards and, from time to time, cursing foully in their own tongue.

The moon tells you that it's night -- in fact it's that celebrated darkest hour which immediately precedes the dawn.

DADA'S uniform is a mass of mud from boot to collar. HE is completely fagged out. His attitude is watchful but horribly dejected and from time

FITZGERALD HAS NEW PLAY COMING

F. Scott Fitzgerald, novelist and short story writer whose only dramatic production to date is "The Great Gatsby," is to have a second play produced by the Lenox Hill players, who were responsible for "The Subway."

The new pieces has two titles — "The Vegetable" and "From President to Postman." It is a satiric comedy.

Casting is now under way at the Cherry Lane theatre, under the direction of Lee Strassburg.

F. Scott Fitzgerald

The Theater
By ARTHUR POLLOCK

The Lenox Hill Players Present "The Vegetable," by F. Scott Fitzgerald, at the Cherry Lane Theater.

DOWN at the Cherry Lane Theater the Lenox Hill Players presented last night a play called "The Vegetable; or, From President to Postman," by F. Scott Fitzgerald. There was no very good reason for their doing so, but they did it nevertheless. Doubtless it is their belief that "The Vegetable" is an important play because it was written some years ago and no professional play-producer has cared to produce it. The minds of those at the head of little theaters work that way. During part of the first act Mr. Fitzgerald's fantastic farce promised to be amusing. After that dullness dropped heavily upon it.

And the Lenox Hill Players, with the ardor of youth, have made it as fantastic as they know how, making it at the same time more absurd than its author ever intended. If it is as fine a play as they believe it to be, they ought to be sensitive enough not to attempt it at all, for they do it very badly. They are boys and girls. Boys and girls of a high school dramatic club would give it a more likable performance, being too shy to play aggressively. But these boys and girls are more ambitious. The first act has the effect of being shouted raucously, the second act is tame and slow and lifeless. At least the play could be acted merrily. Its present effect is unpleasant.

The story concerns a husband who used to have ambitions and now merely remembers them. He had wanted to be a postman. More, he had wanted to be President. Instead, he is an oafish clerk who lets his wife henpeck him thoroughly. His wife last night seemed intent on achieving only noise.

A bootlegger visits him, mixes for him a couple of gallons of synthetic gin and urges him to try it. He does. Whereupon in his stupor he imagines himself President. The next act is laid outside the White House and he is being President as stupidly as such a man would be. His deaf and imbecilic old father he has made Secretary of the Treasury, with the result that out in Iowa voters are crying for the President's resignation. His wife is still shouting at him. A general asks him if he can't start a nice war for him. The bootlegger arrives and, after stealing his scarf pin, his watch and his cigarette case, sells him fictitious islands. And so it goes on.

In this there is, of course, satire. But what feeble satire!

A little girl named Fanny Shack, playing the poor fellow's sister-in-law, gave the impression of being slightly more at home on the stage than the others.

"The Vegetable" would be better dead.

"The Vegetable"

A comedy by F. Scott Fitzgerald. Presented by the Lenox Hill Players at the Cherry Lane Theater. Staged by Lee Strasberg.

THE CAST.

Jerry Frost	Jerome Seplow
Charlotte	Eve Saxen
Dada	Louis John Latzer
Doris	Fanny Shack
Snooks	Mitchell Padraic Marcus
Mr. Jones	Harold Smith
General Pushing	Herman Bandes
Mr. Fish	Harry Jay Marks
Judge Fossile	David Kerman
Detective	Martin K. Altman

Senators—Harry J. Marks, David Kerman and Harold Smith.

Chorus—Syd Brenner, Lilya Slotnikow and Mildred P. Seplow.

The Show Must Go On

PAGE 41
Press photo of Paul and Virginia Gilmore in *Accent on Youth*. 1936.

OPPOSITE
Photojournalist Jerry Cooke captures a photograph of visitors to Paul Gilmore's Cherry Lane Theatre. 1946.

CHERRY LANE THEATRE was barely six years old when the 1929 stock market crash and the resulting Great Depression triggered rampant unemployment, which peaked at 25 percent. Given how often the arts are viewed as a luxury, it was an open question as to how theaters could survive.

Ironically, one of the worst economic times in the nation's history was also the *only* time when there was significant federal funding for the arts. FDR's New Deal and the Works Progress Administration (WPA) put nearly four million Americans across the country to work building roads, bridges, schools, and parks. And the Federal Theatre Project (FTP), one of five cultural programs sponsored by the WPA, marks the only time the US government has ever employed theater workers. Under the direction of Hallie Flanagan, a theater professor from Vassar College, the FTP engaged thousands of out-of-work theater artists: playwrights, actors, technicians, stagehands, directors, and more. Flanagan envisioned a nationwide program that encouraged experimentation and art with a focus on social causes.

She also wanted to make live performance accessible to millions of Americans across the country for the first time ever. The Depression exacerbated the growing threat to the theater posed by motion pictures that had begun during the previous decade. At a time when most Americans struggled to afford basic necessities, they could get a whole evening's entertainment at the cinema for just twenty-five cents, whereas a night at a Broadway theater cost ten times as much.

One of the FTP's productions, *The Bishop Misbehaves* by Frederick Jackson, toured the country with a 1937 stop at Cherry Lane Theatre, then under the stewardship of Paul Gilmore, one of the country's most popular stage and silent screen actors. Gilmore was an outsize character both on and off the stage. He was unafraid of new ideas and innovations, and in 1911 *The New York Dramatic Mirror* announced that he was commissioning a "fleet of automobiles in which he intends not only to carry his company, but also, in a specially constructed car his baggage and entire scenic productions" as a way of avoiding railway trains. And in a 1916 profile by Mary Remington of *The Grand Rapids Press*, he spoke at length about "a Japanese island in the Gulf of Mexico" he was intent on purchasing, as well as about his many investments in real estate, among other businesses. Along with his daughter and fellow actor Virginia, Gilmore

THE SHOW MUST GO ON

BELOW
A holiday card from the Gilmores during the era when they operated Cherry Lane.

OPPOSITE
Paul Gilmore was a master of self-promotion. A number of Cherry Lane's souvenir programs included this collage of Gilmore in character throughout the years.

focused his attention on bringing contemporary scripts to the stage for a diverse audience. In a 1933 invitation for Cherry Lane's production of *Strictly Dishonorable* by Preston Sturges, he wrote, "There are in New York thousands of theatre lovers with a taste and culture yet moderate means. These people need a theatre they can afford . . . It's worth a trip to Greenwich Village just to see our quaint Novel and Intriguing Little Theatre. You will find it like a trip into the Paris Latin Quarters [*sic*]. This is in itself a treat."

Both Gilmores would appear regularly on the Cherry Lane stage throughout this decade—by 1949 they had appeared in over six thousand performances together, including *Strictly Dishonorable* (1933), as well as *A Successful Calamity* (1934), *Dracula* (1936), and *The Bishop Misbehaves* (1937). Ever the self-promoter, Paul Gilmore was quick to tell anyone who was listening (but especially theater critics) about his personal lore and the successes of the theater. In 1934 Ward Morehouse of *The New York Sun* reported, "The Cherry Lane Playhouse is 125 years old and the theatre, under his operation, 'has not been closed one night, winter or summer, for five years. And strange as it may seem (and it does seem strange) each play enjoys an engagement of from six to eight months to capacity.'" By 1934, their successes downtown pushed the Gilmores uptown for a short run managing the 48th Street Theatre and then Daly's 63rd Street Theatre before they returned to Cherry Lane. Gilmore's celebrity, grit, and tenacity kept Cherry Lane not just up and running but moving forward during an incredibly difficult period.

OPPOSITE
Alexander Alland's photo shows *The Gilmores' Cherry Lane Theatre*. The show was put up by the Gilmores after a successful two-year run on Broadway at the Playhouse Theatre. 1937.

ABOVE
Paul Gilmore was committed to staging shows for diverse audiences, and his Mystery Theatre program promised an affordable night of thrills and laughter. 1935.

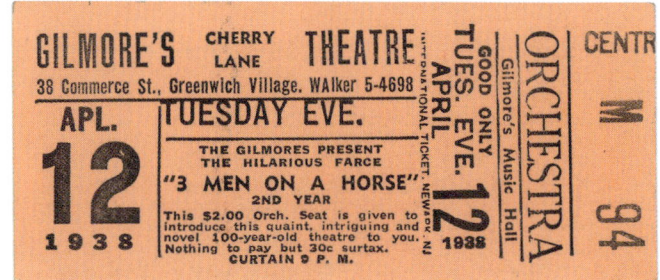

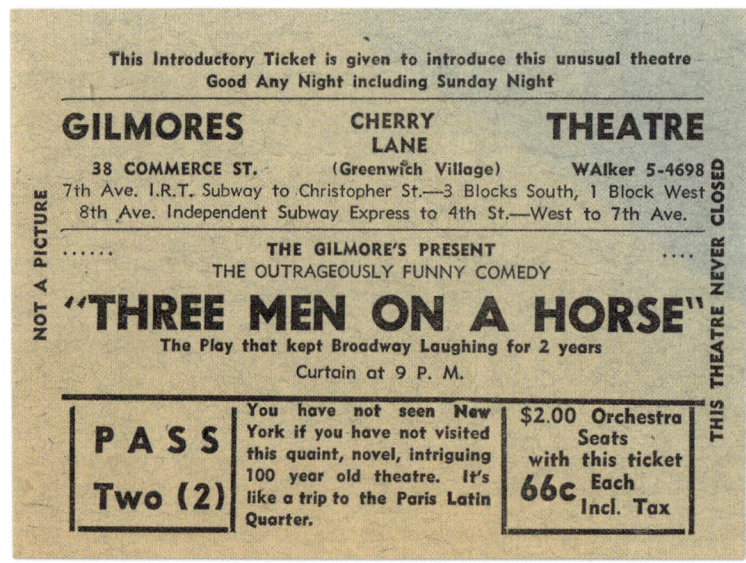

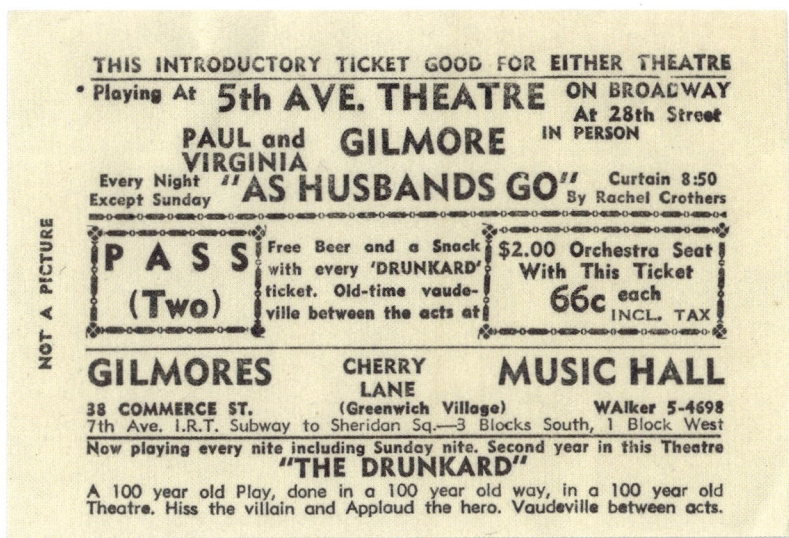

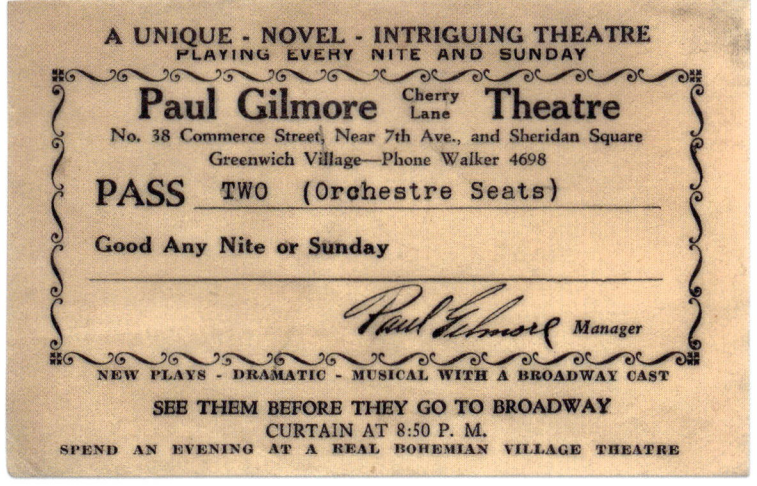

The Bigot
1930

WRITTEN BY
Slater LaMaster

DIRECTED BY
Paul Gilmore

WITH
Rocco Caporaso
Alfred Cooper
Harold Kathman
William H. Malone
Victoria Montgomery
Doris Ryder
Charles Sobel
J. Harrison Taylor
Lauriel Wood

SCENIC DESIGN BY
Harry Smith

SET IN THE HOME of the Crosby family in suburban New Jersey, *The Bigot* tells the story of "how girls are ruined by prohibition," as noted in the promotional material for the play. Written by Slater LaMaster, author of a number of occult mysteries and pulp serials, including *The Phantom in the Rainbow* (1929) and *Cupid Napoleon* (1934), *The Bigot* is a morality play that reflects the ways in which public opinion turned against Prohibition.

A decade after the Eighteenth Amendment was ratified (banning the production, transportation, and sale of alcohol across the United States), the late 1920s saw a rise in anti-Prohibition sentiment largely due to the law's ineffective and uneven enforcement, as well as the rise in violent organized crime. New York's Greenwich Village, with its vibrant nightlife and saloon culture, was at the center of the culture war. By 1929, Pauline Morton Sabin, an heiress and New York's first female representative on the Republican National Committee, resigned from her seat and launched the Women's Organization for National Prohibition Reform, catalyzing 1.5 million anti-Prohibitionists across the country.

Gilmore's staging of *The Bigot* in the heart of the Village stands out for its portrayal of the political tensions of the time; the production forged a strong connection between the theater and the local community. In late 1933, Prohibition was officially repealed, and Gilmore, adept at gauging the mood of his audience, revisited the subject by staging a satirical version of the 1844 temperance play *The Drunkard*. He was inspired by Theatre Mart's wildly successful run of *The Drunkard* in Los Angeles as an audience-participation show: Free sandwiches and beer were passed out and people were encouraged to boo the villain and cheer the hero.

RIGHT
Slater La Master was best known for *Cupid Napoleon* (1928) and *The Phantom in the Rainbow* (1929), which first appeared as serialized novels in the pulp magazine *Argosy All-Story Weekly*.

BELOW
The *Daily News* announces Paul Gilmore's forthcoming show *The Bigot*.

AT CHERRY LANE

Paul Gilmore, having renamed the Cherry Lane theatre the Paul Gilmore Cherry Lane theatre, will offer a new play there Monday. It is "The Bigot," described as a tragi-comedy against prohibition.

Paul Gilmore Little Theatres Inc.

Presents at the

Paul Gilmore Cherry Lane **Theatre**

38 COMMERCE STREET Phone WALker 4698

GREENWICH VILLAGE, N. Y. CITY

"THE BIGOT"

By Slater Le Masters

with

A BROADWAY CAST

PROHIBITION EXPOSED

The Uncle Tom's Cabin of Prohibition Slavery

Innocent "Little Eve" Thrown to the Dogs

How Girls Are Ruined By Prohibition

SEATS by Sub. **1.00**

See It Before It Goes to Broadway

EVERY NITE AND SUNDAY

OPPOSITE AND RIGHT
Poster and playbill for
The Bigot.

PAUL GILMORE CHERRY LANE THEATRE

38 Commerce Street — Near Seventh Avenue and Sheridan Square — **Greenwich Village**

TELEPHONE WALKER 4698 · PAUL GILMORE, Director

PROGRAM PUBLISHED BY THE LITTLE THEATRE PROGRAM COMPANY

FIRE NOTICE: Look around now and choose the nearest exit to your seat. In case of fire, walk (not run) to that exit. Do not try to beat your neighbor to the street.

JOHN J. DORMAN, Fire Commissioner.

Every Evening — at Eight-fifty

PAUL GILMORE

Presents

Signora Poppoec in Songs

"THE BIGOT"

By

SLATER LaMASTER

WILLIAM CROSBY	*J. Harrison Taylor*
MRS. MARY CROSBY	*Victoria Montgomery*
MARGARET CROSBY	*Lauriel Wood*
WINNIE CROSBY	*Doris Ryder*
HARVEY CARLTON	*Rocco Caporaso*
GEORGE NICHOLSON	*Harold Kathman*
JIM NICHOLSON	*William H. Malone*
SAM ABBOTT	*Alfred Cooper*
TONY OLIVERO	*Charles Sobel*

Time—The present.
Place—The living room of the Crosby home at Hillmont, New Jersey, a suburb of New York City.

ACT ONE—One evening.
ACT TWO—A few hours later. (Curtain lowered.)
  SCENE TWO—The next morning.
ACT THREE—The same, months afterward.

Settings by HARRY SMITH

Signora Poppoea Chadwick, who sings before our play, will give vocal instruction at this theatre mornings between ten and twelve.

The Bishop Misbehaves
1937

WRITTEN BY
Frederick Jackson

PRODUCED BY
John Golden

WITH
Sidney Cassel
Jean DeBear
Paul Gilmore
Virginia Gilmore
Fernand Larbaud
Joel Nash
John Regan
Ann Rogers
Frank Thune
Charles Willis

SCENIC DESIGN BY
Ann Rogers

WRITTEN BY AMERICAN PLAYWRIGHT, screenwriter, and novelist Frederick Jackson, *The Bishop Misbehaves* tells the comedic story of the Bishop of Broadminster, a discreet but avid reader of detective fiction who gets entangled in a mystery of his own making. After stumbling into a robbery at the local pub, he meets Hester, a young woman who confesses a secret romance. As the Bishop attempts to solve the crime, he creates comedic chaos as he gets increasingly involved with the personal lives of other characters, leading to mistaken identity, furtive meetings, mix-ups, and misunderstandings.

After a successful run on Broadway at the Cort Theatre in 1935, the play was adapted for the screen in the same year by Metro-Goldwyn-Mayer, directed by E. A. Dupont and starring Edmund Gwenn, Maureen O'Sullivan, and Lucile Watson. A national tour of the play began in 1937 thanks to the support of the Federal Theatre Project, traveling across the country at stops including Cherry Lane Theatre in 1937 and the Mason Opera House in Los Angeles in 1938. The play, featuring an older Bishop and younger cast of women characters, was a great vehicle for Paul and Virginia Gilmore, who frequently sought out and produced shows that allowed them to costar. Despite the fact that Jean DeBear plays the lead in the Cherry Lane production, the show's program gives the Gilmores top billing: "Paul and Virginia Gilmore in last season's sensational success *The Bishop Misbehaves*."

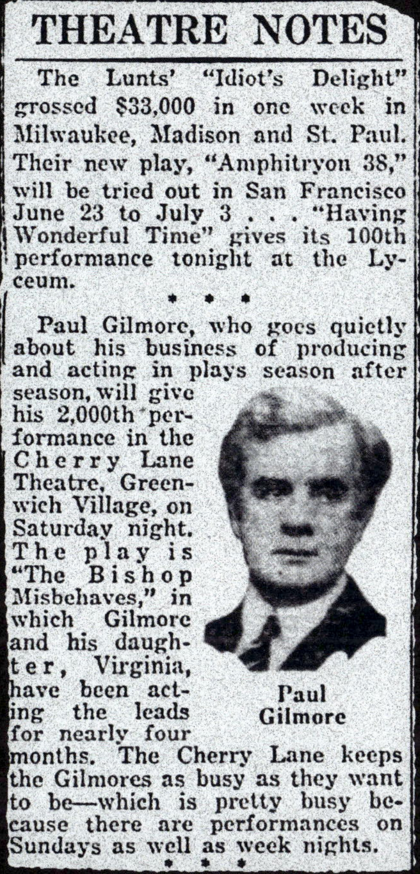

THEATRE NOTES

The Lunts' "Idiot's Delight" grossed $33,000 in one week in Milwaukee, Madison and St. Paul. Their new play, "Amphitryon 38," will be tried out in San Francisco June 23 to July 3 . . . "Having Wonderful Time" gives its 100th performance tonight at the Lyceum.

* * *

Paul Gilmore, who goes quietly about his business of producing and acting in plays season after season, will give his 2,000th performance in the Cherry Lane Theatre, Greenwich Village, on Saturday night. The play is "The Bishop Misbehaves," in which Gilmore and his daughter, Virginia, have been acting the leads for nearly four months. The Cherry Lane keeps the Gilmores as busy as they want to be—which is pretty busy because there are performances on Sundays as well as week nights.

* * *

Paul Gilmore

"The BISHOP Misbehaves

By FREDERICK JACKSON

FEDERAL THEATRE PROJECT USA WORK PROGRAM W.P.A.

ABOVE LEFT
The *Daily News* reports that Paul Gilmore's two thousandth performance at Cherry Lane will be in *The Bishop Misbehaves*. May 18, 1937.

ABOVE RIGHT
A poster for a Federal Theatre Project production of *The Bishop Misbehaves* in Los Angeles. 1938.

PAUL AND VIRGINIA GILMORE IN "ACCENT ON YOUTH"

Paul Gilmore
CHERRY LANE THEATRE

38 Commerce Street
Greenwich Village

At the End of Cherry Lane

There are in New York thousands of theatre lovers with taste and culture yet with moderate means. These people need a theatre they can afford. The above theatre is for those whose income does not permit of luxuries. It's worth a trip to Greenwich Village just to see this quaint, novel and intriguing Little Cameo Theatre. You will find it like a trip into the Paris Latin Quarter. This in itself is a treat, but in addition to all this you will see TRIED and PROVEN BROADWAY SUCCESSES.

PROGRAMME

PAUL & VIRGINIA GILMORE
In Last Season's Sensational Success

THE BISHOP MISBEHAVES
By
FREDERICK JACKSON

As Produced by John Golden on Broadway Last Season

CAST

RED EAGAN	Joel Nash
DONALD MEADOWS	Robroy Farquhar
HESTER GRANTHAM	Nancy Keer
GUY WALLER	Homer Keeney
MRS. WALLER	Elizabeth Newton
THE BISHOP OF BROADMINSTER	Paul Gilmore
LADY EMILY LYONS	Virginia Gilmore
COLLINS	Jack Friedlander
FRENCHY	Fernand Larbaud
MR. BROOKE	Charles Willis

Scenery Designed and Executed by Ann Rogers

SCENES

ACT I. Taproom of The Queen's Head, at Tadworth, in Surrey.

ACTS II and III. Hall of the Bishop's Palace at Broadminster.

The action of the play covers exactly the time it takes to play it.

Stage Mgr.—Robroy Farquhar

THEATRE PARTIES

There is no easier nor more pleasant way to increase the funds of social, charitable and political organizations than by giving a theatre party. Our special rate theatre party plan explains how. Please ask at the box office or write for details.

This Theatre never closed. Open every night including Sunday night.

TEN MINUTES INTERMISSION BETWEEN ACTS
LOUNGE - SMOKING-ROOM - AND REFRESHMENTS
UPSTAIRS

ABOVE AND OPPOSITE
Two sides of the show program for
The Bishop Misbehaves give top billing
to Paul and Virginia Gilmore. 1937.

SOUVENIR PROGRAM

Paul and Virginia Gilmore

Wartime in the Wings

THE 1940s finally saw an end to the Great Depression, but only due to the forces of an even more perilous era—the start of the Second World War. Theaters remained open during the war years, and New York City was often the last destination for thousands of US servicemen before being shipped to the front lines of battle. The American Theatre Wing (which created the Tony Awards in 1947) opened the Stage Door Canteen in 1942 as an entertainment venue for American and Allied servicemen. Hundreds of actors and entertainers performed there for free as a way to support the troops and boost morale. The 1944 Leonard Bernstein musical *On the Town*, featuring the story of three American sailors on shore leave for twenty-four hours in New York, is emblematic of the patriotic spirit alive in New York during the war years. The decade also marks the start of what would later come to be known as the golden age for American musicals. A uniquely American genre, the musical has its roots in operetta and vaudeville, but it was not until Rodgers and Hammerstein's *Oklahoma!* (1943) that a work would carefully combine plot, music, and dance in the service of one integrated story. *Oklahoma!* ushered in an era of growth and innovation for a form that continues to be synonymous with American, and Broadway, theater even today.

Although not American, the operettas of Gilbert and Sullivan (important precursors for American musicals) were prominently featured at Cherry Lane during the 1941–42 residency of the Savoy Opera Guild; eight of the works the storied duo wrote were performed by the Guild during their year-plus at the theater. Other residencies followed, with the Hedgerow Theatre Company in 1945, the Spur in 1946, and On-Stage (which became the Interplayers) from 1946 to 1948—each one providing a temporary artistic home base for itinerant companies. Although these companies can't claim a lasting legacy, their selection of Cherry Lane, as well as the repertoire of plays produced during those years (featuring works by both Eugene O'Neill and Clifford Odets), cemented the theater as an important venue for American playwrights and a destination for new and innovative companies in search of a downtown home.

Perhaps the most significant players to tread the boards at Cherry Lane in this era were three actors who got their start there before finding fame in Hollywood: Jerry Stiller, Bea Arthur, and Tony Curtis. After enlisting in the service, they made their way back to New York in the postwar years to begin their careers in entertainment. All three enrolled

PAGE 59
On-Stage Theatre Company's production of *Gas*, featuring a young Bea Arthur and Jerry Stiller. 1946.

OPPOSITE
Photograph of Cherry Lane. September, 1949.

BELOW
Bob Ramsey (*left*) and Al Hurwitz (*right*), co-founders of On-Stage Theatre Company. 1946–53.

OPPOSITE TOP
On-Stage Theatre Company's production of *Gas*, featuring a young Bea Arthur and Jerry Stiller. 1946.

OPPOSITE BOTTOM
A sign installation for *Dog Beneath the Skin* on Cherry Lane's awning. 1946.

PAGES 64–65
One of On-Stage's most consistent collaborations was with the photographer Alfred J. Balcombe, who took their production stills. Michael Balcombe, his son, writes, "My parents used to tell me that sometimes the Cherry Lane Theatre would pay them for their photos with complementary theater tickets! It was probably, artistically, the most creative period of their marriage." *Clockwise from top left*: *The Watched Pot* by Saki (1947), *Life Sentence* by Philip Van Dyke (1947), *Yerma* by Federico García Lorca (1946), and *No Exit* by Jean-Paul Sartre (1946).

in significant acting schools that had just opened—not in Times Square, as one might expect, but in the West Village—a sign of just how much of a center this neighborhood had become for theater artists. Arthur and Curtis studied under the German director Erwin Piscator, who, fleeing the war, had come to the US and formed the Dramatic Workshop at the New School in 1940. Several blocks away, Stiller apprenticed at the HB Studio under Herbert Berghof and Uta Hagen. Early acting jobs followed quickly. In 1947, Arthur and Stiller performed together at Cherry Lane in *Gas* by Georg Kaiser and *The Dog Beneath the Skin* by W. H. Auden and Christopher Isherwood, both plays staged by Dramatic Workshop alums Bob Ramsey and Al Hurwitz under their On-Stage company. The following year, Curtis was discovered by a scout from Universal Pictures while appearing in the lead role of *Golden Boy* by Clifford Odets. His leap to the screen established Cherry Lane as one of the preeminent launching pads for lustrous careers in the arts—a pattern we will see repeated often in the coming years.

WARTIME IN THE WINGS

Floor Plan
LIFE SENTENCE
CHERRY LANE THEATRE 3/8"~1'
~ BOB RAMSEY ~
1947
LS-1A

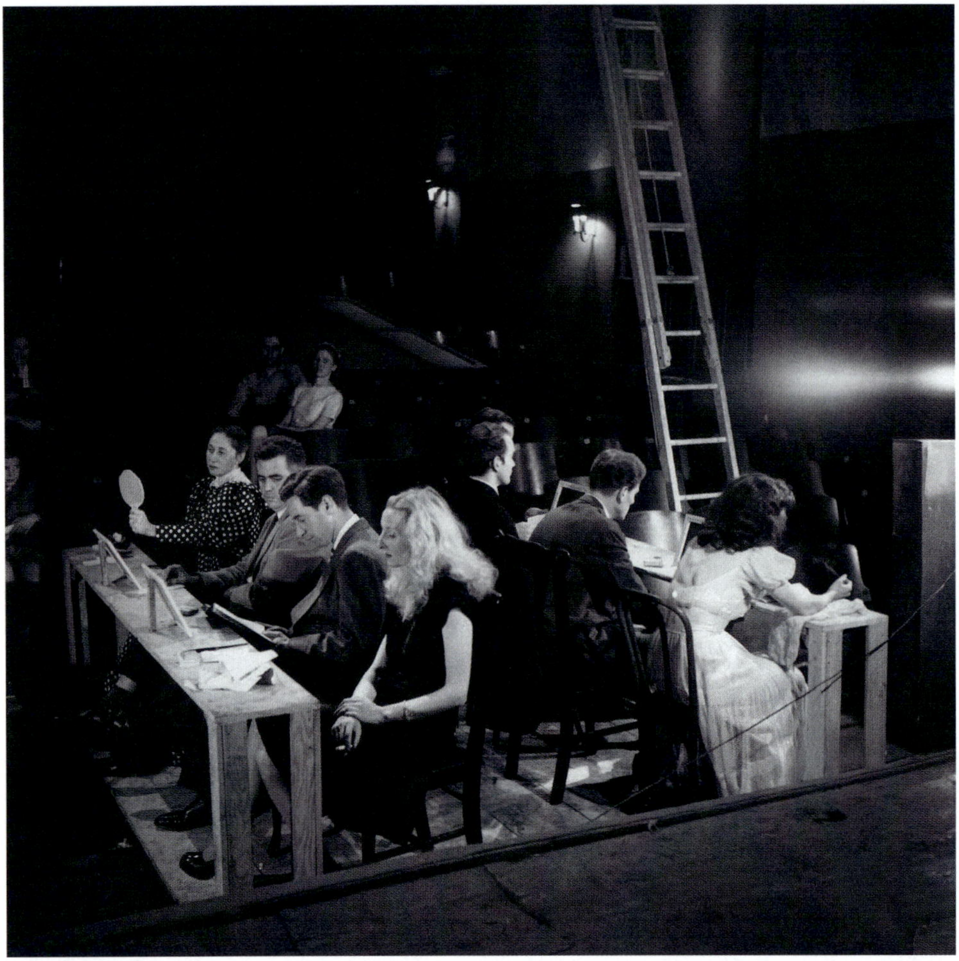

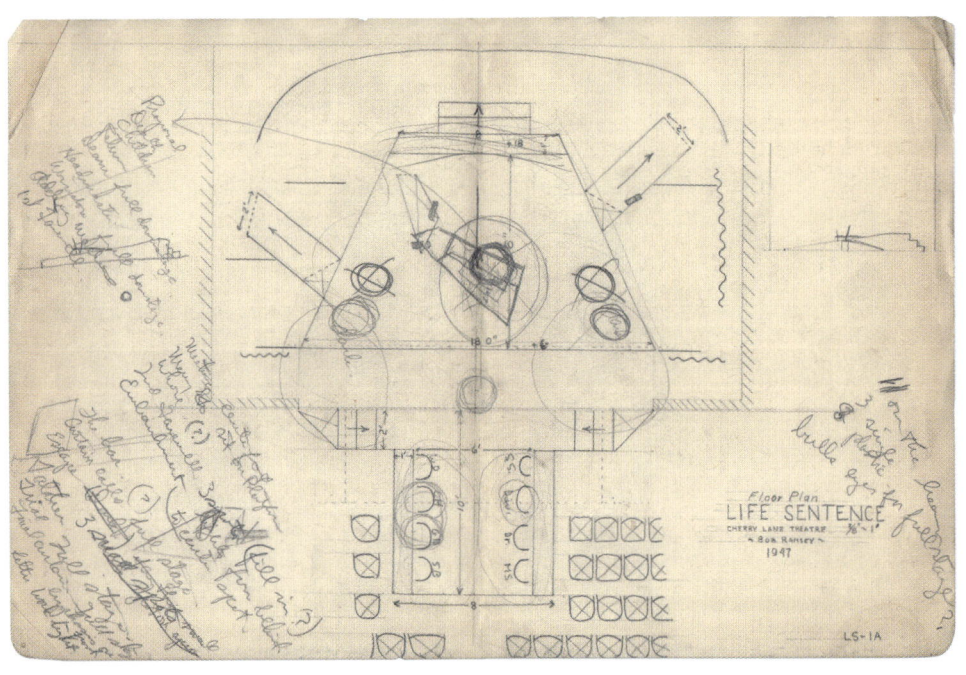

PAGES 64–66
On-Stage Theatre Company rented Cherry Lane beginning in 1946 to produce a number of ambitious shows. Their productions were especially notable for the stage design of co-founder Bob Ramsey, who studied at the Dramatic Workshop of the New School for Social Research.

OPPOSITE TOP
A rehearsal still from *Life Sentence* by Philip Van Dyke. On-Stage's production was the play's New York premiere. 1947.

OPPOSITE BOTTOM
Bob Ramsey's floor plan sketch for *Life Sentence*. 1947.

RIGHT
Rehearsal for *The Watched Pot* by Saki. 1947.

67 WARTIME IN THE WINGS

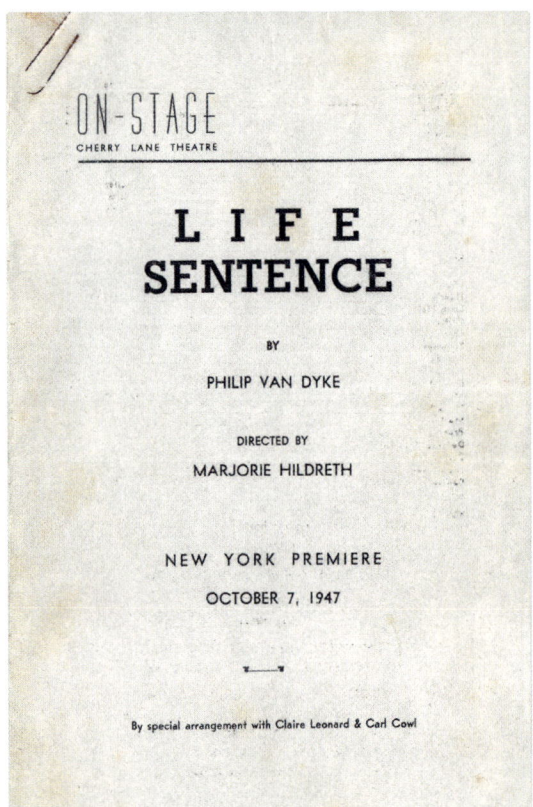
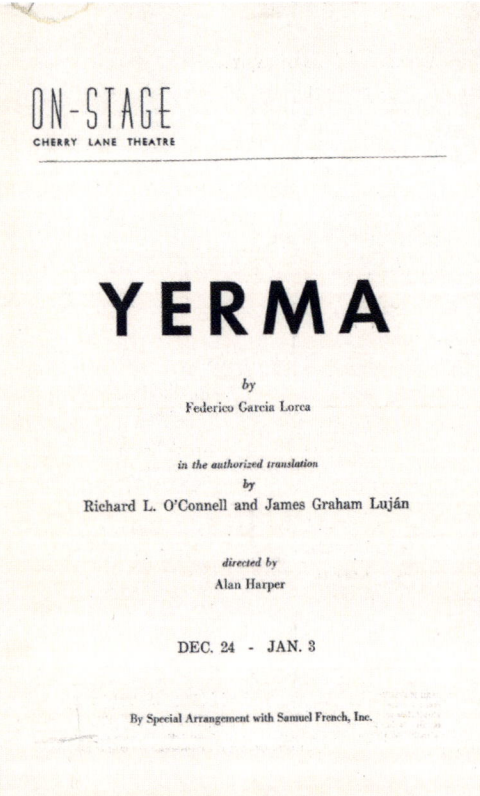
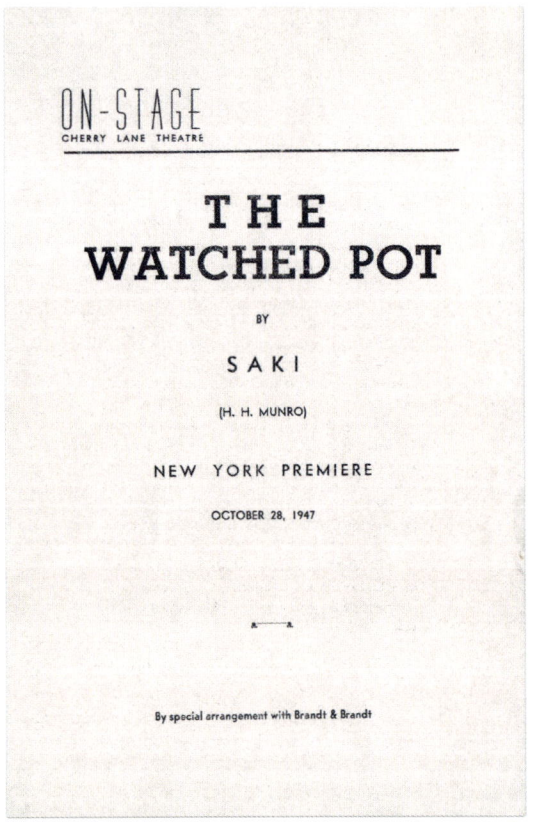

RIGHT
An On-Stage promotional program showing a collage of production stills by Alfred J. Balcombe.

RIGHT
An On-Stage poster promoting the season's productions. 1947.

OPPOSITE
The Watched Pot by Saki. Production stills by Alfred J. Balcombe. 1947.

OPPOSITE AND RIGHT
A young Bea Arthur in *Yerma* by Federico García Lorca. Production stills by Alfred J. Balcombe. 1946–47.

ABOVE
Production still and promotional poster for Jean-Paul Sartre's *No Exit*. Still by Alfred J. Balcombe. 1946.

BY SPECIAL ARRANGEMENT WITH SAMUEL FRENCH, Inc.

ON-STAGE
PRESENTS

NO EXIT
(HUIS CLOS)

By Jean-Paul Sartre

New York Critics Award as Best Foreign Play of 1947

OPENING JUNE 9
AT THE

CHERRY LANE THEATRE
38 COMMERCE ST.

The First of 4 Plays to be Presented this Summer

ON-STAGE, JUNE 9th to AUG. 9th

POPULAR PRICES $1.20 - $1.80 TAX INCL.

Subscription Tickets for the Entire Season $6.20
Write: Ramsey & Hurwitz - 933 2nd Ave., New York 22, N. Y.

BOX OFFICE OPENS JUNE 2

The Savoy Opera Guild

THE SAVOY OPERA GUILD announced their 1941 arrival at Cherry Lane Theatre with a bold proclamation: "Three years ago the founders of the Savoy Opera Guild became convinced that what this country needed more than a good five-cent cigar was a good American repertory company to present Gilbert and Sullivan operas on a permanent year 'round schedule." Over the course of their year-and-a-half residency, the company put on eight of the fourteen comedic musicals from the famed Victorian-era British duo, to glowing reviews from influential critics including Robert Simon in *The New Yorker*, Brooks Atkinson in *The New York Times*, and Eugene Burr in *The Billboard*. In a review of *The Yeomen of the Guard* (1941), Atkinson wrote, "Savoy Opera Guild is keeping the town's Gilbert & Sullivan enthusiasts in fine fettle these evenings . . . should a straying theatre-goer visit the stuffy confines of the Cherry Lane any weekend, he will be treated to some very fine singing."

In order to keep production costs low, the Guild eschewed a full orchestra and kept the instrumentation to a single piano. Ticket sales were just as modest, but what they made "was divided among the players. For many months after the opening on April 15, 1941, this was exactly nothing; then as the reputation of the Guild grew, it gradually increased to the point where receipts would keep the members of the company in their favorite brands of cigarette."

Despite its scrappy reputation, after just one year Burr reported the Guild's productions a resounding success. "Crowds attending the out-of-the-way Cherry Lane, previously regarded as strictly a jinx house, have been heavy." As their residency came to a close, the troupe set its sights a bit higher and started a subscription membership model to fund their move to a larger and more centrally located theater space, described in a promotional pamphlet as "accommodating about eight hundred in a location readily accessible from all sections of the city."

RIGHT
Opening night at Cherry Lane for the Savoy Opera Guild's production of *Pirates of Penzance*. Illustrations by Al Hirschfeld for *The New York Times*. August 23, 1942.

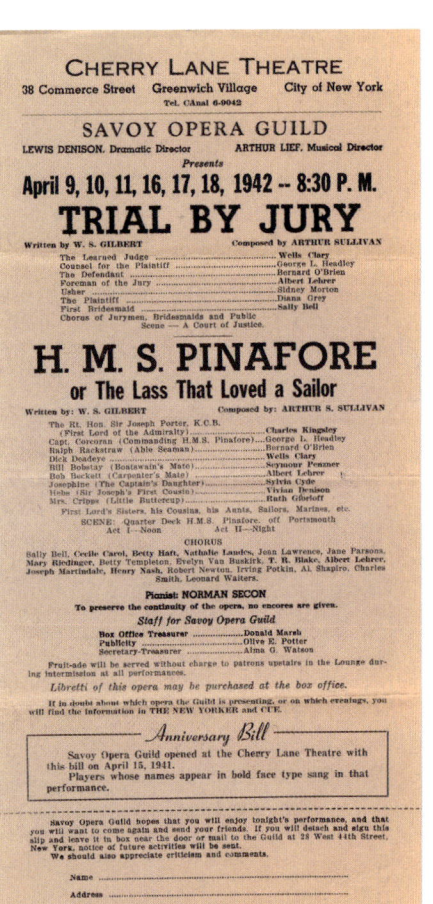
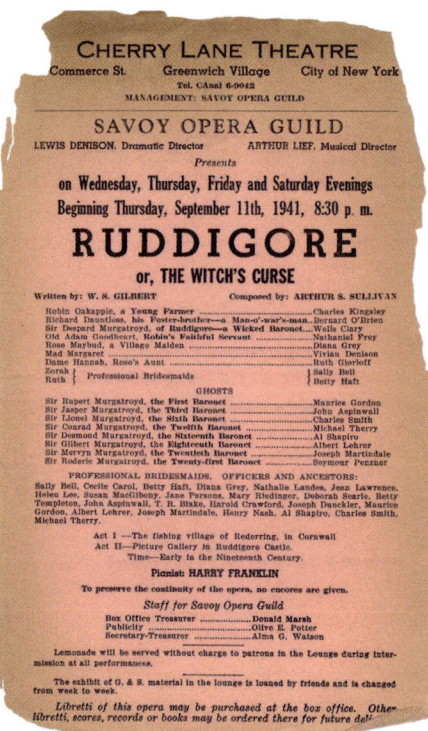
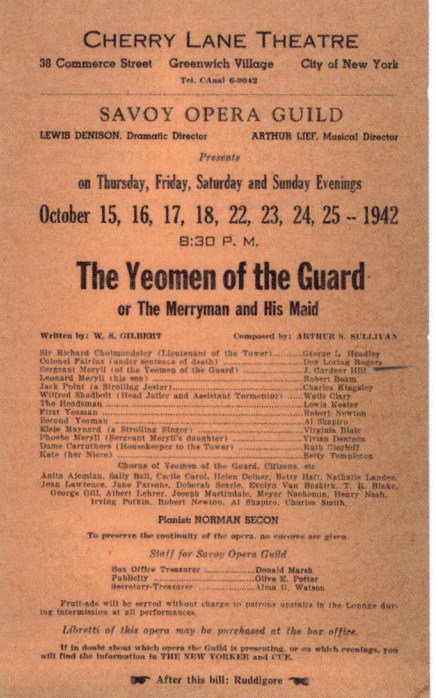
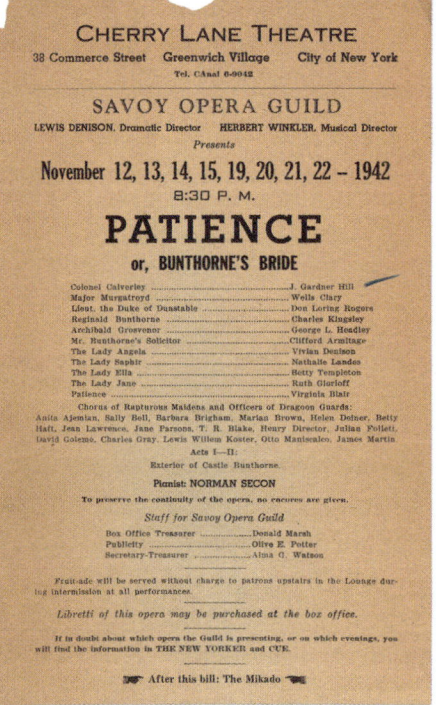

SOG SAGA

VOL. II No. 25   October 15, 1942

MR. BURR VISITS PROVINCETOWN — AND US.

DEBUTANTS

YEOMEN OF THE GUARD marks the debut of 3 people: Virginia Blair as Elsie, Don Loring Rogers as Fairfax, and Joe Hill as a principal in the part of Sergeant Meryll. We expect them to do a grand job and we're all for them.

REITERATION

Thanks again to Evvie for stepping into the breach when Viv was ill. We admit with pride that all week she was an enchanting, delightful, and adorable Cousin Hebe. Quite a trouper she is becoming.

NEW FACES

Despite what the program may say, for the record, the part of Leonard Meryll is being played by Harold Sahl.

The two new choristers are Julian Follett and Henry Director. Long may they be with us!

BUTTS AND REBUTTS

Now that we're all friends again, a suggestion seems to be in order. In the future, if occasion arises requiring the debate of a question (supposing for the nonce that there should be a question) let's have it on the bulletin board with a time set (by the administration) for the debate; and, more important, limit the speakers to three minutes only. Those of us who are not in accord with this more democratic form of governmental procedure can in time perhaps learn to bare all and still bear up; and those who want to go home can go. Thus, we may avoid the recurrence of a near debacle like that of Tuesday night. ..........J.G.H.

The writing of Eugene Burr of BILLBOARD cannot be too often quoted, so, without more ado, here is his latest: "...my attendance had been requested at the Provincetown Playhouse, newly renovated, where the Light Opera Theatre is giving revivals of Gilbert and Sullivan operettas, just a few blocks away from the Cherry Lane, where the Savoy Opera Guild has been offering week-end G & S performances for over a year.

"The bill was THE SORCERER......I had always wanted to see THE SORCERER staged, so I went. I still want to see THE SORCERER staged. The mess they made of it at the Provincetown is quite indescribable. In the first place, they have inexplicably picked costumes that might do for YEOMEN OF THE GUARD instead of Victorian days, and so have utterly ruined the satire of John Wellington Wells....The staging is lackadaisical and painfully unimaginative, and the acting is a bit under the average of a fifth-rate high school club.... the singing.... is for the most part entirely unfitted for the light Gilbert and Sullivan scores-- and some of the singers showed an almost pitiful inability to remain on key. Even the make-up was beyond belief.... And the male chorus turned out to be a tremendous affair composed of just three rather unhappy-looking young men. When four parts had to be sung a principal was drafted to help out..... Some (of the cast) were so hilariously inept that an attempted description would be merely funny-- but not at all funny to any lover of Gilbert and Sullivan.

(Continued on page 2)

........Friday, October 16th, Happy Birthday, Joe Hill, and many of 'em. ....

OPPOSITE
Programs from the Savoy Opera Guild at Cherry Lane. 1941–42.

ABOVE
The SOG Saga, an internal newsletter for the actors and theater artists of the Savoy Opera Guild, published during their residency at Cherry Lane. October 15, 1942.

Tony Curtis, Golden Boy

BEFORE HE WAS Tony Curtis, star of *Sweet Smell of Success* (1957), *Some Like It Hot* (1959), and *Spartacus* (1960), Bernard Schwartz was a kid from the Bronx. It was the movies that gave Schwartz, growing up in a tough neighborhood, a window to a world beyond the five boroughs of New York City. After serving in the navy during World War II (he enlisted after watching Cary Grant on a submarine in the 1943 *Destination Tokyo*), he realized that the GI Bill would allow him to study any subject he wanted, including acting: "The government paid your tuition and gave you $65 a month, a lot of money in 1946." While enrolled in the New School's Dramatic Workshop, where he was in a cohort with Walter Matthau, Elaine Stritch, and Harry Belafonte, he starred in the 1948 school production of Clifford Odets's (also a New School alum) morality story *Golden Boy* at Cherry Lane Theatre. Schwartz's role as Joe Bonaparte, a violinist who becomes a prizefighter to escape poverty, is a study of the price one pays for unchecked ambition.

During this production he was scouted by agent Joyce Selznick, who then brokered a seven-year contract with Universal Pictures, where Schwartz changed his name to Anthony Curtis, developed his craft by learning how to fence and ride horses, and became a star. By 1951, Curtis was cast as the lead in *The Prince Who Was a Thief*, a Technicolor swashbuckler loosely based on an *Arabian Nights* tale, which set him on the path of playing the Hollywood leading man. In 1958 he was nominated for an Academy Award for Best Actor for *The Defiant Ones* (alongside costar Sidney Poitier), and Tony Curtis became one of the most sought-after names in Hollywood.

RIGHT
Tony Curtis in *The Prince Who Was a Thief* (1951), directed by Rudolph Maté.

ABOVE TOP ROW
Tony Curtis as a student at the Dramatic Workshop of the New School for Social Research.

ABOVE BOTTOM ROW
(*From left to right*) Erwin Piscator, founder of the Dramatic Workshop, with an actor. Harry Belafonte, then a student at the Dramatic Workshop. All images photographed by Alfred J. Balcombe.

Henry IV
1947

WRITTEN BY
Luigi Pirandello

TRANSLATED BY
Edward Storer

DIRECTED BY
Alexis Solomos

PRODUCED BY
On-Stage

WITH
Louis Criss
Edward Hussey
Victor Jonston
George Joseph
Glenn McCausland
Michael Mear
Henry Proach
Claire Ramsay
Linda Rhodes
Jean Saks
Kchast Sayers
Walter Witcover

WRITTEN BY ITALIAN dramatist and 1934 Nobel Prize in Literature winner Luigi Pirandello, *Henry IV* is a tragicomic meditation on madness, reality, and identity. The play centers on the story of an Italian aristocrat who falls off his horse and awakes believing he's the Holy Roman emperor Henry IV (no relation to Shakespeare's Henry IV). Twenty years later, the family of "Henry IV" prepares for the arrival of a doctor they hope will finally cure his delusions. A series of comedic events unfolds, ultimately revealing that Henry is not truly mad, but has been merely playing the part. Written in 1921, the play is seen as a forerunner to theater of the absurd and has been translated by a range of writers, from poet Edward Storer (1922) to playwright Tom Stoppard (2004). In 2019, it was ranked by *The Independent* as one of the forty greatest plays ever written.

In 1946, Bob Ramsey and Al Hurwitz, two students from the Dramatic Workshop of the New School for Social Research, founded experimental theater company On-Stage and promptly "scraped together all their available cash" to rent Cherry Lane Theatre. A 1947 profile of the duo in the *Theatre Arts Monthly* by Ian Campbell recounts how "they put the idea for their group before fellow schoolmates at the Dramatic Workshop, former associates at Yale and students and amateurs in other actors' haunts. Soon about thirty people, all in their twenties, had joined the enterprise, willing to work without compensation beyond the experience they would gain and the pleasure they would derive from supporting a project they considered worthwhile." On-Stage opened with Jean-Paul Sartre's *No Exit* on June 9, 1947, followed by the first New York performance of Philip Van Dyke's *Life Sentence*, the New York premiere of Georg Kaiser's *Gas*, and the W. H. Auden–Christopher Isherwood play *The Dog Beneath the Skin*, among an ambitious lineup of productions that same year. In describing Cherry Lane, Campbell wrote, "If a heavy rain comes at performance time people in the front row get wet feet, and a woman once had the disconcerting experience of seeing her shoes carried downstream. Since On-Stage is not a barter theatre, the shoes were returned."

OPPOSITE
Jean (Gene) Saks in the title role of *Henry IV*.

WARTIME IN THE WINGS

ABOVE
Production still from *Henry IV*.

OPPOSITE
Linda Rhodes plays Frida, the daughter of Lady Matilda Spina. Lady Spina's portrait as a young woman hangs behind her. All production stills by Alfred J. Balcombe.

A Safe Haven on Commerce Street

CHERRY LANE HAD BEEN up and running for more than three decades by the time the "off-Broadway" designation was made official in the 1950s. While the roots of off Broadway stretch back to the Little Theatre Movement of the 1910s and 1920s, it was not until the mid-twentieth century that theaters could be officially classified as off-Broadway houses. For starters, size matters: Off-Broadway houses have between 100 and 499 seats—significantly smaller than even the smallest Broadway theater of 600 seats (the majority of Broadway houses have 1,000 or more). More importantly, the ethos of the off-Broadway movement provided a safe haven for experimental and abstract drama, away from the commercial pressures and expenses of Broadway. In 1952 a group of like-minded neighbors, led by lawyer Kenneth Carroad, saved Cherry Lane from demolition by gaining ownership of the building. In 1956, *The Village Voice* launched the Obie Awards to honor excellence in off-Broadway theater—a major milestone. The year prior, the Tony Awards (which are limited to Broadway productions) bestowed a Special Tony Award on Proscenium Productions, then in residence at Cherry Lane, making it the first off-Broadway company to be recognized.

The postwar period had a chilling effect on culture and media. The Red Scare stoked fears of Soviet espionage and communist influence on American institutions, and Senator Joseph McCarthy and the hearings conducted by the House Un-American Activities Committee (HUAC) stifled the creative freedom of artists who feared the blacklist. These pressures, coupled with the censorship restrictions of the Hays Code in Hollywood, may have inspired artists to seek refuge in the relative freedoms of off Broadway. In fact, away from the scrutiny of HUAC, off Broadway and Cherry Lane were flourishing.

Two major moments for experimental theater occurred at the little theater on Commerce Street. First, in 1951, the Living Theatre, one of the most influential experimental theater troupes of the twentieth century, took out a two-year lease on Cherry Lane. Cofounded by Judith Malina and Julian Beck, the Living Theatre exploded the boundary between player and audience and staged bold, unapologetically political pieces that were radical in form and content. American poet William Carlos Williams wrote to Beck and Malina after seeing their first production at Cherry Lane: "I am walking in a dream, the aftermath of what I saw and heard at your Cherry Lane Theatre last evening . . . It is so far above the level of commercial

PAGE 87
Press photo of the Cherry Lane production of *Endgame* by Samuel Beckett. Photograph by Gjon Mili/The LIFE Picture Collection. 1958.

OPPOSITE
A woman hanging a sign on the awning of the Cherry Lane. 1956.

BELOW
Playbill featuring an illustration by Pablo Picasso for the inaugural season of the Living Theatre at Cherry Lane. 1951.

OPPOSITE
Photos from the Living Theatre's production of *R.U.R.* by Karel Čapek, 1953.

theatre that I tremble to think it may fade and disappear." Other notable Living Theatre productions during this time include *A Night of Bohemian Theatre*, featuring work by Gertrude Stein, Pablo Picasso, and T. S. Eliot; and the proto-absurdist epic *Ubu the King*, by Alfred Jarry (both 1952).

Then, at the end of the decade, Samuel Beckett's *Endgame* (1958) jump-started a foray into the theater of the absurd movement that would continue for the next decade, bringing with it an association with a young, new American playwright who quickly earned himself the moniker of American Absurdist and would go on to win three Pulitzer Prizes for drama: Edward Albee.

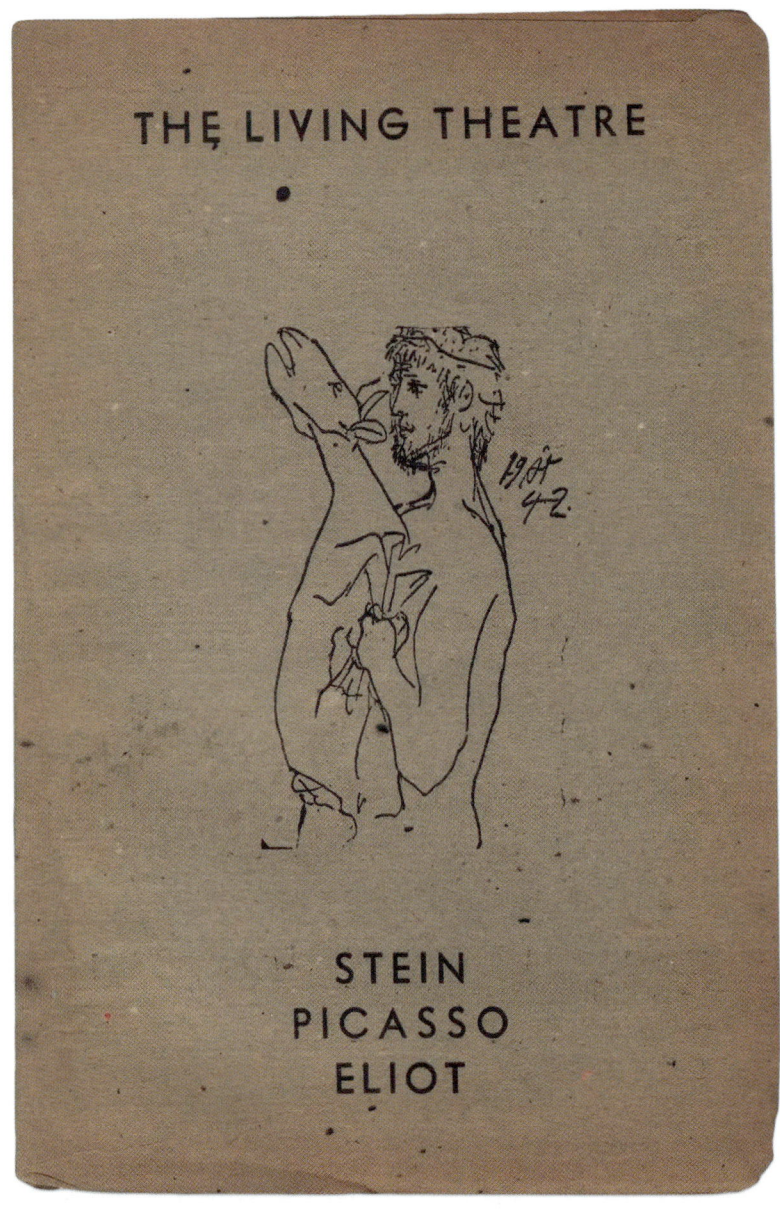

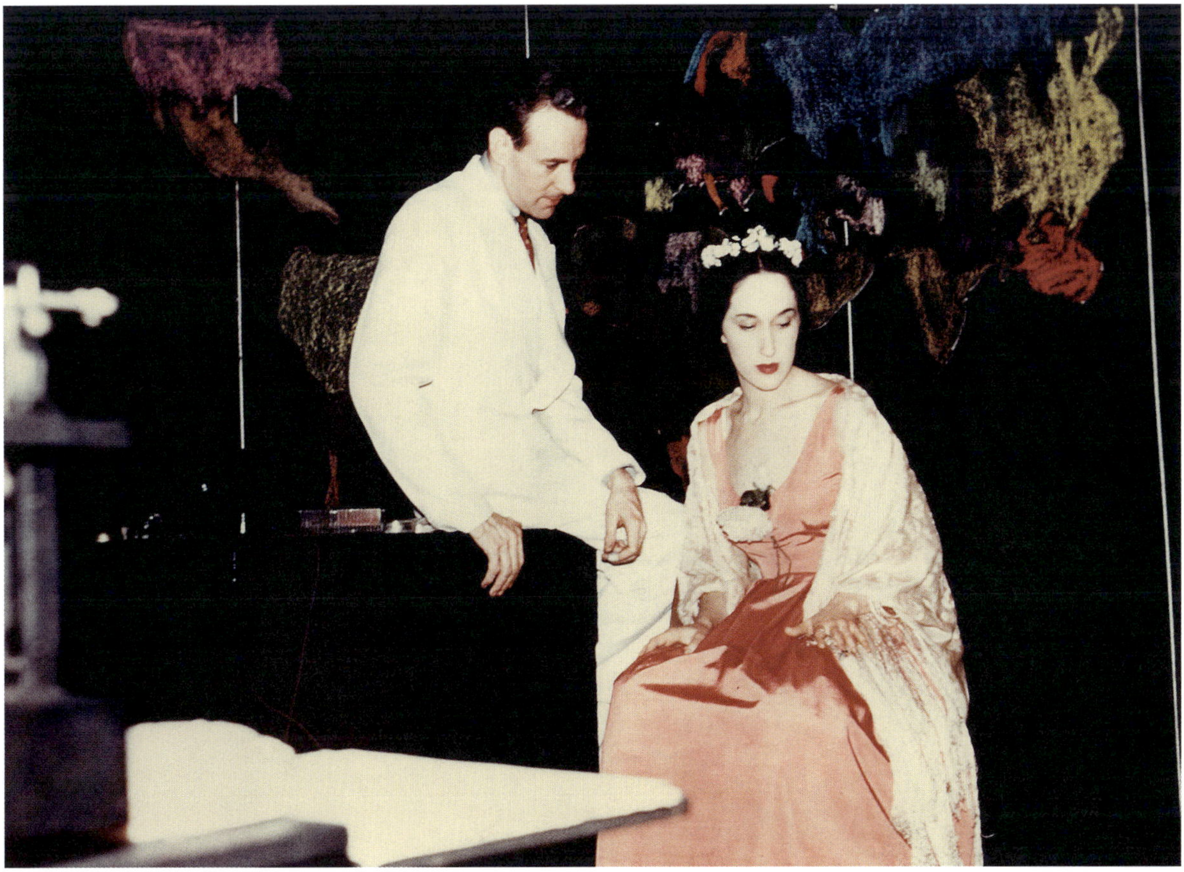

A SAFE HAVEN ON COMMERCE STREET

OPPOSITE
Rehearsal stills from *Endgame* by Samuel Beckett. *Top photo, from left to right*: Director Alan Schneider and actors Alvin Epstein as Clov, Nydia Westman as Nell, P. J. Kelly as Nagg, and Lester Rawlins as Hamm. *Bottom photo, from left to right*: Nydia Westman and P. J. Kelly. Photographs by Eileen Darby. 1958.

RIGHT TOP
Brooks Atkinson's review of *Endgame* for *The New York Times*. "Thanks to the bitterness of the direction and acting, Samuel Beckett's second play turns out to be quite impressive." January 29, 1958.

RIGHT BOTTOM
Advertisement for *Endgame* in *The New York Post*. January 29, 1958.

The Theatre: Beckett's 'Endgame'

4-Character Play Opens at the Cherry Lane

By BROOKS ATKINSON

THANKS largely to the bitterness of the direction and the acting, Samuel Beckett's second play turns out to be quite impressive. Impressive in the macabre intensity of the mood, that is.

For "Endgame," which opened at the Cherry Lane last evening, deals in tones and perversities of expression. Like "Waiting for Godot," it never comes precisely to the point. But Mr. Beckett is wise in choosing the form of the myth in which to sound his tocsin on the condition of human society. Since his theme is unearthly, the unearthly form becomes it.

•

The stage represents a gloomy brick cavern with spectral light, two grotesque windows that can be reached only by a ladder, scabrous walls, rubble, decay. There are four characters—an irascible, blind tycoon in a hard hat and rags, sitting in a battered pulpit chair; his shuffling, groaning slave who drags himself around the stage on futile errands; an elderly man and an elderly woman who live in two ashcans. Once or twice during the course of Mr. Beckett's harangue of disgust they poke their death-like faces above the rims of the ashcans and act as a grisly chorus to the main theme.

Apparently, the place is somewhere between life and death, and the time is just short of the night of the earth's last whimper. Don't expect this column to give a coherent account of what—if anything—happens. Almost nothing happens in the sense of action.

But Mr. Beckett, destitute of hope, is flinging a shroud across earth's last revels. He is painting a portrait of desolation, lovelessness, boredom ruthlessness, sorrow, nothingness. Looking out of the window through a telescope, Clov reports what he sees: "Zero, zero and zero." Mr. Beckett is preparing us for oblivion.

•

Whether or not his theme is acceptable or rational, his director, Alan Schneider, has had the grace to take him at his own evaluation and stage his play seriously. Although there is not much physical movement in it, it has con-

Lester Rawlins, left, and Alvin Epstein in "Endgame"

The Cast

ENDGAME, a drama by Samuel Beckett. Staged by Alan Schneider; designed by David Hays; presented by Noel Behn and the Rooftop Productions (Jerome Friedman, Barry Hyams and David Brooks). At the Cherry Lane Theatre.
Clov .... Alvin Epstein
Hamm .... Lester Rawlins
Nagg .... P. J. Kelly
Nell .... Nydia Westman

tinuous tension and constant pressure. The words are the sounds of fluctuations in temper—from scorn and despair to sardonic humor, from hopelessness to hatred.

In "Endgame," as in "Waiting for Godot," the central character is a tyrant. Here he is called Hamm. Lester Rawlins acts the part with astonishing variety and vigor. Seated on his silly throne, he gives the whole play a driving harshness that is baleful and mad, and that stings the nerves of the audience. In view of the elusiveness of the dialogue, the fierce clarity of the characterization he draws is a superb stroke of theatre.

The part of Clov, the slave, is well played by Alvin Epstein, who is another versatile actor. As he trudges around the stage, dragging a ladder, dropping the telescope, blundering this way and that, Mr. Epstein creates another intelligible image—inventive, drawn between duty re-vulsion, between obedience and contempt. It is excellent work.

"Comedy" may be too cheerful a word to describe the episodes in the ashcans. They are part of Mr. Beckett's grim joke on the futility of life. But it is a pleasant thing to see Nydia Westman poke her bonneted head out of one ashcan and listen to her quavering voice, and it is also pleasant to see P. J. Kelly's pointed features appear out of the refuse and hear his Irish inflections. Think of the years of work and study that have prepared Miss Westman and Mr. Kelly to practice art in an ashcan!

•

What Mr. Beckett has to say is contrary and nihilistic. But he is a writer. He can create a mood by using words as incantations. Although the dialogue is often baffling, there is no doubt about the total impression. We are through, he says. Nature has forgotten us. The jig is up.

Under Mr. Schneider's bustling and perceptive direction, inside David Hays' stage design of doom, Mr. Beckett is getting an intelligent hearing. This is how he feels. The actors have given him the privilege of saying what he feels with no equivocating. No one on the stage is asking him to be reasonable.

A SAFE HAVEN ON COMMERCE STREET

The Living Theatre

BORN IN 1947 in the living room of an Upper West Side apartment, the Living Theatre, founded by husband-and-wife duo Julian Beck and Judith Malina, became one of the most influential avant-garde theater companies of the twentieth century.

Their long-term lease at Cherry Lane Theatre began in 1951 and gave the company their first theatrical home, where they staged poetic dramas, including Gertrude Stein's *Doctor Faustus Lights the Lights* (1951), and proto-absurdist comedies, including Alfred Jarry's *Ubu the King* (1952)—although the latter was abruptly closed by the fire department, supposedly due to the flammable materials used onstage. The inspection and subsequent shuttering of the production was understood as a veiled attempt to silence the Living Theatre and their bohemian influence. According to Cherry Lane lore, Judith Malina chased the fire inspector out of the theater and down Commerce Street with a bamboo spear, a stage prop from *Ubu*. Unhappy with the tensions brought by the often disorganized troupe, Kenneth Carroad, then the owner of Cherry Lane, decided to end their lease and expel the troupe in 1952. The group struggled throughout the rest of the decade with meager finances and an itinerant existence, producing little-known and experimental work that failed to find an audience.

The Living Theatre's breakout success came with the 1959 production of *The Connection*, a drama about drug addiction by Jack Gelber, which toured in Europe, followed by Kenneth H. Brown's *The Brig* (1963), a play depicting the military as brutally dehumanizing. The political views of Beck, Malina, and others in the group tended toward nonviolent political protest and anarchy. Despite their growing notoriety, the company was

RIGHT
Portrait of Julian Beck photographed by Carl Van Vechten. August 22, 1951.

OPPOSITE
Helen Jacobs (*left*) and Judith Malina (*right*) in a production of Gertrude Stein's *Ladies Voices*, photographed by Carl Van Vechten. August 22, 1951.

A SAFE HAVEN ON COMMERCE STREET

OPPOSITE
Production stills of *Doctor Faustus Lights the Lights* by Gertrude Stein. Photographs by Carl Van Vechten. *Clockwise from top left*: Remy Charlip as the Viper, Louis Spencer as Boy and Girl, Donald Marye as Doctor Faustus, Sudie Bond as Dog, and Michael Wright as Chorus. December 7, 1951.

BELOW
Promotional material for the Living Theatre's full season at Cherry Lane featuring *Doctor Faustus Lights the Lights* by Gertrude Stein, *Beyond the Mountains* by Kenneth Rexroth, and *Faustina* by Paul Goodman. 1951.

continually plagued by financial mismanagement and precarity, ultimately resulting in Beck and Malina being tried, convicted, and briefly jailed for violating tax law.

Following their release from prison, Beck, Malina, and members of the company set off for voluntary exile in Europe in 1964, where their work grew increasingly radical in its desire to abolish the boundary between art and life, performer and audience. This ethos was best embodied by *Paradise Now* (1968), a four- to five-hour ritual and performance spectacle involving nudity, drugs, and audience confrontation. The experimental piece aimed to spark an anarchic revolution during which spectators and performers alike could ascend a ladder to paradise.

The group performed throughout the twentieth century. Beck died in 1985 and Malina continued their legacy with new partners until her death in 2015. Today, the company is guided by Garrick Beck, son of Julian and Judith.

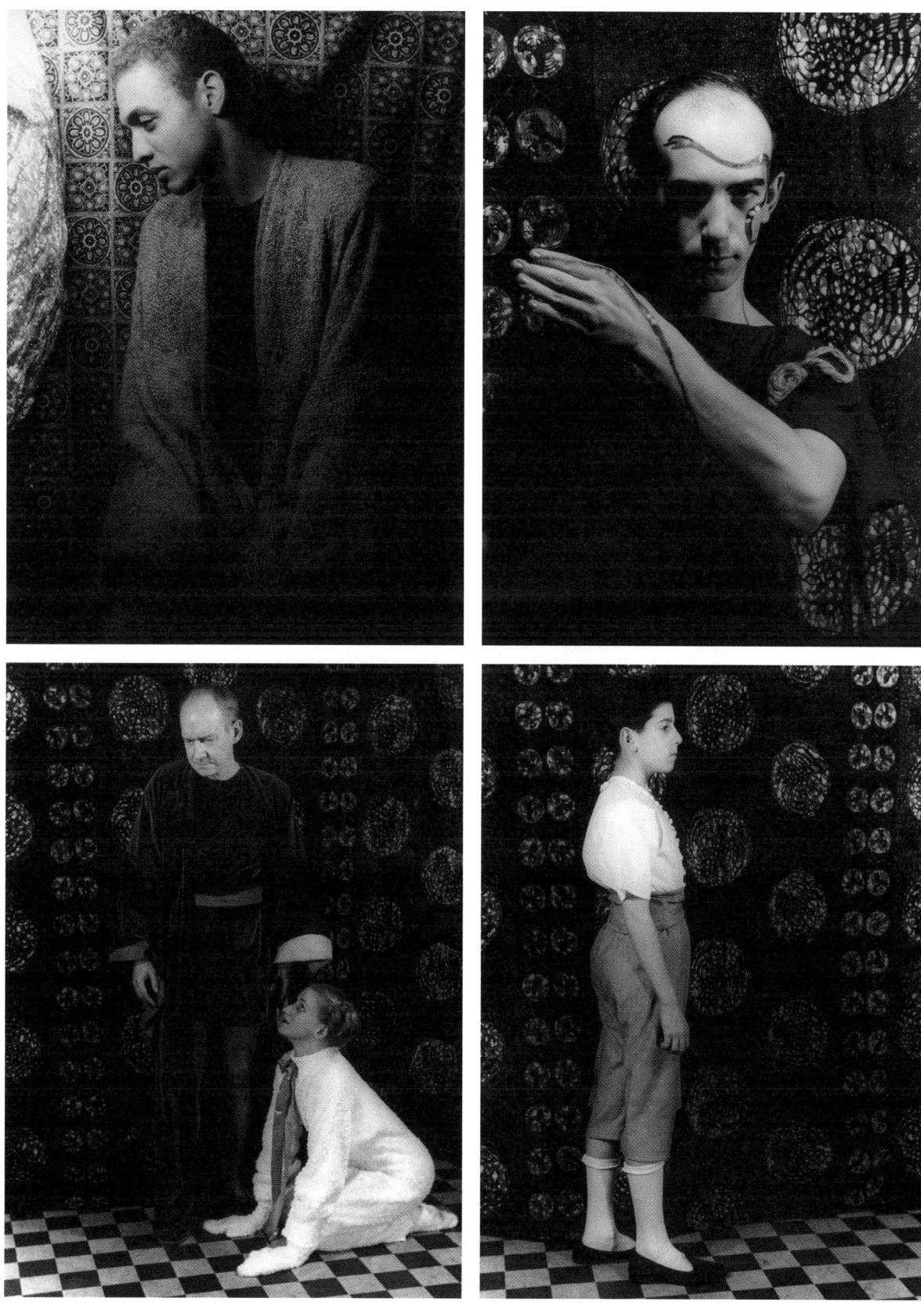

ABOVE
Poster artwork for *Ubu the King*. 1952.

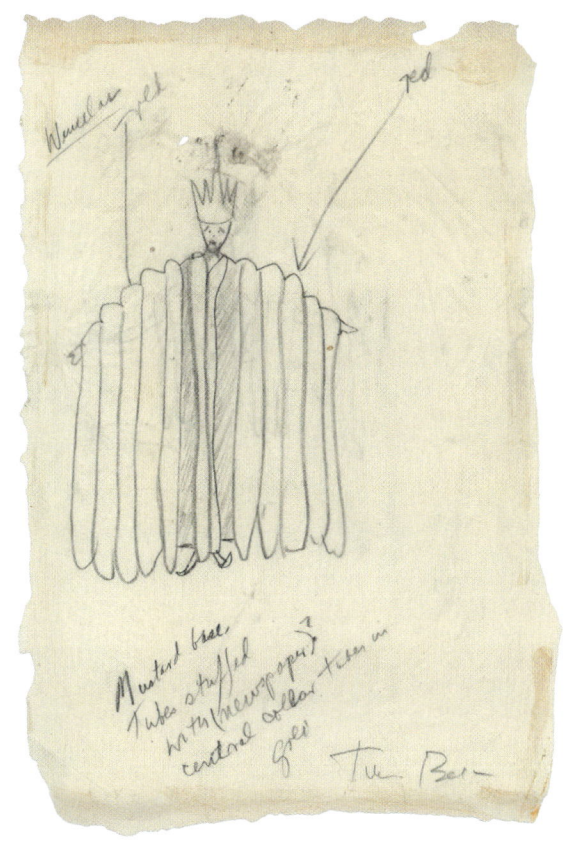

ABOVE
Poster artwork for *Ubu the King*. 1952.

RIGHT
Costume sketch by Julian Beck for the character Wenceslas in *Ubu the King*. August 1952.

A SAFE HAVEN ON COMMERCE STREET

ABOVE
A chart for *Paradise Now* conceived by Julian Beck and Judith Malina to illustrate the structure of the production and handed out to the audience. It is designed to be read horizontally from left to right, then vertically. "This chart is the map. The essential trip is the voyage from the many to the one. The plot is the revolution." 1968.

OPPOSITE
Production stills from *Paradise Now*. After its premiere at the Festival d'Avignon in France, the festival banned the company from performing the play again as scheduled. The production then traveled across Europe with stops including London and Berlin. 1968.

A SAFE HAVEN ON COMMERCE STREET

James Dean Doodles

IN THE 1950s, Cherry Lane Theatre hosted a number of productions staged by two local schools: the Dramatic Workshop, founded by Erwin Piscator and incubated by the New School for Social Research beginning in 1940, and the Actors Studio, founded by Elia Kazan, Cheryl Crawford, and Bobby Lewis in 1947. Given their proximity, the two schools had a lot of crossover among their students and staff. Lee Strasberg, who helmed the Actors Studio beginning in 1951, was also a faculty member of the New School; Judith Malina, cofounder of the Living Theatre, was also a drama professor at the New School.

Teachers, students, and playwrights from these schools called Cherry Lane their home. This included a young James Dean while he was a student at the Actors Studio. Photos from a 1954 reading of Sophocles's *Women of Trachis*, translated by Ezra Pound and staged by Eli Wallach and Julie Harris, show Dean and Wallach on the Cherry Lane stage, along with castmates Anne Jackson, Adelaide Klein, Earle Montgomery, and Joseph Sullivan. The show was produced by the New School.

During downtime on set, Dean liked to doodle on the backs of his theater programs—this one is from *Women of Trachis*.

RIGHT
James Dean (*right*) sits on stage with Eli Wallach (*left*) at a Cherry Lane rehearsal. Photograph by Roy Schatt. 1954.

OPPOSITE
Doodles by James Dean on the back of the *Women of Trachis* flyer. 1954.

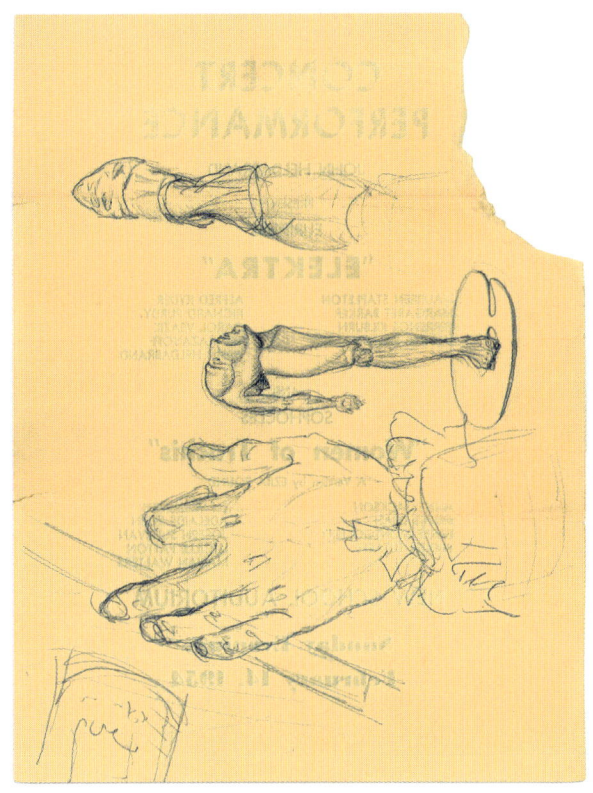
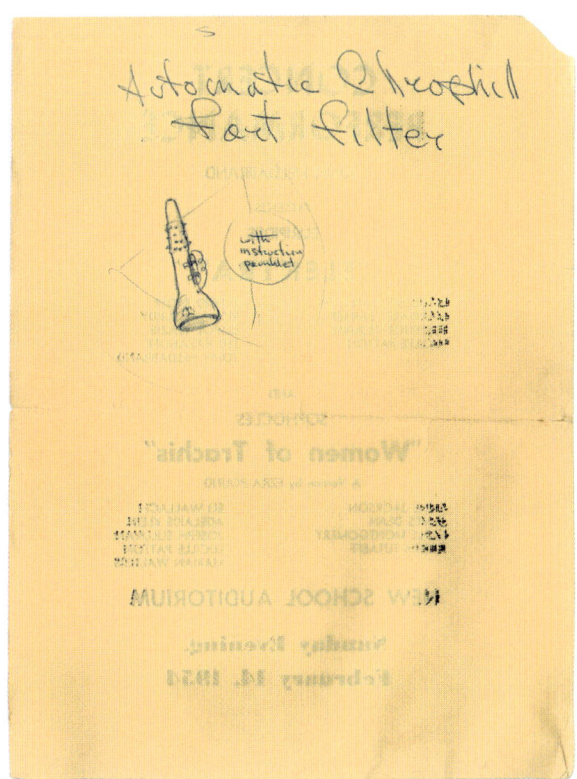

A SAFE HAVEN ON COMMERCE STREET

NEW SCHOOL FOR SOCIAL RESEARCH - 66 West Twelfth Street, New York 11, N. Y.

PLAY READINGS #1   JOHN HELDABRAND (co-ordinator)

Program for Sunday evening, February 14, 8-11 PM

Euripides'
ELECTRA*

(The Cast in order of speaking)

PEASANT (Electra's husband)	TED KAZANOFF
ELECTRA	MAUREEN STAPLETON
ORESTES	ALFRED RYDER
WOMEN OF ARGOS	(CAROL VEAZIE
	(LUCILLE PATTON
OLD MAN	RICHARD PURDY
MESSENGER	TERRANCE KILBURN
CLYTEMNESTRA	MARGARET BARKER
CASTOR	JOHN HELDABRAND

Directed by EDWARD G. GREER

(ELECTRA will be read without Intermission)

INTERMISSION
15 minutes

Sophokles'
WOMEN OF TRACHIS
A version by EZRA POUND**

DAYSAIR	ANNE JACKSON
NURSE	ADELAIDE KLEIN
HYLLOS	JAMES DEAN
GIRLS OF TRACHIS	(LUCILLE PATTON
	(JUDITH TUTAEFF
	(MARRIAN WALTERS
A MESSENGER	JOSEPH SULLIVAN
LIKHAS	EARLE MONTGOMERY
HERAKLES ZEUSON	ELI WALLACH

Directed by HOWARD O. SACKLER

Instrumentalists in WOMEN OF TRACHIS: Cello
                                                           Tympany

Assistants to Director: JEFF LONG, BARBARA BRAND

* Translated by Gilbert Murray
** Copyright 1953, by Hudson Review, Inc.
    Reading by permission of Hudson Review

OPPOSITE
Playbill for the New School for
Social Research's reading of
Sophocles's *Women of Trachis*
with James Dean playing Hyllos.
February 14, 1954.

ABOVE
The full cast of *Women of Trachis*
rehearses at Cherry Lane.
Photograph by Roy Schatt. 1954.

A Curious Evening with Gypsy Rose Lee

ON OCTOBER 24, 1960, *A Curious Evening with Gypsy Rose Lee* opened for a limited three-night run at Cherry Lane Theatre. The format, described in the promotional materials as "a silent film on her life, assembled and narrated by Miss Lee herself," gave audiences a rare peek at the legendary burlesque entertainer's archive of personal films and photos. "She sits on a stool and there is the throaty voice, the statuesque figure, the good humor and the abundant charm," writes Milton Esterow in the *New York Times* review. "On the screen unfolds the saga of Gypsy—completely bare at the age of 1, when she took top prize in a beauty contest, to the world of diamond bracelets, bubble baths and bonbons."

The performance followed the success of Lee's 1957 book, *Gypsy: A Memoir*, which was then adapted by Stephen Sondheim, Jule Styne, and Arthur Laurents into the hit Broadway musical *Gypsy* in 1959. After its brief stint at Cherry Lane, *A Curious Evening* transferred to the Mayfair Theatre on Broadway in 1961. Despite the fact that she made her name and fortune elevating the art of striptease, Lee's one-woman show was panned by *The New York Times* for lacking tension, "a cross between a documentary and an intellectual strip teaser's home movies."

RIGHT
Gypsy Rose Lee started her stage career as a child, dancing in vaudeville acts. 1922.

ABOVE
Gypsy Rose Lee on the road with a Rolls Royce and showgirls. 1957.

RIGHT
Striptease certificate for Gypsy Rose Lee issued by Minsky's Theatre. 1937.

A SAFE HAVEN ON COMMERCE STREET

Gyp No Strip

Gypsy Rose Lee comes to the Cherry Lane tomorrow night but not for reasons of old. Instead of disrobing, she'll show and comment upon films (both still and in motion) depicting various stages of her career. The offering, titled "A Curious Evening With Gypsy Rose Lee," will be repeated on the following two Mondays.

ABOVE TOP
Publicity photograph of Gypsy Rose Lee in the stage production *Star and Garter*. Photograph by Florence Vandamm, a British photographer who became the official photographer for the Theatre Guild. Vandamm shot over two thousand theatrical productions over her five-decade career. 1943.

ABOVE BOTTOM
A Curious Evening with Gypsy Rose Lee at Cherry Lane announced in the *Daily News*. October 23, 1960.

OPPOSITE TOP
Gypsy Rose Lee signing an autograph outside the Mayfair Theatre during the Broadway run of *A Curious Evening with Gypsy Rose Lee*. 1961.

OPPOSITE BOTTOM
Jerome Robbins, Stephen Sondheim, Gypsy Rose Lee, Arthur Laurents, and Jule Styne during rehearsals for the stage production *Gypsy*. Photograph by Friedman-Abeles. 1959.

A SAFE HAVEN ON COMMERCE STREET

Endgame
1958

WRITTEN BY
Samuel Beckett

DIRECTED BY
Alan Schneider

PRODUCED BY
Noel Behn and
Rooftop Productions

WITH
Alvin Epstein
P. J. Kelly
Lester Rawlins
Nydia Westman

SCENIC DESIGN BY
David Hays

MAKING ITS AMERICAN PREMIERE at Cherry Lane Theatre in 1958, Samuel Beckett's *Endgame* is an absurdist meditation on human suffering, survival, and the meaninglessness of life. Set in a nondescript room, *Endgame* revolves around a family as they navigate living in an inhospitable, dystopian wasteland. Hamm is a cruel, blind, chairbound crank; his parents, Nagg and Nell, are both legless and living in trash cans; Clov, the only able-bodied person of the family, was taken in by Hamm as a child. Through bleak humor and nonsensical utterances, Beckett weaves together the horror of a world that is full of death and nothingness. "Nature has forgotten us," Hamm declares. Clov corrects him, replying, "There's no more nature."

Much has been written about Beckett's disillusionment following the trauma of World War II. "Apparently, [*Endgame*] is somewhere between life and death, and the time is just short of the night of the earth's last whimper," Brooks Atkinson wrote in his 1958 *New York Times* review of the Cherry Lane production. As the title of the play alludes, there is a sense that the characters are mere chess pieces in the final stages of a game, headed toward an inevitable defeat. As a key figure in the development of the theater of the absurd, Beckett had an undeniable influence on modern theater; he received the Nobel Prize in Literature in 1969, and he considered *Endgame* his masterpiece.

OPPOSITE
Press photo of Lester Rawlins as Hamm (*left*) and Alvin Epstein as Clov (*right*) in the Cherry Lane production of *Endgame*. Photograph by Gjon Mili/The LIFE Picture Collection. 1958.

A SAFE HAVEN ON COMMERCE STREET

OPPOSITE
Press photo by Gjon Mili/The LIFE Picture Collection. 1958.

ABOVE
Production still by Alix Jeffry. 1958.

A New Generation Takes the Stage

5

THE 1960s were an undeniably tumultuous decade in American life and culture, defined by growing social movements (civil rights, Black power, women's liberation, Pride, anti-war protests) and a seismic countercultural shift. It was the age of Dylan and folk music, of Warhol and pop art, and New York City, specifically Greenwich Village, served as the hub for bohemian artists of all disciplines.

This was an extraordinarily fertile period at the little theater on Commerce Street, where dozens of new, groundbreaking works were staged each year. Heavily influenced by the theater of the absurd movement, which began in postwar Europe, the productions of this era are characterized by an anti-realist aesthetic and an avant-garde sensibility.

Although theater of the absurd was never a formally organized movement, the bizarre, genre-defying plays written by playwrights such as Samuel Beckett, Eugène Ionesco, Harold Pinter, and others in the late 1950s and 1960s would quickly come to inhabit this new moniker. These plays shared similarities such as nonlinear plots, nonsensical language, generalized settings, and archetypal characters not seen in more traditional or realistic plays. According to Edward Albee, the only American playwright in the bunch, "The word absurd is not to be construed to mean ridiculous. Instead, it denotes what its practitioners regard as the contemporary human condition." At a time when nuclear warfare was still a recent memory, it felt natural to foreground the futility and fundamental absurdity of the human experience.

Albee's first plays, including *The American Dream*, *The Zoo Story*, and *The Sandbox*, all had productions at Cherry Lane during this time as part of the 1962 *Theatre of the Absurd* festival, put up by Theater 1962, a producing collective formed by Albee and two professional partners, Richard Barr and Clinton Wilder. *The Sandbox* appeared alongside a formidable list of plays by European playwrights, including Samuel Beckett, Jean Genet, and Eugène Ionesco.

In order to nurture a new generation of playwrights, Albee, Barr, and Wilder formed the Albarwild Playwrights Unit (a portmanteau of their last names), giving scores of young American writers mentorship, networking opportunities, and a venue to present their works. The list of playwrights whose work was staged at Cherry Lane during this decade reads as a roster

PAGE 115
Lee Kissman as Young Man in Sam Shepard's *Up to Thursday*, presented by Albarwild's Theater 1965 Evening of New Playwrights. February 1965.

OPPOSITE
Publicity photo of Harold Pinter under the Cherry Lane awning. 1962.

A NEW GENERATION TAKES THE STAGE

BELOW
Showcard featuring a young Edward Albee. Photograph by Alix Jeffry. 1964.

OPPOSITE TOP
Playwrights Sam Shepard, Paul Foster, and Lanford Wilson in front of the Cherry Lane awning. Photograph by Alix Jeffry. Jeffry moved to New York from Chicago in 1952 and began documenting off-Broadway theater and performances. Much of her work from the 1950s and 1960s captures the early productions of Edward Albee. 1964.

OPPOSITE BOTTOM
A "family" portrait from the workshop production of *Dutchman* by LeRoi Jones, produced by Theater 1964 and Albarwild's Playwrights Unit. *Seated, foreground*: principal actors Al Freeman Jr. and Jennifer West. *Standing*: LeRoi Jones (later known as Amiri Baraka) and Edward Albee. *Seated, background*: Edward Parone, director, centered; extras are seated around him. Photograph by Alix Jeffry. 1964.

of luminaries of twentieth-century American theater: LeRoi Jones (later known as Amiri Baraka), Adrienne Kennedy, Lorraine Hansberry, Lanford Wilson, Sam Shepard, Terrence McNally, A. R. Gurney, and more. With Albarwild, Cherry Lane Theatre secured its enduring legacy as an incubator that nurtured experimental work and new talent.

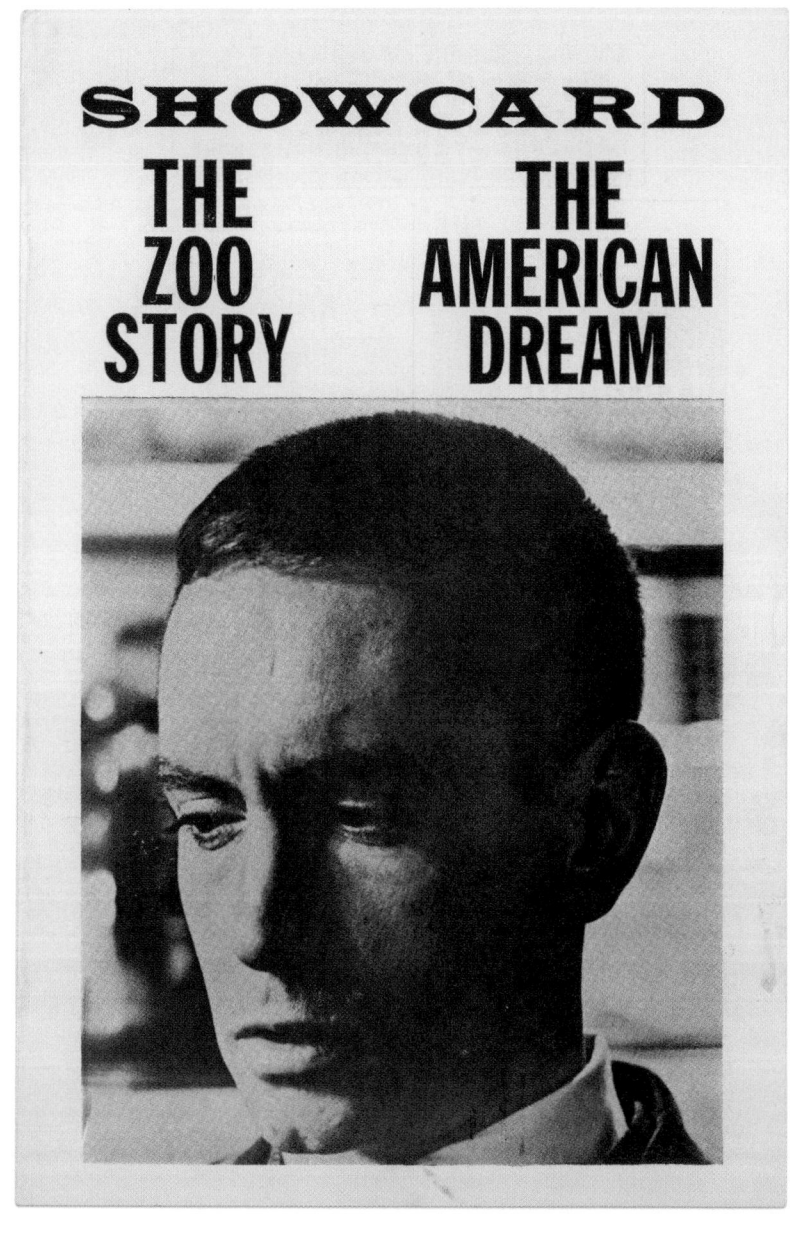

A NEW GENERATION TAKES THE STAGE

OPPOSITE
Gene Hackman and James Coco in the stage production *The Basement*. Photograph by Friedman-Abeles. 1967.

ABOVE
Illustration by William Auerbach-Levy of James Earl Jones as Jesse Prince and Royce Wallace as Marianne Prince in the Cherry Lane production of *The Pretender* by Lionel Abel. 1960.

WITH a stern woodcut of Bertold Brecht staring down at him, Edward Albee lounged on a comfortable sofa in his W. 12th St. apartment — complete with plants, modern art, and three cats — and reported that it took a "quadruple play" to get his first play, "The Zoo Story," staged.

Albee, now 33, had just finished two and a half years as a Western Union messenger boy in the spring of 1958. "I was pushing 30. And I felt I hadn't done anything with my life," Albee said. "My play, 'The Zoo Story,' was going to change all that. I finished it during the summer and sent it to several Broadway producers. In essence, they said, 'It's interesting, but why don't you send us your work when you've written a full-length play?'"

At the suggestion of a composer friend, William Flanagan, Albee sent his script to composer David Diamond in Italy. Diamond sent the play on to Pincus Braun in Zurich. Braun liked the script so much he made a tape recording of the two-character play and sent it, along with the script, to a woman named Hunzinger who ran the drama department of a publishing house in Germany.

"Zoo" was finally staged in Germany as part of a double bill which included Samuel Beckett's "Krapp's Last Tape." Six months after he had written the play, Albee found himself sitting in the opening night audience, a $400 advance in his pocket. It was September, 1959, and he was feeling completely frustrated.

"I couldn't make any sense out of my play at all," Albee said. "I don't understand German. But every opening night is like that. I don't hear or see anything..."

From Germany, the twin bill went on to play 582 performances off-Broadway. "Zoo" is still playing in repertory at the Cherry Lane — along with other Albee plays, such as "The Sandbox" and "The American Dream."

Albee has turned down eight offers to make "Zoo" into a movie. "They won't let me have script control," he says. He won't be staged on Broadway for the

Edward Albee
He lives to write.

same reason. "Uptown, the playwright is the last man in the theatre. It shouldn't be that way..."

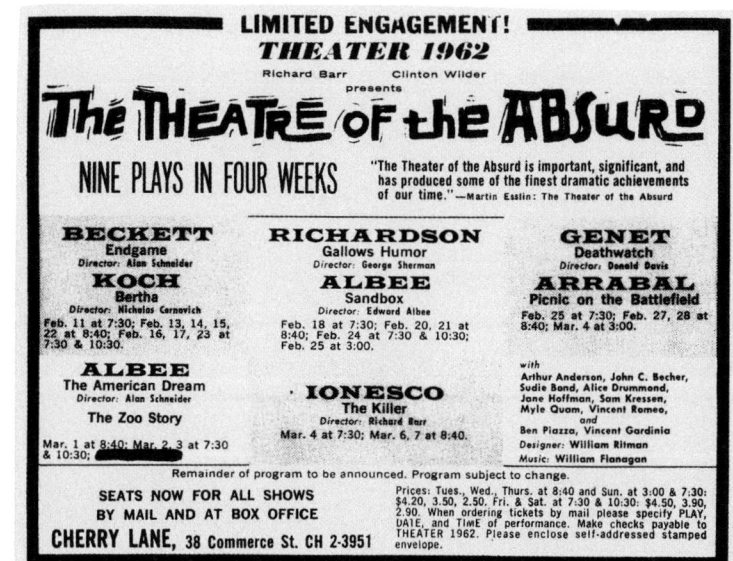

Alix Jeffrey

"KRAPP'S LAST TAPE" — George Bartenieff, in the title role, strains to hear his tape. The play is given with "Zoo Story" at the Cherry Lane Theater.

OPPOSITE LEFT
Edward Albee profiled for *The Daily News*. The caption under his photo declares, "He lives to write." March 11, 1962.

OPPOSITE TOP RIGHT
Newspaper ad for Theater 1962's *Theatre of the Absurd* showcase at Cherry Lane. February 1962.

OPPOSITE BOTTOM RIGHT
Photo of George Bartenieff in *Krapp's Last Tape* by Samuel Beckett. Photograph by Alix Jeffry. 1965.

ABOVE
Production still from Edward Albee's *The Sandbox*. Photograph by Alix Jeffry. 1962.

Albarwild

By Dr. Natka Bianchini

ALBARWILD THEATRE ARTS, Incorporated, was *not* named, as it may seem, for some Middle Earth character straight out of Tolkien, but as a portmanteau of the last names of its three founders: Edward Albee (1928–2016), Richard Barr (1917–1989), and Clinton Wilder (1920–1986). This collaboration—between two leading theatrical producers and the Pulitzer Prize–winning American playwright they're credited with discovering—dominated one of the most generative decades in Cherry Lane's history. It also included the development workshop the Playwrights Unit, which Albarwild ran from 1961 to 1971, and which remains one of its most significant legacies.

Barr's and Wilder's theatrical careers had inauspicious beginnings. As young, Ivy League–educated men, both aspired to a professional life in the theater—Barr as an actor and then a director, and Wilder, who had terrible stage fright, as a stage manager. Neither found much success in those early roles. During a trip to Europe, Barr experienced firsthand works by the burgeoning avant-garde playwrights of the late 1950s: Samuel Beckett, Eugène Ionesco, Jean Genet, and Fernando Arrabal. He longed to be the first to produce that type of work for American audiences, who were accustomed to the kitchen-sink realism and domestic dramas prevalent at the time. A colleague handed him a copy of Albee's first play, called *The Zoo Story*, a curious piece with two actors that takes place on a bench in Central Park, which was having its world premiere at the Schiller Theater in Berlin. Barr immediately acquired the rights to produce it in the United States and presented it on a double bill along with Beckett's *Krapp's Last Tape* at the Provincetown Playhouse in 1960, an event that became a landmark in off-Broadway history: The double bill ran for more than eighteen months and nearly six hundred performances. It cemented Barr's reputation as a major producer, introduced Edward Albee to American audiences, and caught the attention of Wilder, who agreed to join Barr in producing Albee's next play, *The American Dream*, at Cherry Lane.

On the heels of these successes, the Playwrights Unit was born. The three men combined forces (and some of their personal funds) to create a formal program where emerging playwrights could be mentored and their work professionally staged. Barr and Wilder shared a vision of off Broadway as a training ground for new work. "I wanted to do what was not possible on Broadway. Give authority to the playwright. Turn the theatre back to the playwright," Barr remarked.[1] The Playwrights Unit created a professional workshop series dedicated to the cultivation of new work. For many young playwrights, it was one of the only places they could hope to have their work properly staged at a real theater, as opposed to the basement cafés or Greenwich Village storefronts that were common at that time in the semiprofessional off-off-Broadway ecosystem.

The Playwrights Unit was unique in the amount of control it gave to the playwrights—most of the developmental programs for young writers that existed at the time were run by actors or directors. "We hope the

OPPOSITE
Albarwild (*from left to right*) — Edward Albee, Clinton Wilder, and Richard Barr — in front of the Playwrights Unit at the Village South Theatre. Photograph by Alix Jeffry. 1968.

---

1   David Crespy, *Richard Barr: The Playwright's Producer* (Southern Illinois University Press, 2013), 79.

OPPOSITE TOP
George Grizzard, Uta Hagen, and Arthur Hill in the Broadway production of Edward Albee's *Who's Afraid of Virginia Woolf?*, produced by Richard Barr and Clinton Wilder at the Billy Rose Theatre. Photograph by Friedman-Abeles. 1962.

OPPOSITE BOTTOM
Leslie Rivers as the Mother, Ellen Holly as the Duchess of Hapsburg, Cynthia Belgrave as Queen Victoria, and Norman Bush as Jesus in the Albarwild production of Adrienne Kennedy's *Funnyhouse of a Negro*. Photograph by Alix Jeffry. 1964.

playwrights themselves will dictate the operation," said Albee. "What we're going to do is to provide a theatre to work in, a stage, actors, a director, whatever we can do to be helpful. We are not going to say anything about the kind of work that should be done. If a man wants to do something that seems completely incomprehensible to us, fine."[2]

Albarwild took out a five-year lease on Cherry Lane in August 1962 and used the theater as the home base of the Playwrights Unit, often producing readings of new work on Monday evenings, the traditional dark day in professional theater. While the innovation and creativity of off Broadway fueled them, they simultaneously produced work on Broadway as well. In fact, it was the success of Albee's *Who's Afraid of Virginia Woolf?*, a major Broadway hit for Barr and Wilder in the fall of 1962, that kept the Playwrights Unit funded for several years.

The Playwrights Unit was committed to producing diverse voices. Two early successes: *Dutchman* by LeRoi Jones (later Amiri Baraka) and *Funnyhouse of a Negro* by Adrienne Kennedy were staged in 1964. These plays, which debuted during the civil rights movement, ask probing questions about the nature of race and identity in the United States; both won awards at that year's Obie Awards. Actor Robert Hooks, who originated the role of Clay in *Dutchman*, subsequently founded the Negro Ensemble Company in 1967—one of the first professional theatrical groups in the country run by and for Black people.

All three members of Albarwild identified as gay men. In this pre-Stonewall era, the degree to which each was open about that aspect of their identity differed. Nonetheless, their own lived experiences outside the mainstream undoubtedly influenced their desire to champion work by writers exploring challenging topics and less traditional worlds.

Running the Playwrights Unit was costly, and the trio hoped to replicate the *Who's Afraid of Virginia Woolf?* model with subsequent Albee premieres on Broadway, using the profits to continue to fund the Unit. The trouble was, with the exception of *A Delicate Balance* in 1966, Albee did not produce a reliable hit for decades. Several expensive failures hastened the end of the program, which limped along in the second half of its decade-long existence before finally shuttering after the 1971 Broadway flop of Albee's *All Over*.

Despite its brief tenure, the Playwrights Unit created a lasting impact. In its final year, director Robert Moss served as the Unit's managing director. When the program disbanded, he took the Unit's mailing list, then housed in a shoebox, and founded Playwrights Horizons, a professional theater in Manhattan dedicated to the development of contemporary American playwrights, which still exists today. Closer to home, the Mentor Project at Cherry Lane, which began under Angelina Fiordellisi in 1998, is a direct descendant of the Playwrights Unit.

---

2   Crespy, *Richard Barr*, 124.

A NEW GENERATION TAKES THE STAGE

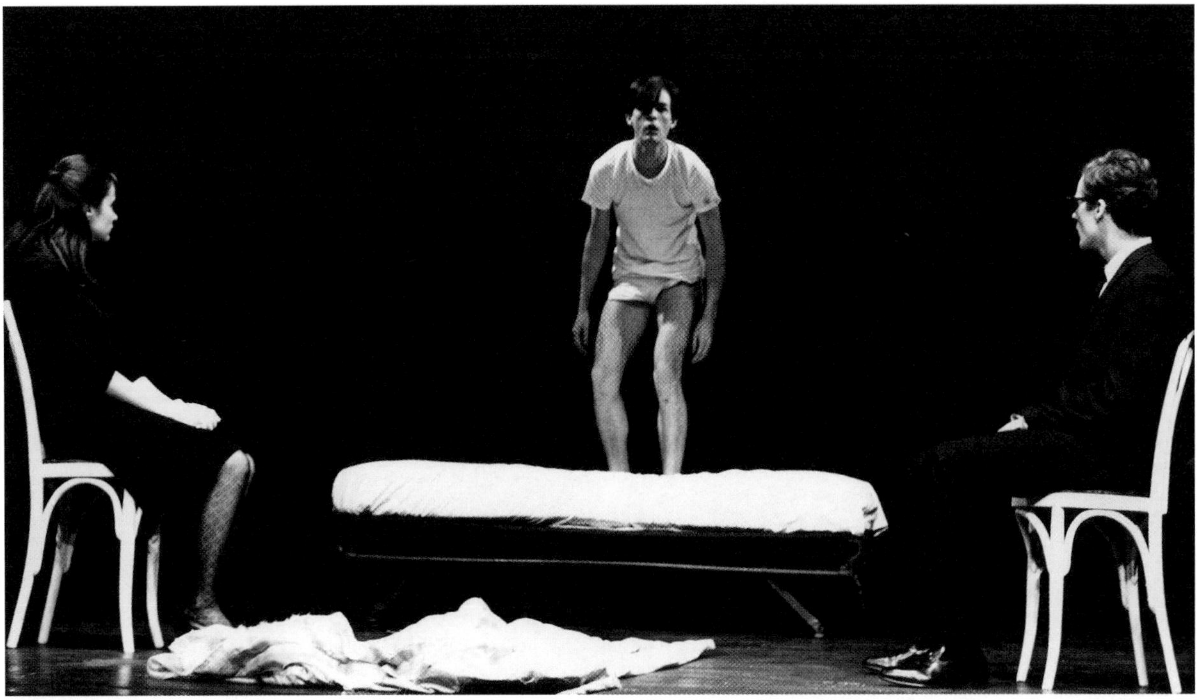

CHERRY LANE THEATRE

Trio of 1-Acters at Cherry Lane

By LEONARD HARRIS
Of the World-Telegram Staff

Weird. Funny. Self-Conscious.

Three one-act plays, ranging from the absurd to the ridiculous, were presented at the Cherry Lane Theater last night by Theater 1965, the producing entity that comprises Richard Barr, Clinton Wilder and Edward Albee.

They are the first of several programs in which Theater 1965 will introduce the works of 10 new playwrights. I think we're in for some fun.

"Balls" is a weird opus by Paul Foster, who is 33; "Up to Thursday" a funny bit of symmetry by Sam Shepard, 21, and "Home Free!" a self-conscious piece of pathology by 26-year-old Lanford Wilson.

In "Balls," the only things visible on-stage are two ping-pong balls suspended from strings. Swinging from side to side, they appear from the wings, are drawn slowly to

Sam Shepard
"Up to Thursday"

the center until they almost touch and then separate and disappear into the wings.

They represent two dead men in their graves, heard as off-stage voices. Other voices are heard, but the stage is untouched by human feet.

Foster achieves some fascinating verbal effects, but why he deliberately chooses to sacrifice the visual impact a stage piece should have is beyond me. A second drawback is the sound system, which, in making the voices sepulchral, occasionally makes them inaudible as well.

"Up to Thursday" is the evening's success. Delightfully nonsensical, uninhibitedly committed to absurdity, it is graphic, humorous and neatly geometric.

* * *

And it is visual. Where you have to strain forward to reach for Foster's opener, Shepard's "Up to Thursday" leaps off the stage to entertain you. It even has people on-stage, and they are all excellent, particularly Lee Kissman, Joyce Aaron, Stephanie Gordon, Robert F. Lyons and Kevin O'Connor.

"Home Free!" is a shapeless, self-conscious attempt at amorality. Reminiscent of Jean Cocteau's "Les Enfants Terribles,"—brother and sister live together and play their own secret game — it tries to shock shock shock by being sick sick sick.

* * *

It tries too hard and the effort sticks out all over. The sister is pregnant by the brother — and they're not even married. They speak to two fey, hallucinatory creatures. And into all these pseudo-weirdo antics, Wilson is not above tossing whatever pedestrian jokes come to mind.

Five years ago Barr and Wilder discovered Albee. Now the three are on another talent hunt. I suggest you join them. There aren't too many Albees extant, but the woods still yield some rare fauna.

OPPOSITE TOP
Lee Kissman as Young Man in Sam Shepard's *Up to Thursday*, presented by Albarwild's Theater 1965 Evening of New Playwrights. February 1965.

OPPOSITE BOTTOM
Production still from Edward Albee's *The Zoo Story*, produced by Richard Barr and Clinton Wilder. 1963–65.

ABOVE
Review of Theater 1965's triple-bill presentation at Cherry Lane, which included Sam Shepard's (*pictured*) *Up to Thursday*. World Telegram. 1965.

RIGHT
Showcard for three one-act plays by Thornton Wilder presented by Albarwild at Cherry Lane. 1966.

OPPOSITE
Production stills from *The Long Christmas Dinner* (top row), *Queens of France* (middle row), and *The Happy Journey to Trenton and Camden* (bottom row). Photographs by Alix Jeffry. 1966.

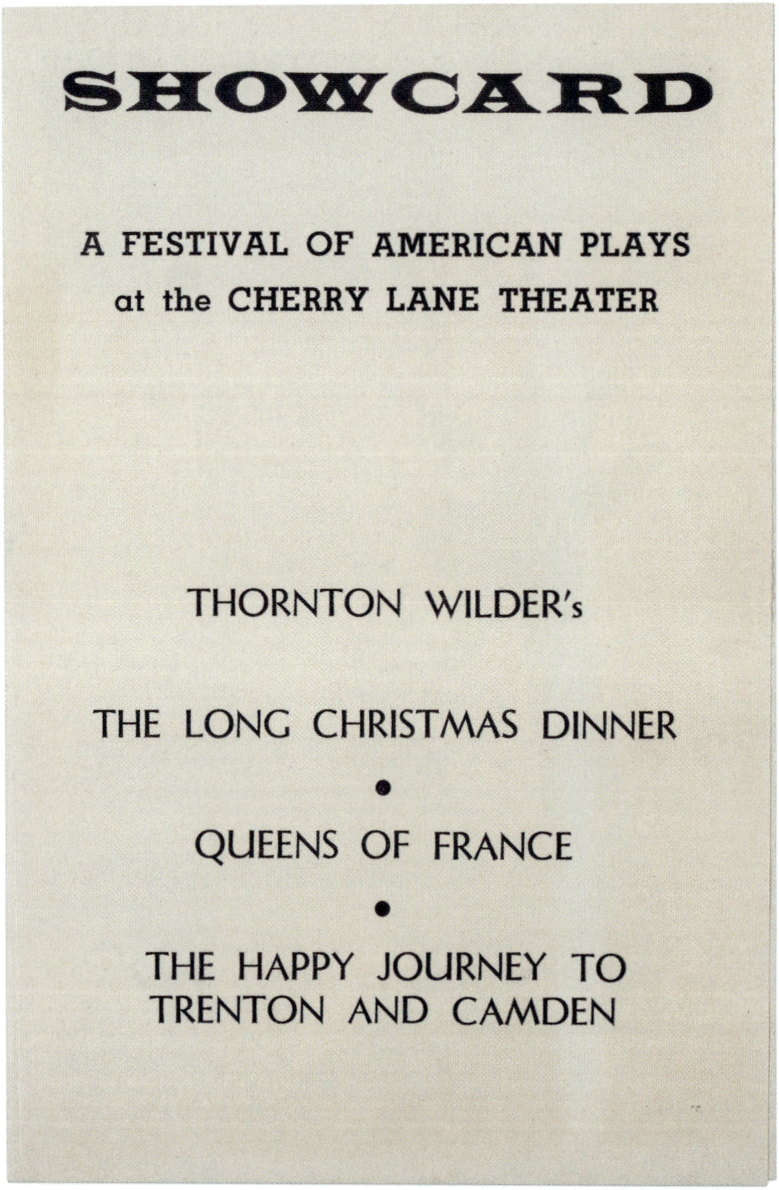

SHOWCARD

A FESTIVAL OF AMERICAN PLAYS at the CHERRY LANE THEATER

THORNTON WILDER's

THE LONG CHRISTMAS DINNER

•

QUEENS OF FRANCE

•

THE HAPPY JOURNEY TO TRENTON AND CAMDEN

A NEW GENERATION TAKES THE STAGE

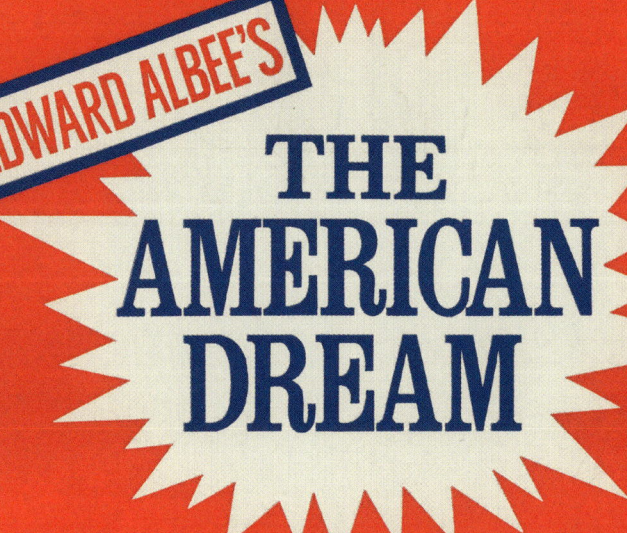

OPPOSITE AND RIGHT
Posters promoting double bills from Theater 1964 (*left*) and Theater 1965 (*right*) at Cherry Lane.

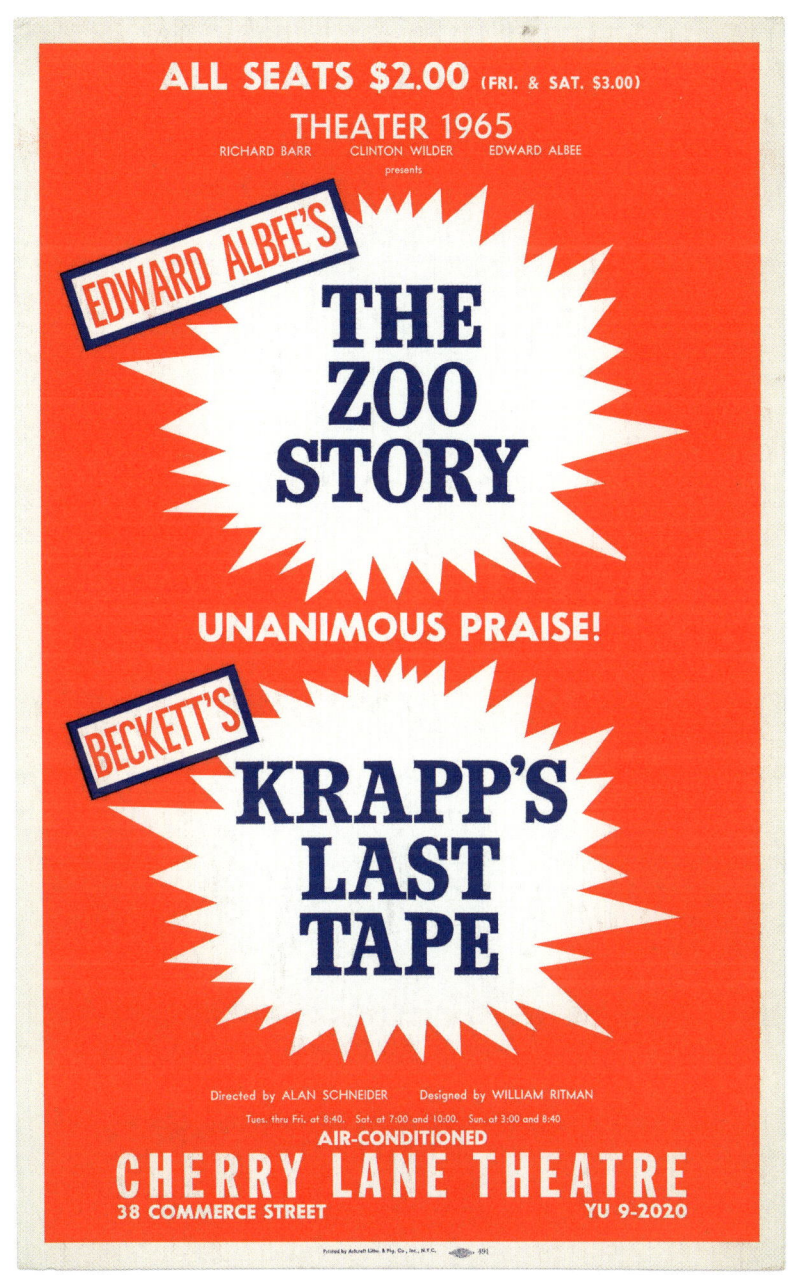

The American Dream
1962

WRITTEN BY
Edward Albee

DIRECTED BY
Alan Schneider

PRODUCED BY
Theater 1962

WITH
John C. Becher
Sudie Bond
Alice Drummond
Jane Hoffman
Ben Piazza

"Is the play offensive? I certainly hope so; it was my intention to offend—as well as amuse and entertain. Is it nihilist, immoral, defeatist? Well, to that let me answer that *The American Dream* is a picture of our time—as I see it of course."

—Edward Albee, preface to *The American Dream* and *The Zoo Story*

CONSIDERED A LANDMARK WORK in American theater, *The American Dream* by Edward Albee is a seething indictment of America's idolization of the nuclear family, obsession over social standing, and consumerism as a replacement for human connection. The one-act play opens with Mommy and Daddy waiting for the arrival of a visitor and discussing putting Grandma, Mommy's mother, into a nursing home. We soon discover a grotesque history of events that occurred in their home and a dark web of relationships between a series of unexpected visitors, culminating in the arrival of Young Man, whom Grandma refers to as "the American Dream."

First performed at York Playhouse in January 1961, *The American Dream* received mixed reviews from critics—"There was much debate as to whether the work had value," Celine Rafferty wrote for the Edward Albee Society. Despite its uneven start, the play drew a steady crowd and was staged at least five times at Cherry Lane Theatre between 1962 and 1964. Its first appearance there was for Theater 1962's *Theatre of the Absurd* festival in the early spring of 1962. *The American Dream* is often performed in a double bill with *The Zoo Story*, another Albee one-act. The play was revived again at Cherry Lane in the fall of 1962 (by Theater 1963*), included in a double bill with Albee's *The Death of Bessie Smith* (1962), then again with *The Zoo Story* in 1963 (Theater 1964), and with LeRoi Jones's *Dutchman* in the fall of 1964. In 2008 Albee oversaw a revival of the play at Cherry Lane starring Judith Ivey in a double bill with *The Sandbox*, another one-act from 1959.

The American Dream ushered in a new wave in American theater. It was awarded Best Play of 1960–1961 Season by the Foreign Press Association.

OPPOSITE
Publicity photo for *The American Dream* featuring Edward Albee (foreground) and Ben Piazza. Photograph by Friedman-Abeles. 1961.

* Albee and two professional partners, Richard Barr and Clinton Wilder, came together to form a producing collective called Theater 1960, even though it was 1959. Each year on June 30, the collective would change the name to reflect the next year and convey the group as forward-looking and avant-garde, "pushing the year ahead," as Barr recalled

A NEW GENERATION TAKES THE STAGE

ABOVE
Sudie Bond, Nancy Cushman, Ben Piazza, Jane Hoffman, and John C. Becher in a production still from *The American Dream*. Photograph by Friedman-Abeles. 1961.

OPPOSITE
Production still with Jane Hoffman (*left*) and Sudie Bond (*right*) from *The American Dream*. Photograph by Friedman-Abeles. 1961.

A NEW GENERATION TAKES THE STAGE

Dutchman
1964

WRITTEN BY
LeRoi Jones (Amiri Baraka)

DIRECTED BY
Edward Parone

PRODUCED BY
Edward Albee
Richard Barr
Clinton Wilder
with Rita Fredericks

WITH
Robert Hooks
Jennifer West

SCENIC DESIGN BY
William Ritman

SET ON A NEW YORK CITY subway train, *Dutchman* is a political allegory exposing the bitter racial tensions simmering in the shadow of the civil rights movement in mid-1960s America. Developed under the Playwrights Unit, LeRoi Jones's one-act play centers on an explosive encounter between Clay, a young Black man in a three-piece suit, and Lula, a loud, older white woman who preys on Clay in a series of aggressive, erratic interactions that oscillate between flirtatious innuendo and racist insults. The play culminates in a monologue by Clay about double consciousness, a concept introduced by W. E. B. Du Bois that describes the tension of "always looking at one's self through the eyes of others"—the tension of being Black and American.

Despite the fact that Jones felt uncertain whether people would be interested in watching a play about race in New York City, the show went into production and debuted on a triple bill with *Play*, by Samuel Beckett, and *The Two Executioners*, by Fernando Arrabal. Reviews were mixed: Howard Taubman opened his *New York Times* review with "Everything about LeRoi Jones' *Dutchman* is designed to shock . . . it is an explosion of hatred rather than a play." But a month later, Taubman's colleague Lewis Funke wrote a glowing profile of Jones, calling him one to "watch." *Dutchman* won an Obie for Best New American Play in the 1963–64 season.

At the time of its first staging, Jones was twenty-nine years old and known in New York's downtown circles as a poet, writer, and publisher who embodied the consciousness of the emerging Black nationalist movement. The play was also an expression of the politics and social tensions of a larger cohort of thinkers and artists who were working and living in Greenwich Village. While acting in *Dutchman*, Robert Hooks began teaching theater to local Black youths. That early work laid the foundation for the Negro Ensemble Company, which was based at the nearby St. Mark's Playhouse. Hooks cofounded the company with actor and playwright Douglas Turner Ward, whom he met while touring in the road company of Lorraine Hansberry's *A Raisin in the Sun*.

The assassination of Malcolm X in 1965 spurred Jones (along with Askia Touré and others) to found the Black Arts Repertory Theatre/School (BART/S) in Harlem. The program was intended to promote Black self-determination and celebrate Black culture, history, and identity through the dramatic arts and is widely recognized as the first initiative

BELOW
Production still with Robert Hooks as Clay and Jennifer West as Lula in *Dutchman* at Cherry Lane Theatre. Photograph by Alix Jeffry. 1964.

of the Black Arts Movement. To further reflect his Black nationalist identity, Jones changed his name to the Bantu Muslim name Imamu Ameer Baraka (later Amiri Baraka) in 1967. The success of *Dutchman* represents the power of off Broadway as a place for artistic risk-taking and exploring complex, powerful ideas.

Dutchman was reprised at Cherry Lane in 2007.

A NEW GENERATION TAKES THE STAGE

ABOVE
Harvey Selsby, Sue Carol Davis, and Richard Mansfield as passengers in *Dutchman*. Photograph by Alix Jeffry. 1964.

OPPOSITE
Robert Hooks as Clay and Jennifer West as Lula. Photograph by Alix Jeffry. 1964.

A NEW GENERATION TAKES THE STAGE

To Be Young, Gifted and Black: The World of Lorraine Hansberry
1969

ADAPTED BY
Robert Nemiroff

DIRECTED BY
Gene Frankel

PRODUCED BY
Harry Belafonte/Chiz Schultz
Edgar Lansbury

WITH
Barbara Baxley
John Beal
Rita Gardner
Gertrude Jeanette
Janet League
Stephen Strimpell
Cicely Tyson
Andre Womble

SCENIC DESIGN BY
Merrill Sindler

LIGHTING BY
Barry Arnold

SOUND AND PRODUCTION STAGE MANAGEMENT BY
Gigi Cascio

MUSICAL COORDINATION BY
William Eaton

PHOTOGRAPHIC EFFECTS BY
Stuart Bigger

"MY NAME IS LORRAINE HANSBERRY. I am a writer." Adapted from Lorraine Hansberry's unpublished writings, *To Be Young, Gifted and Black* opens with an unembellished statement that unspools into a triumphant ode to the late writer's life and works. After her premature death in 1965, her ex-husband and collaborator Robert Nemiroff collected Hansberry's letters, interviews, poems, and journal entries into a play that charts her life and words from childhood to her death. In 1959, at just twenty-nine, Lorraine Hansberry became the youngest American, the first woman, and the first Black playwright to receive the New York Drama Critics' Circle Award for Best Play of the Year, for her groundbreaking work *A Raisin in the Sun*. She was also the first Black woman playwright to have a show on Broadway.

After *New York Times* journalist Nat Hentoff saw *To Be Young, Gifted and Black* with his school-aged daughter, he reflected on the "kaleidoscopic fusion of autobiography, invention, intentions, doubts, and affirmation." The play "kept us both, for a while after we left, silent and thinking about possibility." With Harry Belafonte as a producer, and a cast list that assembled key players of Black American theater at the time, *To Be Young, Gifted and Black* opened on January 2, 1969, to almost universal praise. The play ran for 380 performances at Cherry Lane Theatre before being adapted to an autobiography and film, as well as memorialized in the civil rights anthem by Nina Simone in a song of the same name.

OPPOSITE
Lorraine Hansberry (*left*) and Nina Simone (*right*) singing together at a benefit event for the Student Nonviolent Coordinating Committee. 1963.

ABOVE
Publicity photo for *To Be Young, Gifted and Black*. Photograph by Martha Swope. 1968–69.

A NEW GENERATION TAKES THE STAGE

CHERRY LANE THEATRE

OPPOSITE
All images from the liner notes of *To Be Young, Gifted and Black*'s three-record album. Caedmon Records (TRS 342). 1971. *From top to bottom*: Bruce Hall, Andre Womble, and Janet League; Micki Grant as the Playwright and Dolores Sutton as Juno; Barbara Baxley and Janet League. 1969.

ABOVE
Cicely Tyson, James Baldwin, a guest, and Harry Belafonte attend the *To Be Young, Gifted and Black* gala at Cherry Lane. Belafonte was a producer for the show. Photograph by Ron Galella. January 2, 1969.

Keeping the House Lights On

CHERRY LANE THEATRE

THE FREE LOVE of the late 1960s soon gave way to the grittier, harsher reality of life in the 1970s. In New York, economic crisis and skyrocketing crime drove nearly a million Manhattanites out to the surrounding suburbs. For those who remained, the city's deterioration was perhaps epitomized by a Times Square packed with strip clubs, sex workers, and illegal drugs. While the commercial theater industry on Broadway suffered, a regional not-for-profit theater movement took shape—creating high-quality, professional venues in cities across the country and shifting the theatrical locus away from New York.

Cherry Lane Theatre persisted during these years under challenging circumstances, with productions closing early, the building falling into disrepair, and general financial precarity threatening its existence. Despite a local newspaper declaring, "Cherry Lane Theatre makes clear . . . that for all intents and purposes, Off Broadway is dead," it continued to house significant artists and productions throughout the decade.

Pulitzer Prize–winning playwright David Mamet made his New York debut at Cherry Lane with the 1976 productions of *Sexual Perversity in Chicago* and *Duck Variations*, both of which featured future Oscar winner F. Murray Abraham. Mamet's explicit scripts resonated with the cultural roughness of the times—and with critics. Both *Sexual Perversity in Chicago* and Mamet's *American Buffalo* won the Obie that year for Best New American Play.

Cherry Lane also staged less challenging fare. The 1971 production of *Godspell*, with music and lyrics by Stephen Schwartz (who composed *Pippin* and, much later, *Wicked*), was a holdover of the late 1960s spirit of the bohemian community. A series of parables based on the Gospel of Matthew, *Godspell* played briefly at La MaMa (an off-off-Broadway theater in the Village), followed by Cherry Lane, before heading to the Promenade, where it ran for an astonishing five years and 2,100-plus performances. During its run at Cherry Lane, production had to make do with the less-than-ideal digs. As Schwartz put it to one interviewer, it was a place where "there was a leak, there were rats running around." Still, the success of his production was one of the few bright spots for the theater during an otherwise difficult time.

PAGE 147
Production still from Stephen Schwartz's *Godspell*. Photograph by Martha Swope. 1971.

OPPOSITE
Models outside Cherry Lane as part of a menswear feature in *The New York Times Magazine*. Photograph by Michael Mauney. September 19, 1976.

RIGHT TOP
David Mamet's *Duck Variations* at Cherry Lane. Paul Sparer (*left*) as Emil Varec and Michael Egan (*right*) as George S. Aronovitz. Photograph by Rena Hansen for *After Dark* magazine. August 1976.

RIGHT BOTTOM
Publicity photo of Michael Egan as George S. Aronovitz and Mike Kellin as Emil Varec for *Duck Variations* at Cherry Lane. 1976.

ABOVE
Cherry Lane's playbill for David Mamet's double bill featuring *Sexual Perversity in Chicago* and *Duck Variations*. 1976.

OPPOSITE
Godspell promotional poster for the Broadway production at Broadhurst Theatre. 1976.

RIGHT
Sonia Manzano, Lamar Alford (kneeling), Stephen Nathan, David Haskell, Herb Braha, and Robin Lamont in *Godspell*. Photograph by Kenn Duncan. 1971.

Godspell
1971

BOOK BY
John-Michael Tebelak

MUSIC AND LYRICS BY
Stephen Schwartz

DIRECTED BY
John-Michael Tebelak

PRODUCED BY
Joseph Beruh
Stuart Duncan
Edgar Lansbury

WITH
Lamar Alford
Peggy Gordon
David Haskell
Joanne Jonas
Robin Lamont
Sonia Manzano
Gilmer McCormick
Jeffrey Mylett
Stephen Nathan
Herb Simon

COSTUME DESIGN BY
Susan Tsu

LIGHTING BY
Lowell B. Achziger

LOOSELY BASED ON the Gospel of Matthew, *Godspell* is a two-act musical of parables that began as John-Michael Tebelak's student project at Carnegie Mellon. At the time, Tebelak was conflicted about pursuing theater or dedicating his life to the church. *Godspell* came out of his interest in writing a play that would, according to composer Stephen Schwartz in an interview for Masterworks Broadway, "explore the joy and humor that he thought had been leached out of religion." It was enough to interest producers Joseph Beruh and Edgar Lansbury, who saw the off-off-Broadway student production at Café La MaMa and decided to invest in the show, but not without a major adjustment—they brought in twenty-three-year-old composer Stephen Schwartz to write new music and lyrics for *Godspell*'s run at Cherry Lane.

"A lot of the *Godspell* score is a resetting of Episcopal hymns," Schwartz told Masterworks Broadway. The musical is largely about the friendship and betrayal of the Jesus and Judas characters, underscored by the importance of building community—a set of both bohemian and biblical values, dressed up in flamboyant costumes. "It is a whimsical view of Jesus, who is made into a pure simpleton clown, with a red nose, a red heart painted on his forehead and a Superman shirt," Clive Barnes wrote in his opening-night review in *The New York Times*. "It is an honest attempt to make Jesus into a musical comedy star, and there may well be those who will find freshness and originality here where I could discover only a naive but fey frivolity." Tebelak was onto something, however; 1971 became the year of the Jesus rock musical when Andrew Lloyd Webber and Tim Rice debuted *Jesus Christ Superstar* on Broadway in the fall. Despite a tepid *Times* review, *Godspell* went on to become a cult classic: It was adapted into a film in 1973 and remains Schwartz's most frequently recorded score.

ABOVE
Actors David Haskell (*left*) and Stephen Nathan (*right*) in *Godspell*. Photograph by the acclaimed performing arts photographer Martha Swope. Swope arrived in New York to attend the School of American Ballet and began her career as a performance photographer when her classmate Jerome Robbins asked her to photograph rehearsals for *West Side Story*. The New York Public Library's collection of her work consists of over 1,520,000 images. 1971.

ABOVE
Actors Peggy Gordon, Sonia Manzano, Joanne Jonas, Gilmer McCormick (*top from left to right*), and Robin Lamont (*center*) in *Godspell*. Photograph by Martha Swope. 1971.

OPPOSITE
Actors David Haskell and Stephen Nathan (*center*) surrounded by castmates from *Godspell*. Photograph by Martha Swope. 1971.

KEEPING THE HOUSE LIGHTS ON

Sexual Perversity in Chicago
1976

WRITTEN BY
David Mamet

DIRECTED BY
Albert Takazauckas

PRODUCED BY
Larry Goossen
Jeffrey Wachtel

WITH
F. Murray Abraham
Jane Anderson
Peter Riegert
Gina Rogak

SCENIC AND
COSTUME DESIGN BY
Michael Massee

LIGHTING DESIGN BY
Gary Porto

MUSIC BY
George Quincy

BETWEEN BAR BANTER and pillow talk in the summer of 1976, *Sexual Perversity in Chicago* examines the ways in which language shapes and complicates love, sex, and relationships. Two men, Danny and Bernard, and two women, Deborah and Joan, are navigating the nuances of dating in their late twenties. They couple off, with Danny and Deborah eventually moving in together, and Bernard and Joan locked in a cycle of insults and frustration. A commentary on the shifting power dynamics within erotic relationships, *Sexual Perversity* "is a glittering mosaic of tiny, deadly muzzle-flashes from the war between men and women among the filing cabinets and singles bars," wrote Richard Eder in a 1976 review of the play for *The New York Times*.

    Despite its cynical take on a risqué topic and its aggressive, profanity-laden dialogue, *Sexual Perversity* won a 1976 Obie for Best New American Play with its off-off-Broadway production by St. Clement's Theatre company at St. Clement's Church. The company then took the production to Cherry Lane Theatre, where it ran for 273 performances, with Eder writing, "The production is flawless . . . [the cast] are all splendid."

OPPOSITE
Peter Reigert as Danny Shapiro and F. Murray Abraham as Bernard Litko in David Mamet's *Sexual Perversity in Chicago* at Cherry Lane. Photograph by Shaun Considine, Burke Photos. 1976.

RIGHT TOP
Gina Rogers as Joan Webber and Jane Anderson as Deborah Soloman in David Mamet's *Sexual Perversity in Chicago* at Cherry Lane. Photograph by Shaun Considine, Burke Photos. 1976.

RIGHT BOTTOM
Full cast of *Sexual Perversity in Chicago* at Cherry Lane. Photograph by Shaun Considine, Burke Photos. 1976.

OPPOSITE
Poster for David Mamet's double bill at Cherry Lane for *Sexual Perversity in Chicago* and *Duck Variations*. 1976.

The Passion of Dracula
1977

WRITTEN BY
Bob Hall
David Richmond

DIRECTED BY
Peter Bennett

PRODUCED BY
Bob Hall
Eric Krebs
David Richmond

WITH
Brian Bell
Christopher Bernau
Michael Burg
Samuel Maupin
K. Lype O'Dell
Giulia Pagano
Elliott Vileen
Alice White
K. C. Wilson

SCENIC DESIGN BY
Allen Cornell
Bob Hall

COSTUME DESIGN BY
Jane Tschetter

OPPOSITE
Production still of actors Giulia Pagano and Christopher Bernau in *The Passion of Dracula* at Cherry Lane. Photograph by Bernard Gotfryd. 1977.

SET IN RURAL ENGLAND in 1911, *The Passion of Dracula* injected a vital dose of comedy and camp into the Cherry Lane lineup after a string of more serious productions. Loosely based on Bram Stoker's *Dracula*, the play combines melodrama with whodunit frivolity to tell the story of the titular vampire, a trio of doctors, a young reporter, and an English lord, all of whom vie for the attention of a young heroine against a backdrop of flickering candlelight.

    Reviews were mixed. "What is funny becomes silly; what is silly becomes boring," Richard Eder wrote in *The New York Times*. "For the first two acts or so, its cheerful incongruities coupled with several interesting performances keep things reasonably entertaining." Beyond the critics' circle, the play was a hit and ran for 718 performances. *The Passion of Dracula* remains beloved in the theater community for its over-the-top theatricality and sheer spectacle. The show also launched the career of Eric Krebs, the prolific off-Broadway producer, who went on to produce Tony-nominated shows including *Electra* (1998), *It Ain't Nothin' But the Blues* (1999), and *Bill Maher: Victory Begins at Home* (2003).

SHOWBILL

CHERRY LANE THEATRE

ABOVE LEFT
Actors Alice White and Christopher Bernau, with K. C. Wilson (*on the floor*). Photograph by Bernard Gotfryd. 1977.

ABOVE RIGHT
Actors Sam Maupin, Christopher Bernau, and Michael Burg. Photograph by Bernard Gotfryd. 1977.

All Roads Lead to Cherry Lane

7

BY THE 1980s, the regional theater movement had permanently shifted the center of American theater from Broadway to cities across the country. Now that professional, high-caliber theater companies could be found all over the map, it was no longer necessary to travel to New York to catch a Broadway production or to wait for a Broadway tour to come to a city near you in order to see the best shows. Now, just as often, productions that were incubated in regional theaters then headed to New York. Unsurprisingly, Cherry Lane Theatre was at the vanguard of this transition as well.

Steppenwolf Theatre Company is one of the few regional theaters in the country founded by actors. Since the mid-1970s, Steppenwolf has maintained a storied presence in Chicago; its core acting ensemble remains at the heart of the group's mission and governance. Actors Gary Sinise and John Malkovich, two of the founding ensemble members, costarred in a 1982 production of Sam Shepard's *True West*, directed by Sinise at the company's 211-seat theater in North Chicago. This production moved to Cherry Lane later that year—the first of many times a Steppenwolf production went on to New York. The *New York Times* theater critic Mel Gussow called the production "an exhilarating confluence of writing, acting and staging." Sinise and Malkovich were both honored with Obies, and Cherry Lane played a prominent role in launching the New York career of Malkovich, whose star quickly rose both onstage and onscreen.

After sixty years, Cherry Lane was now respected as one of the oldest cultural institutions in the city. Actors including Kevin Bacon, Joan Cusack, and Dennis and Randy Quaid all took to the stage on Commerce Street. The breadth of work presented during this era reflected a commitment to a broad range of styles and genres, from innovative new work from playwrights like Sam Shepard and Joe Orton to musical comedy (*Nunsense*, 1985) and revivals of absurdist masterpieces (Samuel Beckett's *Endgame*). In an ever-changing theatrical landscape, Cherry Lane's savvy and nimble approach to programming allowed it to reach diverse audiences and remain the stalwart cultural center of downtown theater.

PAGE 167
Actors Gary Sinise and John Malkovich in a scene from the Steppenwolf production of Sam Shepard's *True West* at Cherry Lane. Photograph by Martha Swope. 1982.

OPPOSITE
Property tax photo of 38 Commerce Street for New York City's Department of Taxes. 1985.

ABOVE
Playbills for the Cherry Lane productions of *Brilliant Traces* (1989) by Cindy Lou Johnson and *Album* (1980) by David Rimmer.

OPPOSITE TOP
Production still with actors Joan Cusack and Kevin Anderson in *Brilliant Traces*. 1989.

OPPOSITE BOTTOM
Production still with actors Keith Gordon as Boo and Kevin Bacon as Billy in *Album*. 1980.

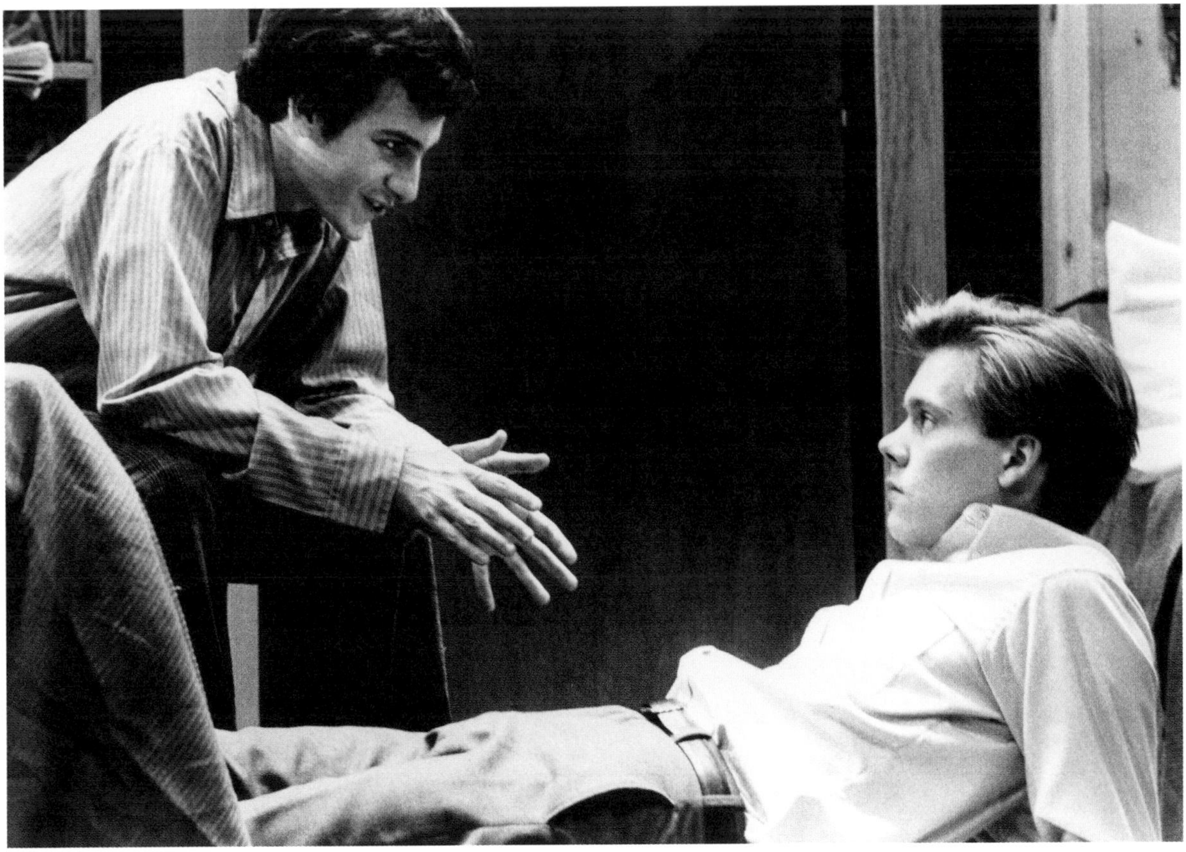

ALL ROADS LEAD TO CHERRY LANE

ABOVE
Actors Alice Drummond, James Greene, Alvin Epstein, and Peter Evans in a scene from the Cherry Lane revival of Samuel Beckett's *Endgame*. Photograph by Martha Swope. 1984.

OPPOSITE
Poster for the Cherry Lane revival of *Endgame*. 1984.

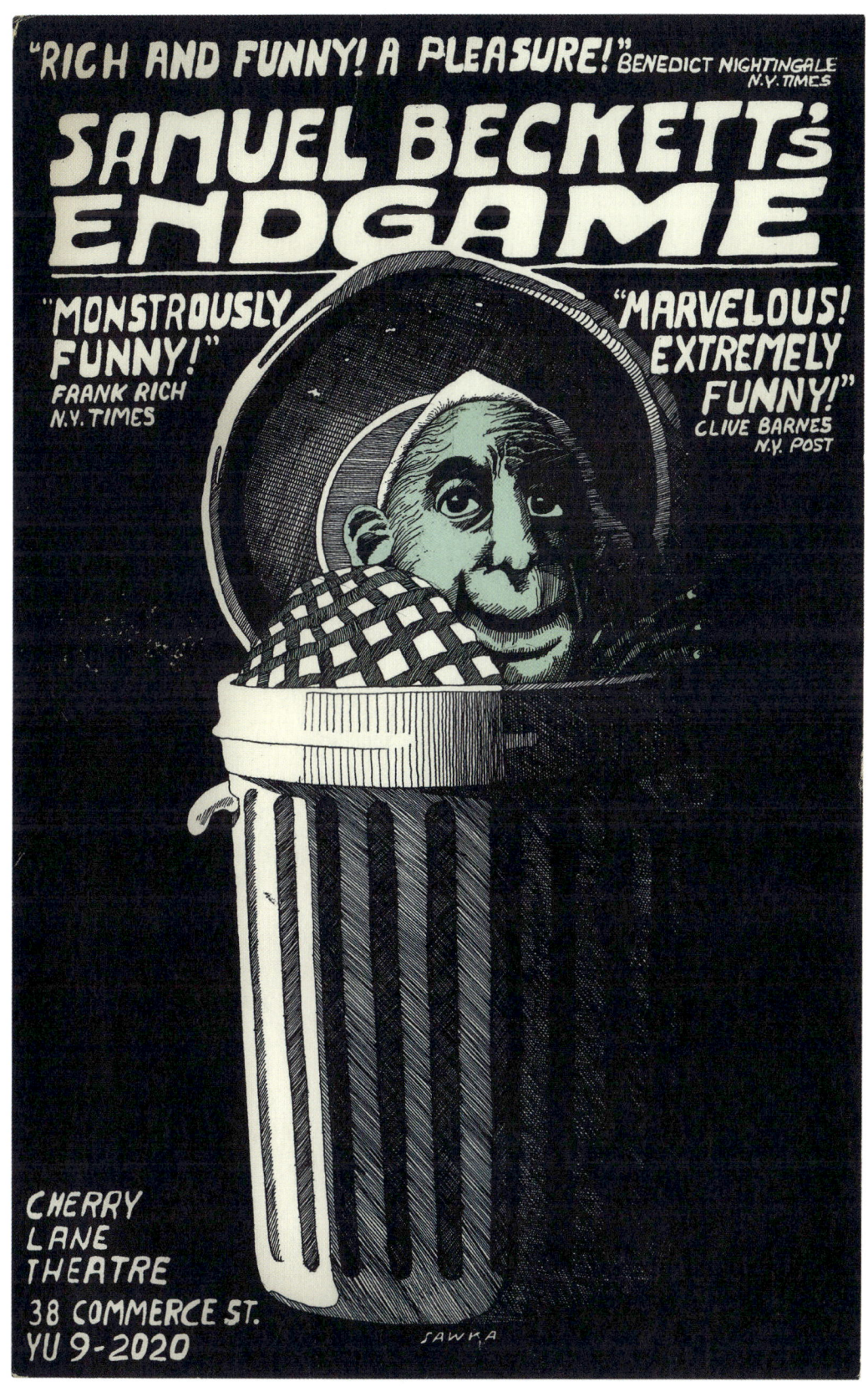

OPPOSITE
Poster for the Cherry Lane production of Sam Shepard's *True West*. 1982.

ABOVE
Exterior shot of the theater. Photographer unknown. 1982.

PAGES 176–177
Productions of *True West* at Cherry Lane have starred John Malkovich and Gary Sinise, Jim Belushi and Gary Cole, Dennis Quaid and Randy Quaid, and Tim Matheson and Daniel Stern. The show ran for 762 performances. All photographs by Martha Swope. 1982.

CHERRY LANE THEATRE

ALL ROADS LEAD TO CHERRY LANE

True West
1982

WRITTEN BY
Sam Shepard

DIRECTED
Gary Sinise

PRODUCED BY
Wayne Adams
Harold Thau

STARRING
John Malkovich
Gary Sinise

WITH
Sam Schacht
Margaret Thomson

SCENIC DESIGN BY
Deb Gohr
Kevin Ridgon

CENTERED ON THE relationship between estranged brothers Lee and Austin, *True West* wrestles with themes of sibling rivalry, masculinity, and the American dream. When Lee, a desert grifter and thief, and Austin, a successful Hollywood screenwriter, find themselves housesitting for their mother in the suburbs of Los Angeles, old grievances flare as they attempt to put aside their differences and collaborate on a script.

True West helped define Cherry Lane Theatre in the 1980s as a place to launch careers and celebrate a wide range of stories and experiences on the stage. After the show's failed 1980 debut at the Public Theater, *The New York Times* called the Cherry Lane revival "an act of theatrical restitution and restoration." The show ran for 762 performances from 1982 to 1984, with multiple casts featuring emerging actors at the time like Jim Belushi, Gary Cole, Dennis Quaid, and Randy Quaid. The original production with John Malkovich and Gary Sinise marked their New York stage debuts and put the Chicago-based Steppenwolf Theatre Company in the national spotlight. The Steppenwolf production also marked the return of Sam Shepard to Cherry Lane—the prolific playwright got his start with Albarwild Playwrights Unit in the 1960s, and *True West* showcased the writer at the height of his career.

In 1983, John Malkovich won an Obie for his performance and a Clarence Derwent Award (from the Actors' Equity Association) for most promising male actor. *True West* was a finalist for the Pulitzer Prize for Drama the same year.

OPPOSITE
Actors Gary Sinise as Austin (*left*) and John Malkovich as Lee (*right*) in a scene from Sam Shepard's *True West* at Cherry Lane. Photograph by Martha Swope. 1982.

CHERRY LANE THEATRE

OPPOSITE
The Steppenwolf production of *True West* at Cherry Lane earned a number of awards for the 1982 season, including 1983 Obies to John Malkovich for performance and Gary Sinise for direction; the 1983 Clarence Derwent Award to John Malkovich for most promising male performance in a supporting role; and a 1983 Theatre World Award for John Malkovich. Photograph by Martha Swope. 1982.

ABOVE
Actors Mary Rausch, Gary Sinise, and John Malkovich in *True West*. Photograph by Martha Swope. 1982.

Nunsense
1985

WRITTEN & DIRECTED BY
Dan Goggin

PRODUCED BY
Bill Crowder
Joseph Hoesl
The Nunsense Theatrical Company

WITH
Christine Anderson
Vicki Belmonte
Semina DeLaurentis
Marilyn Farina
Suzi Winson

MUSICAL STAGING & CHOREOGRAPHY
Felton Smith

SCENIC DESIGN BY
Barry Axtell

LIGHTING DESIGN BY
Susan A. White

MUSICAL DIRECTION BY
Michael Rice

NUNSENSE IS A MUSICAL COMEDY about the fictitious order of the Little Sisters of Hoboken, New Jersey, that began, oddly enough, as a line of novelty greeting cards featuring a nun offering pointed one-liners. The cards' popularity snowballed into a cabaret show and then a full-length theatrical production that premiered at Cherry Lane Theatre in December 1985. Set in a high school gym, *Nunsense* follows five nuns who put on a variety show in order to raise money so they can afford a proper burial for the sisters accidentally poisoned by the convent cook.

Universally beloved, the show had multiple extensions at other off-Broadway theaters. The glowing *New York Times* review called the show "hysterical," "wacky fun," with "side-splitting jokes." By the end of its initial theatrical run, *Nunsense* boasted a total of 3,672 performances, becoming the second-longest-running off-Broadway show at the time. It was then adapted for television (starring Rue McClanahan, another Cherry Lane alum), followed by six sequels, and it has the distinction of being translated into over twenty-six languages with multiple international adaptations. Dan Goggin and many of the original cast and crew continue to be familiar faces on Commerce Street as supporters and extended Cherry Lane family. *Nunsense* was revived by Cherry Lane in 2010 as part of the Heritage Series.

ABOVE
Publicity photo for *Nunsense* by Dan Goggin featuring actors Marilyn Farina, Edwina Lewis, Suzi Winson, Susan Gordon-Clark, and Christine Anderson. Photograph by Adam Newman. 1985.

ABOVE
Production still from *Nunsense* at Cherry Lane. Photograph by Stephen Aucoin. 1986.

OPPOSITE
Playbill from the Cherry Lane production.

PLAYBILL

CHERRY LANE THEATRE

The Sum of Us
1990

WRITTEN BY
David Stevens

DIRECTED BY
Kevin Dowling

PRODUCED BY
Dowling Entertainment
Gintare Sileika Everett
Duane Wilder

STARRING
Tony Goldwyn
Richard Venture

WITH
Neil Maffin
Phyllis Somerville

SCENIC DESIGN BY
John Lee Beatty

COSTUME DESIGN BY
Therese A. Bruck

LIGHTING BY
Dennis Parichy

THE SUM OF US follows Harry, a widower, and his gay son, Jeff, as they both search for love in suburban Melbourne. The play debuted at the height of the AIDS crisis, and its poignant depiction of family dynamics and the humanity of its gay characters rallied the Greenwich Village community around Cherry Lane Theatre and sparked a wider conversation about family, queerness, and romantic relationships.

It opened to warm reviews and ran for 335 performances. During its first week, *The New York Times* wrote, "The direction and the acting in the production . . . are exceptional in their understatement and precision."

The Sum of Us marks the conclusion of Australian playwright David Stevens's *A Currency Trilogy*. It won the Outer Critics Circle Award for Outstanding Off-Broadway Play, and Tony Goldwyn won an Obie for his performance as Jeff. Recently, Goldwyn, writing in memory of fellow cast member Richard Venture, singled out *The Sum of Us* as "one of the greatest creative experiences of my life."

ABOVE
Cast photo from *The Sum of Us*.
Photograph by Carol Rosegg. 1990.

RIGHT
Playbill featuring Tony Goldwyn and Richard Venture from the original Cherry Lane production of *The Sum of Us*. 1990.

OPPOSITE
Poster for the Cherry Lane production of *The Sum of Us*. 1990.

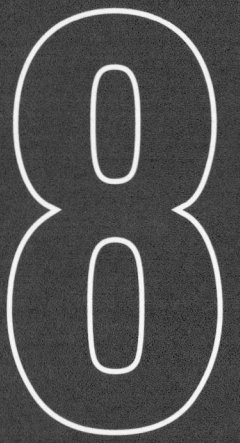

New Mentors
New Voices

IN 1996, Cherry Lane Theatre was just shy of celebrating its seventy-fifth anniversary when a visionary leader took the helm. Angelina Fiordellisi, an actor, director, and producer, purchased the theater and became its artistic director, a position she held for more than two decades until she stepped down in 2017. Her stewardship included bold new programs that expanded the theater's reach and secured its legacy as the premier destination for emerging voices in American playwriting.

When Fiordellisi arrived, she quickly established Cherry Lane Alternative, a not-for-profit production company, and opened the Cherry Lane Studio, a small black box theater that sat adjacent to the main stage. The addition of a second performance venue allowed Fiordellisi a space to support the Mentor Project, a program she (and producing partner Susann Brinkley) launched in 1998 to cultivate the next generation of American playwrights.

Drawing inspiration from the Albarwild Playwrights Unit of the 1960s, Fiordellisi and Brinkley solicited applications from early-career writers, selecting just a handful each year out of hundreds of submissions. From there, playwrights were connected to a mentor—an established writer who could support both the dramaturgical development of the script and the professional development of the writer. All mentees received guidance during the writing phase, a staged reading of their work in progress, and, most crucially, a fully staged production in the Studio. The list of mentors and mentees from this era reads as a who's who of American theater, with award-winning writers such as Edward Albee, David Henry Hwang, Tony Kushner, Marsha Norman, and Wendy Wasserstein serving as mentors in the first few years of the program. The list of mentees, equally impressive, includes a number of writers who would go on to find commercial success—as well as critical acclaim—on Broadway and in film and television, such as Katori Hall, Rajiv Joseph, Antoinette Nwandu, and Jen Silverman.

In 2016, toward the end of her tenure, Fiordellisi launched the Founder's Project as a way to support the careers of older theater makers. She also oversaw the Heritage Series, a set of revivals of beloved productions from Cherry Lane's nearly century-long existence. The 2002 revival of Samuel Beckett's *Happy Days*, which had its world premiere at Cherry Lane in 1961, was filmed by the Lincoln Center library and lauded by critics and audiences alike. Other main-stage productions in this era

PAGE 191
Production still from *99 Histories* by Julia Cho, mentored by David Henry Hwang. 2002.

OPPOSITE
A crowd gathers outside Cherry Lane to celebrate the opening night of *This Beautiful Future* by Rita Kalnejais. Photograph by Emilio Madrid. 2022.

BELOW
Production still from Cherry Lane revival of *American Dream* by Edward Albee. Photograph by Gabe Evans. 2008.

OPPOSITE
Posters from Fiordellisi's era as artistic director. *Clockwise from top left*: 1998 revival of *The American Dream* and *The Sandbox* by Edward Albee, 2007 revival of *Dutchman* by LeRoi Jones (later known as Amiri Baraka), 2002 revival of *Happy Days* by Samuel Beckett, 2015 one-man show *The New York Story* by Colin Quinn.

were Bridgette Wimberly's *Saint Lucy's Eyes* (2001), a play that explores illegal abortions in a pre-*Roe* America and that was incubated during the first season of the Mentor Project; an eclectic mix of comedy shows, including *Black Humor: The Comedy of Lewis Black* (1998); and revivals of both *Dutchman* (2007) and *The American Dream*—which Albee directed himself in 2008. Fiordellisi's artistic directorship of Cherry Lane during this era will always be remembered for the way in which it secured the theater's legacy both by honoring its past and looking boldly toward its future.

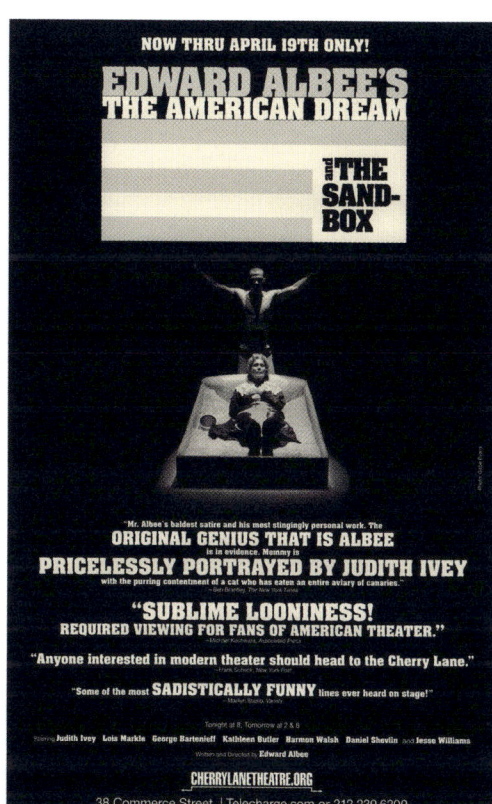

NEW MENTORS NEW VOICES

OPPOSITE
Dulé Hill as Clay and Jennifer Mudge as Lula in a scene from the Cherry Lane revival of *Dutchman* by LeRoi Jones (later known as Amiri Baraka). Photograph by Gabe Evans for *The New York Times*. 2007.

ABOVE
Joyce Aaron as Winnie in the Cherry Lane revival of *Happy Days* by Samuel Beckett. Photograph by Dennis Kleiman. 2002.

ABOVE
Susann Brinkley (*left*) and
Angelina Fiordellisi (*right*)
outside Cherry Lane. Circa 1996.

Angelina Fiordellisi on Building the Cherry Lane Theatre Company

From her purchase of the theater in 1996 until its sale to A24 in 2023, Angelina Fiordellisi charted a course for Cherry Lane as a home for visionary work: building the sixty-seat Cherry Lane Theatre Studio, supporting emerging playwrights with the Mentor Project, and honoring the history of the theater with revivals of iconic plays from Cherry Lane's extensive canon. For over twenty seasons, Fiordellisi served as the artistic director of Cherry Lane Theatre and founded Cherry Lane Alternative, a nonprofit entity with a mission to support emerging playwrights.

WHEN I FIRST WALKED into Cherry Lane Theatre in June 1996, it was a mess. There were plumbing issues; when it rained, the first four rows of seats would flood before the water eventually ran down into the basement. It looked as though it hadn't been cleaned in a decade. There was old broken furniture upstairs where the dressing rooms were, and off the lobby, an anteroom was filled with sawdust and old restaurant equipment.

Even in its funky, uncared-for state, I saw what it could be in six months, one year, ten years, twenty years. I had this distinct feeling that I belonged in this space and was going to do a lot of good work there. That feeling floored me. I wasn't entirely ready for it, but with the support of my husband, Matt Williams, a playwright, and my dear friend Susann Brinkley, an amazing director who ran an off-off-Broadway theater, I started the Cherry Lane Theatre Company.

At first, there was a backlog of unpaid bills and violations to deal with. The neighbors were not happy. The theater had been dark for many years and they didn't want to deal with the public descending upon their quiet cul-de-sac. I listened as they complained and called the buildings department, but I pressed on. I was there 24/7, sweeping in the front, cleaning the windows, polishing the poles . . . I was doing everything. I was even fixing clogged toilets in the beginning.

I knew nothing about running an off-Broadway theater, but Susann and I knew some of the theater owners in town and we took them to lunch. They were very generous and shared legal documents and financials and advice on how to structure a theater package, which includes everything from your house manager and box office treasurer to the toilet paper in the bathrooms—all the costs involved in running a theater. At the time my total "house package" came to $4,500 a week, and we were able to charge $3,500 a week for rent. We kept it lean and mean with only minimal staff, and I tried to hold it there for as long as possible so that nonprofits and young producers could afford to rent it.

Cherry Lane Theatre Company managed the Cherry Lane main stage. I wanted a "company" because in my undergrad studies at the University of Detroit the company did everything: costumes, hair, makeup, lighting, stage management, box office, house management, etc. When you invest your full self—mentally, physically, spiritually—into a space, people respond to that energy when they walk in. And most importantly, you could feel the spirit of the extraordinary artists who were launched and flourished there. I thought that if I had a company with that kind of intensity and commitment to the spirit of the theater, it would set the stage for an elevated viewing experience.

Of course, Cherry Lane had a rich history before I arrived. When I first bought the theater and talked to people about it, most of them would put their hands over their hearts. Cherry Lane is beloved to those who know its history—it's the soul of the theater community. One of my favorite eras was the late 1960s, when Edward Albee, Richard Barr, and Clinton Wilder started Albarwild, a company that produced the work of emerging playwrights. Among Albarwild's early productions were plays by Amiri Baraka (then known as LeRoi Jones), Adrienne Kennedy, and Sam Shepard.

We were renting out the main stage at the time, which allowed me to pay the bills, develop the staff, and keep up the historic building. But I wanted to develop new American plays and support playwrights, so I started a nonprofit called Cherry Lane Alternative that enabled us to present their plays and hire supporting artists and staff.

I recognized that many playwrights were given amazing productions at the university level but when they arrived in New York they would get *bubkes*, nothing at all. Some of them were fortunate enough to get a reading at a popular institution, but no one would produce the plays because no one wanted to take the risk. Albarwild wasn't around anymore, and there were no programs producing early-career playwrights in 1996. None! So I thought, we can serve this niche and pair emerging writers with master (and in most cases Pulitzer Prize–winning) writers to launch the next generation of American playwrights.

I asked Edward Albee to be involved in the Mentor Project because he was my dream mentor, the mentor's mentor. One of the greatest gifts of my artistic directorship was sitting in on his master classes. These young playwrights would come in having read each other's plays and sit there with sandwiches and talk about the plays. Edward, who was a bit of a curmudgeon, was so tender and loving with these young playwrights. His pure heart came forth in those master classes; I remember Edward teasing Rajiv Joseph with questions about his play. Edward led those classes for about sixteen years.

We've launched so many writers who've gone on and done so well. When we produced the plays we developed in the Mentor Project, everyone in the industry would come to see them: agents, theater owners, young writers. These audiences played a vital role in the development of these plays. And afterward, they would gather and talk. It became a really beautiful community gathering.

Sitting at my desk and talking to playwrights was the best part of my job at Cherry Lane, and my greatest relationships were with artists with whom I felt safe with my heart. This list includes: Gretchen Cryer, David Henry Hwang, Alfred Uhry, Charles Fuller, Pete Gurney, Wendy Wasserstein, and Marsha Norman, though many of them are gone now. It was such an honor to work with them.

I had been snubbed by the industry and people who didn't take me seriously because I had a very mothering approach. People came in and saw that I was naive and tried to take over in the beginning of my tenure. Everyone wanted my job. It took a long time to develop a tough skin and learn who to trust, and these artists taught me how to have boundaries in

BELOW
Staff photo outside
Cherry Lane. 2003.

this business. I learned that when my heart feels safe, that's where I want to go. I want to lead with my whole heart and spend time with the people that operate at the same frequency.

Cherry Lane was a great proving ground not only for the playwrights but also for the directors, young stage managers, and designers. Faye Armon-Troncoso started with us as a house manager and decided she wanted to try making the props. She went on to become the first prop designer to win an Obie, and now she's on Broadway and doing film and television. Mary Geerlof, who began as an intern, is now the managing director of the theater. That is the history of Cherry Lane, too: a safe place to learn and invest in the people. I felt a responsibility to be a steward and expand the Cherry Lane family.

CHERRY LANE THEATRE

Mentor Project

IN 1998, two years after she became Cherry Lane Theatre's artistic director, Angelina Fiordellisi established the Mentor Project, a program dedicated to launching the next generation of American dramatists. Inspired by the success of Albarwild Playwrights Unit, the collaboration between producers Richard Barr and Clinton Wilder and playwright Edward Albee, and its model of providing production opportunities for early-career dramatists in the 1960s, the Mentor Project worked to support the future of American drama by incubating and producing new works by emerging playwrights.

The Mentor Project engaged leading playwrights in one-on-one mentoring relationships with early-career writers. Over the course of a season, mentors guided writers through the challenging process of new play development, from readings, rewrites, and casting to rehearsals and performance. The program culminated each spring in fully staged workshop productions, following Cherry Lane's belief that "there is no better teacher for a playwright than experiencing your play as it was intended: in living, luminous shape on stage, from your seat in the company of an audience."

The Mentor Project launched new works by more than sixty emerging playwrights, including Anne Washburn, Katori Hall, Rajiv Joseph, and Sheila Callaghan—all of whom later returned to the program to serve as mentors. Because of COVID-19, the final season of the Mentor Project ended in March 2020. Below are listed the names of the mentees and mentors; each mentee's name is listed above the name of their mentor.

OPPOSITE TOP
Production still from *Nollywood Dreams* by Jocelyn Bioh, mentored by Branden Jacob-Jenkins. Photograph by Russ Rowland. 2017.

OPPOSITE BOTTOM
Production still from *Peerless* by Jiehae Park, mentored by Kwame Kwei-Armah. Photograph by Chasi Annexy. 2015.

2020
Shawn Randall
  Diana Oh

2019
C. A. Johnson
  Martyna Majok
Kareem M. Lucas
  Craig "muMs" Grant
Matthew Paul Olmos
  Taylor Mac

2018
Sam Chanse
  Midgalia Cruz
Kate Cortesi
  Anne Washburn

2017
Jocelyn Bioh
  Branden Jacob-Jenkins
Ren Dara Santiago
  Lucy Thurber
Nathan Yungerberg
  Stephen Adly Guirgis

2016
Sarah Einspanier
  Sheila Callaghan
Christopher Gabriel Núñez
  Rajiv Joseph
Antoinette Nwandu
  Katori Hall

2015
Jesse Jou
  Barry Edelstein
Jiehae Park
  Kwame Kwei-Armah
Kristina Poe
  Chay Yew

2014
Lina Patel
  David Henry Hwang
Jen Silverman
  Lynn Nottage
Awoye Timpo
  Lisa Peterson

2013
Nastaran Ahmadi
  Kia Corthron
Elizabeth A. Davis
  Edna Walsh
Natalia Naman Temesgen
  Eduardo Machado
Lisa Ramirez
  Cynthia Hopkins

2012
Patricia Buckley
  Jean-Claude van Itallie
Anne DeSalvo
  David Rambo
Elizabeth Rose
  Gretchen Cryer

2010
Nate Rufus Edelman
  Charles Fuller
Ruth McKee
  David Henry Hwang
Winter Miller
  Craig Lucas

2009
Jakob Holder
  Charles Mee

2008
Greg Keller
  Gretchen Cryer
Deirdre O'Connor
  Michael Weller
Samuel Brett Williams
  Charles Fuller

2007
Peter Gil-Sheridan
  Michael Weller
Colin McKenna
  Lynn Nottage
Molly Smith Metzler
  Jules Feiffer

2006
Sheila Callaghan
  Michael Weller
Katori Hall
  Lynn Nottage
Megan Mostyn-Brown
  Theresa Rebeck

2005
Courtney Baron
  David Auburn
Sam Forman
  Michael Weller
Rajiv Joseph
  Theresa Rebeck

2004
Alexandra Bullen
  Ed Bullins
Joseph Fisher
  A. R. Gurney
Kendra Levin
  Michael Weller

2003
Bathsheba Doran
  Michael Weller
Anton Dudley
  Ed Bullins
Allison Moore
  Marsha Norman

2002
Julia Cho
  David Henry Hwang
Eliam Kraiem
  Michael Weller
Deborah Zoe Laufer
  Marsha Norman

2001
David Adjmi
  Craig Lucas
Ross Berger
  Michael Weller
Glyn O'Malley
  Alfred Uhry
Cybele Pascal
  Marsha Norman
David Wiener
  David Henry Hwang

2000
Hunt Holman
  Michael Weller
Ward Just
  Wendy Wasserstein
Rosemary Moore
  A. R. Gurney
Anne Washburn
  Craig Lucas
Gary Winter
  Alfred Uhry

1999
Peter Buchman
  Michael Weller
Heather Hill
  A. R. Gurney
Lizzie Olesker
  Tony Kushner
Christopher Shinn
  Charles Fuller
Bridgette Wimberly
  Wendy Wasserstein

Edward Albee (Mentor's Mentor)

NEW MENTORS NEW VOICES

NEW MENTORS NEW VOICES

PAGES 206–207
Production stills from the Mentor Project. *Clockwise from top left*: *Urgent Fury* by Allison Moore, mentored by Marsha Norman (2003); *three girls never learnt the way home* by Matthew Paul Olmos, mentored by Taylor Mac (2019); *The Parents' Evening* by Bathsheba Doran, mentored by Michael Weller (2003); *The Climb* by C.A. Johnson, mentored by Martyna Majok (2019).

ABOVE
Production still from *Esai's Table* by Nathan Yungerberg, mentored by Stephen Adly Guirgis. Photograph by Rob Strong. 2017.

Stephen Adly Guirgis and Nathan Yungerberg on Mentorship

NATHAN YUNGERBERG IS a storyteller and Afro-surrealist who writes for theater, TV, and scripted podcasts. His play *Esai's Table* was featured in the 2017 Cherry Lane Theatre Mentor Project. Stephen Adly Guirgis won the 2015 Pulitzer Prize for Drama for his play *Between Riverside and Crazy* (2014) and is a member and former co–artistic director of LAByrinth Theater Company.

Paired for the 2017 season of the Mentor Project, Yungerberg and Guirgis reflect on the role the program played in their work, and how it shapes their practice today.

* * *

NATHAN YUNGERBERG: I initially learned about the Mentor Project as an emerging writer. I attended as an audience member two seasons in a row, and I was really excited about the fact that Cherry Lane did what appeared to be a full production of these plays.

By the time I got into the theater world, a lot of developmental opportunities already started drying up. The Mentor Project is one of the few programs in the country that actually gives you an opportunity to see your play fully realized with all the bells and whistles while protecting the work from critical review. I made it my mission to get connected with the people over there. Getting to see a fully realized production of a work is very rare—it's a luxury.

STEPHEN ADLY GUIRGIS: That's true. LAByrinth [the New York City–based ensemble theater company] was in residence at Cherry Lane and I got to meet and work with the team there. I always knew of the Mentor Project, and I'd heard stories of legendary playwrights mentoring at Cherry Lane. When they asked me if I wanted to do it, I didn't have any expectations around the role—I just wanted to be available and to be of service.

NY: I was excited about getting matched with a seasoned professional. I invited Seri [Lawrence, former Cherry Lane literary manager] to a reading of *Esai's Table* and she showed up. That same day I got an email from her to submit the play for the Mentor Project.

SAG: My memory of you is that you were really humble, but very proactive. You had a career before you became a writer—you're a multitalented dude. So anything that I can do to help stoke the flames of your passion is a good thing. I did whatever I thought would be helpful. If you asked for anything, I would try to do it.

NY: We had our first meeting at your place. You asked me a couple questions, and one of them became a catalyst for the major work I did on the play. You asked me, "Who do you see playing Esai in your dream cast?" I said, "Ron Cephas Jones." You said to me, "If you want someone like Ron, you're going to have to shake this character up and make him more dangerous."

SAG: It's like with directing: What do I say to Nathan that will activate him to go in the direction that the character ought to go to, but [how do I] say it in such a way that he feels like he's coming up with it himself or that it's like we arrived at it together? It's a bit like therapy.

I've mentored outside of Cherry Lane. When you reach a certain age, people are going to reach out to you for connections or a little inspiration. I try to show up and be helpful. Writing is definitely a solo act, but you need to come up for air and connect with other people, and it's hard. You don't always get the opportunity to do that amongst peers. I'd love to send my play to people and say, "Hey, can you read this? Can you help?," but that doesn't really happen.

With the Mentor Project, I tried to be helpful and honest and encouraging. I remember the reading we did went really well . . .

NY: It did! The first reading with Danya [Taymor, director] and Kristen [Robinson, scenic designer] was really magical. For one, I was still really new to theater. Getting paired with Stephen, knowing your background and experience, and being invited into your home, was already incredible. Then, sitting there with a breathtaking view of the river, surrounded by such talented people, it all felt like one of those "pinch me" moments. Having them read *Esai's Table* and being able to listen to it with their energy was thrilling.

Then we did a second read of the revised script at your dining table with actors. It was the first time that I heard a revised version of the play within the context of this mentorship relationship. To this day, having a table read can be scary. It's like standing in your underwear and reading out of your journal to strangers. It's really, really an awkward feeling because it's so vulnerable. But then there's the flip side of being excited to finally hear the voices outside your own head, and it's really helpful.

SAG: It goes both ways because when you mentor somebody, it's a way of being of service. But once everybody goes home, I have to ask myself, "Am I doing the things I'm suggesting for Nathan? Am I holding my feet to the fire as well?" But *you* have to do it yourself. It was a really positive experience for me.

I didn't have any formal training as a writer. I learned by doing, and also from studying acting and thinking about who and what I wanted to see on a stage. Creating a good theater experience for an audience can be rough, but I always have people that I look up to.

Lynn Nottage, for example, took me under her wing early on and affirmed that I was a writer, a real writer. She was always very supportive. In my mind, that's what you're supposed to do. You're supposed to bring someone into your home and affirm them. It doesn't feel like an extraordinary act.

NY: Even though you gave me one big note, the amount of work I had to do in order to address it was the equivalent of a home renovation, where you rip everything down to the studs and build it up again. I hadn't done that before.

SAG: I do it all the time. I go back under the hood and make a copy that I call the "fucked-up version," and then I let myself dig into it as much as needed.

One good thing about computers is that you can make a copy and mess with it as much as you want. If you make it worse, you still have the old one.

NY: At one point I removed so much stuff that I was freaking out and not really sure what to do; I reached out to you, and you were there to reassure me: "Just trust yourself. You got this." To this day, I still use that practice where I take my sword and clear out all this stuff and then rebuild from the ground floor. Having a mentor, someone who could share that experience, was really beneficial to my practice.

SAG: We always need new playwrights and new voices to tell their stories and our stories. It's hard now because you have a lot of folks who might do one play, and then if it's in any way successful, they head to Hollywood or write for television. There's nothing wrong with that—that's certainly one of the only ways to make money—but it's important to build up a body of work. When I was growing up, anytime Martin Scorsese or Francis Ford Coppola or Woody Allen had a new movie, you automatically went to see it. To have playwrights that constantly return to theater is important.

NY: It goes back to this lack of developmental opportunities in the United States. Now we're down to just two prominent ones: the New Dramatists in New York and the Playwrights' Center in Minneapolis. All the others have shuttered. It's so rare to get produced and or do workshop production.

Also, the visibility that comes with working with a prominent institution and playwright is extremely valuable. When the announcement went out for *Esai's Table*, that's when people started listening and agents and artistic directors started calling. Those connections are really difficult to get as a newer writer.

SAG: Historically, Cherry Lane has been extremely dedicated to developing new writers and voices in the theater. I'm glad to hear that was your experience, too.

NY: When it was over, you told me our relationship wasn't going to end, and I should continue to reach out. And I did. Not long after, I was having one of many existential crises as a writer, and I reached out to talk. And now, many years later, you're still my reference for fellowships and grants and developmental programs. Plus, I update you with pictures of my kids from time to time.

SAG: We don't talk all the time, but I consider you part of my artistic family, and if I get a call, I'm going to respond. The door is always open. I'm just glad that Cherry Lane prioritizes a program like this because it's invaluable. A lot of times when you're the person initially on the receiving end, you feel grateful that someone is going out of their way for you. But the other person also gets something. We may go on to not interact that much, or we could end up on a trip down the Amazon. These relationships are circular and ultimately very positive.

Saint Lucy's Eyes
2001

WRITTEN BY
Bridgette Wimberly

MENTORED BY
Wendy Wasserstein

DIRECTED BY
Billie Allen

PRODUCED BY
Cherry Lane Theatre
Angelina Fiordellisi

STARRING
Willis Burks II
Ruby Dee

WITH
Toks Olagundoye
Sally A. Stewart

SCENIC DESIGN BY
Beowulf Boritt

COSTUME DESIGN BY
Alvin B. Perry

LIGHTING DESIGN BY
Jane Reisman

MUSIC AND SOUND BY
Michael Wimberly

OPPOSITE
Production still from *Saint Lucy's Eyes* by Bridgette Wimberly, mentored by Wendy Wasserstein. 2001.

SPANNING TWELVE YEARS, *Saint Lucy's Eyes* is a powerful drama centered around Grandma, a back-alley abortionist working out of a tenement apartment in 1968 Memphis, Tennessee. With the civil rights movement roiling in the background, Grandma's story embodies the historical narrative, illuminating the human cost behind life-and-death decisions. In his review for *Variety*, Charles Isherwood described Ruby Dee's portrayal of Grandma as a "sympathetic portrait of a distinctive woman struggling to reconcile her ideas of right and wrong with those of society and the church."

Saint Lucy's Eyes is a hallmark of Cherry Lane Theatre, reflecting its history of nurturing talent and fostering transformational ideas. After it was developed in the first season of the Mentor Project, with Bridgette Wimberly mentored by Wendy Wasserstein, the show was moved to the main stage for its 2001 production. The show won a 2002 AUDELCO Award, which honors excellence in African American theater in New York City, for Beowulf Boritt's scenic design, and Dee was awarded a Lucille Lortel Award for Outstanding Lead Actress.

The production also exemplifies Cherry Lane as a company of artists: Wimberly started in the Mentor Project and went on to serve on the board of directors until her passing. Ruby Dee and director Billie Allen were icons within the cultural landscape of the Cherry Lane; their supportive presence and generous spirit were felt throughout the theater company, where they constantly lent their voice and offered advice—no ask was too big or small. For over a decade, the creative energy of all three people uplifted the work of Cherry Lane—the theater community lost Dee in 2014, Allen in 2015, and then Wimberly in 2022.

CHERRY LANE THEATRE

OPPOSITE
Ruby Dee as Grandma and Willis Burks II as Bay in *Saint Lucy's Eyes*. Photograph by Carol Rosegg. 2001.

ABOVE
Ruby Dee as Grandma and Toks Olagundoye as Young Woman in *Saint Lucy's Eyes*. 2001.

Hoodoo Love
2007

WRITTEN BY
Katori Hall

MENTORED BY
Lynn Nottage

DIRECTED BY
Lucie Tiberghien

PRODUCED BY
Cherry Lane Theatre

WITH
Keith Davis
Marjorie Johnson
Angela Lewis
Kevin Mambo

SCENIC DESIGN BY
Robin Vest

COSTUME DESIGN BY
Rebecca Bernstein

LIGHTING DESIGN BY
Pat Dignan

MUSIC BY
Daniel Baker

SET AGAINST THE backdrop of "mojo bags and wailing banjos" in 1930s Memphis, Tennessee, *Hoodoo Love* centers on Toulou, a young, poor recent arrival from rural Mississippi with dreams of becoming a blues singer. After meeting and falling in love with Ace of Spades, a rambling bluesman, Toulou plots to entrap him with a little bit of help from her neighbor and local hoodoo practitioner, Candylady.

Developed in 2006 as part of the Mentor Project under the mentorship of Lynn Nottage, *Hoodoo Love* was Katori Hall's debut play. Reviewers singled out her dialogue and evocative writing, with Tom Sellar of *The Village Voice* writing, "Hall's ear for unusual language makes her a new writer worth watching." Its critical success propelled Cherry Lane Theatre to extend its run, making it one of only a few Mentor Project shows to transition from the Cherry Lane Studio, the smaller black box theater space, to the historic main stage.

The show celebrated Black artistry both onstage and behind the scenes, and was nominated for three AUDELCO Awards, which honor excellence in African American theater in New York City, for Best Actress (Angela Davis), Best Supporting Actress (which Marjorie Johnson won), and the August Wilson Playwright Award. The play is regularly produced, with notable runs with the Ruby Theatre in Los Angeles (2012), Sound Theatre Company at Center Theatre in Seattle (2017), and the Collective Theatre at Raven Theatre in Chicago (2019).

ABOVE
Production still of Marjorie Johnson as Candylady and Angela Lewis as Toulou in *Hoodoo Love* by Katori Hall, mentored by Lynn Nottage. Photograph by Jaisen Crockett. 2007.

OPPOSITE TOP
Portrait of Katori Hall at Cherry Lane for *The New York Times*. Photograph by Nicole Bengiveno. October 14, 2007.

OPPOSITE BOTTOM
Cast and crew of *Hoodoo Love*. 2007.

RIGHT
Poster for *Hoodoo Love*. 2007.

First Love
2018

WRITTEN BY
Charles Mee

DIRECTED BY
Kim Weild

WITH
Angelina Fiordellisi
Taylor Harvey
Michael O'Keefe

SCENIC DESIGN BY
Edward Pierce

IN *FIRST LOVE*, Edith and Harold, who are in their seventies, have a contentious encounter on a park bench and then fall in love—for the first time ever. The two grapple with finding their way to one another and realizing the last chance for love they'll ever have, all while navigating the weight of the baggage of their lives. In her review for *The New York Times*, Laura Collins-Hughes called it a "pleasingly jagged romantic comedy."

    Set in the "world of Magritte," as Mee writes in his stage directions, *First Love* is notable for its vivid set pieces, costumes, and props, reflecting his vision of being "indoors and out at the same time." The revival was part of the Founder's Project, a program started by Cherry Lane's owner and artistic director Angelina Fiordellisi (who also starred as Edith) in 2016. The Founder's Project celebrated artists and playwrights aged sixty-five and over, "mature theater-makers [who] have contributed their genius to the American stage—and still have much to share—but find fewer substantial opportunities." When *First Love* was mounted, Mary Geerlof, then the director of community engagement, remembers, "Charles Mee was an amazing presence, ever generous of his time and positive spirit. As a playwright who is confined to a wheelchair, he gave visibility to artists with disabilities who are often underrepresented."

ABOVE
Production still of Taylor Harvey as Waitress, Angelina Fiordellisi as Edith, and Michael O'Keefe as Harold in *First Love* by Charles Mee. Photograph by Monique Carboni. 2018.

ABOVE
Production still with Vanessa Redgrave as Maria and Jesse Eisenberg as David from *The Revisionist* by Jesse Eisenberg. Photograph by Sandra Coudert. 2013.

Epilogue

By Jesse Eisenberg

MY FIRST TWO PLAYS were produced at Cherry Lane Theatre. In between the productions, I moved into an apartment across the street. Of course, I really just wanted to live inside the theater.

I'd always had a little stage fright, but when I started writing and performing in my own plays, it became debilitating. I would spend my days in a panic, not being able to get out of bed or eat anything until the show was over. I had nightly terrors about forgetting my lines or breaking character, looking into the audience, and revealing every gross thought I'd ever had. My therapist, Dr. Hess, said I was punishing myself because "having power made me feel unstable due to childhood fears of abandonment," and also because I had "general personality problems."

But one night, I was backstage at my first show, *Asuncion* (2011), with our cast and stage managers, and I had an epiphany. I had just finished acting in a Hollywood movie—the kind where you wait in your trailer for four hours to say one line and run past a green screen—and I realized that being in a Hollywood movie felt like being on a yacht with your friends, and working on a play felt like being on a life raft with your fellow castaways after your ship was torpedoed. It was scary, but we had meaning. It wasn't stable, but it was agile. And you had to be nimble—everything was unknown, and you were navigating in the dark. It was impossible to be creative on a yacht—the boat's too big, and there are too many people to make any interesting decisions. And I felt much more at home on the life raft.

My second show, *The Revisionist* (2013), starred Vanessa Redgrave in her first off-Broadway appearance in decades. I thought she'd be a diva or unflappably aloof, but she immediately folded into the Cherry Lane family. In fact, she was just as nervous as I was. She would show up to the theater three hours before each performance and anxiously pore over her script while picking at a supermarket rotisserie chicken. The two of us would share a cigarette on the fire escape before the show—passing it back and forth with our shaky hands—and a shot of vodka after the show, relieved that the thing was finally over and we had twenty-two full hours before the next one. Vanessa was there because she wanted to share a life raft, too.

My first movie as a writer/director was with A24, and the movie I'm currently making—which is a fever dream about a shy woman who finds her voice at a small theater—is also lucky enough to be at A24. The movie is a veiled autobiographical story of me finding myself in the terrifying, thrilling world of off-Broadway theater. When I heard A24 was partnering with Cherry Lane, it made complete sense. A24 is a life raft. They are nimble and smart, and they produce without a net.

When I would get really panicky before a show, I'd tell myself that, yes, I'm terrified to be onstage, but I'd be even more terrified to be home in my apartment across the street, knowing it was all happening without me.

RIGHT
Cherry Lane Theatre on the cover of *The New Yorker*. May 14, 1960.

Cherry Lane Theatre Production History

NOTE
This is the most current list of mainstage Cherry Lane Theatre productions based on what we have on record. We recognize that some productions have been lost to history and will continue to add to this list as documentation emerges.

Opened Fall 1923

<u>1924</u>

Produced by the Cherry Lane Players:

SATURDAY NIGHT
By Robert R. Presnell
Directed by Reginald Travers
With Herbert Ashton Jr., Marie Chambers, Lyle C. Clement, Fay Courtenay, Juliette Day, Vincent Duffy, George Haller, Ida Fitzhugh, William Friend, Luis Frohoff, Della Trout, Lester Vail
This production was the first theatrical presentation to be reviewed at Cherry Lane Theatre.

THE PRINCE OF ONCE UPON A TIME
By Erno Szep
Directed by William A. Rainey, Reginald Travers, or Evelyn Vaughan

THE MAN WHO ATE THE POPOMACK: A TRAGI-COMEDY
By W. J. Turner
Directed by Reginald Travers
Produced by the Cherry Lane Players
With Esther Belford, Neal Caldwell, Dennis Cleugh, Lionel Ferrend, Thurston Macauley, Ethel Martin, Walter Plunkett, William Rainey, Arthur William Row, Vera Tompkins, Reginald Travers, Sarah Truax, Charles Welsh-Homer, Bert Young, Elizabeth Zachary

TYRANTS: A COMEDY IN FOUR ACTS
By Benjamin F. Glazer and Thaddeus Rittner
Adapted by Benjamin F. Glazer
Presented by Inter-Theatre Arts Inc.
With Charles Cardon, Leonard Carey, Dennis Cleugh, Harda Daube, A. V. Floud, Edmund Forde, Harry Wagstaff Gribble, William Kirkland, Joseph Mullen, Josephine Royle, J. D. Souther, Raymond Walburn, Charles Welsh-Homer
Scenic design by Inter-Theatre Arts Inc.

THE WAY OF THE WORLD
By William Congreve
Produced by the Cherry Lane Players
With Esther Belford, Gertrude Bryan, Margaret Campbell, Edmund Forde, Marie Hassell, Murray Kinnell, Auriot Lee, Bruce de Lette, Florence Miller, Jeanne Owen, William S. Rainey, William H. St. James, Vera Tompkins, Lawrence Tulloch
120 performances

THE LEAP
By Jessi Trimble and Eugenie Woodward

MUD
By Katherine Browning Miller

<u>1925</u>

LOGGERHEADS
By Ralph Cullinan
Produced by Whitford Kane and Barry Macollum
With Earl House, Gail Kane, Whitford Kane, Barry Macollum, Joanna Roos

WILD BIRDS
By Dan Totheroh
Directed by John Wray
With Donald Duff, George Farren, Edmond Forde, Mina C. Gleason, Thomas MacLarnie, Mildred MacLeod, Florence Miller, Dodson L. Mitchell, Laurence Tolloch, Mildred Whitney

THE CRICKET ON THE HEARTH
By Boris Suskevitch

POLLY: AN OPERA IN THREE ACTS
Second part of *The Beggar's Opera*
By John Gay
Directed by Gorden Davis and William S. Rainey
With Richard Abbott, Maude Allan, Oscar Amundsen, Margot Andre, Zoe Barry, William Broderick, Dorothy Brown, William Burke, Marion Cowen, Orde Creighton, David d'Arcy, Edmund Forde, Geneva Harrison, Michael Kilborn, Kathryn Mulholland, Eunice Osborne, Jeanne Owen, William S. Rainey, Grace Searles, Charles Trout, Helen White
Scenic design by Joseph Mullen
Lighting by Mr. Edison
Musical arrangements by Dr. Pepusch, credited to Kate McComb
Piano by William Irwin

225   PRODUCTION HISTORY

AN INTIMATE REVUE
Book by Marita Resler and
   James Reynolds
Music by Herman Hupfeld
With Edith Meiser

DRIFT
By Hyman Adler and Maurice V. Samuels
With Hyman Adler

SO THAT'S THAT
By Joseph Byron Totten
With Charles Gilpin

1926

SHELTER
By Harry Chapman Ford
With Reginald Barlow, Barry Macollum, Janet McLeavy

THE MOON IS A GONG
By John Dos Passos
Directed by Edward Massey
Produced by Juliet Barrett Rublee
With William Challee, Helen Chandler, William Edwards, Agnes Gildea, Hazel Gladding, Frances Hyde, Allyn Morgan Joslyn, Harold Kennedy, Max Leavitt, Benjamin Osipow, George N. Price, Renita Randolph, Edward Reese, James Shute, Glen Snyder, Joseph Thayer, F. B. Wells
Scenic design by Mordecai Gorelik

'TIS PITY SHE'S A WHORE
By John Ford
Directed by C. Edwin Brandt
Produced by the Lenox Hill Players
50 performances

1927

THE BELT
By Paul Sifton
Directed by Edward Massey
Produced by the New Playwrights' Theatre
With Jane Barry, Herbert Bergman, Lawrence Bolton, Edward Buckman, Gail De Hart, Lionel Ferrend, Moss Fleisig, Murray Franklin, Edward Franz, Ross Matthews, Herman Nandes, Benjamin Osipow, George N. Price, Irwin Swerdlow, Charles P. Thompson, Franchot Tone, Parker Totten, Willard Williams
Scenic design by John Dos Passos

THE CENTURIES
Written and directed by Em Jo Basshe
Produced by the New Playwrights' Theatre
With Herman Bandes, Jane Barry, Ellen Bartlett, Herbert Bergman, Lawrence Bolton, Peter Brocco, Edwin Clare, Mary Doerr, Sylvia Feningston, Lionel Ferrand, Murray Franklin, Edward Franz, Albert Gilman, Miriam Gumble, Felix Jacoves, Marion Johnson, Max Leavitt, Mona Lewis, Cecile Lifter, Samuel Schneider, Sheba Strunsky, Irwin Swerdlow, Franchot Tone
Scenic design by John Dos Passos

STIGMA
By Donald Duff and Dorothy Manley
Produced by Donald Duff and Edmond Rickett
With Donald Duff, Edmond Rickett, Joanna Roos, Doralyne Spence

SUBURB
By John Dos Passos
Produced by the New Playwrights' Theatre

SINGING JAILBIRDS
By Upton Sinclair
Produced by the New Playwrights' Theatre

1928

THE INTERNATIONAL
Written and directed by J. H. Lawson
With Herbert Bergman, Miriam Gumble, George Price, Franchot Tone

HOBOKEN BLUES
Book by Michael Gold
Directed by Edward Massey
With Lawrence Bolton, Murray Franklin, Mona Lewis, Sheba Strunsky

THE WALTZ OF THE DOGS
By Leonid Andreyev
Directed and produced by Celia Avramo
With Jules Artfield, Samuel Baron, Antoinette Crawford, Edward England, Sylvia Hoffman, Harold Johnsrud, Douglas B. Krantzor

DARK MIRROR
By Irving Stone
Directed by Adele Gutman Nathan
Produced by the Lenox Hill Players
With Lillian Azair, Syd Brenner, A. J. Field, Milton Gendel, Mary Hallett, Louis John Latzer, Jesse Loewenthal, Mitchell Padraic Marcus, Ben Nelson, Adeline Ruby, Evah Schwab, Jerome Seplow, Fanny Shack, Harold Smith

A LANTERN TO SEE BY
By Lynn Rigg
Directed by Adele Gutman Nathan
Produced by the Lenox Hill Players

1929

THE SUBWAY
By Elmer Rice
Directed by Adele Gutman Nathan
Produced by the Lenox Hill Players
With Herman Bandes, E. Brooks Dascomb, Peter Gwyn, Jane Hamilton, Harry J. Marks, Louis John Latzer, Rudolph Lovinger, Mitchell Padraic Marcus, Ben Nelson, Adeline Ruby, Evah Schwab

PLAYING WITH LOVE
By Arthur Schnitzler
With Lewis Leverett, Catherine Roma, Everett Sloan

A TRIP TO SCARBOROUGH
By Richard Brinsley Sheridan
Directed by Bushnell Cheney
Produced by the Jitney Players
With Bushnell Cheney, Harrison Dowd, David Elliott, Ferris Hartman, Alice B. Keating, William Lovejoy, Gene Magnus, Julia Parlow, Robert R. Parsons, Jack Rennick, Ralph W. Shattuck, Frances Simpson, Elizabeth Zachary
Scenic design by James Reynolds

THE DRAGON
By Lady Augusta Gregory
Directed by David Elliot
Produced by the Jitney Players
With Bushnell Cheney, Harrison Dowd, David Elliott, Ferris Hartman, Alice B. Keating, William Lovejoy, Gene Magnus, Robert R. Parsons, Juliette Phillips, Jack Rennick, Ralph W. Shattuck, Frances Simpson

THE VEGETABLE: OR FROM PRESIDENT TO POSTMAN
By F. Scott Fitzgerald
Directed by Lee Strasberg
Produced by the Lenox Hill Players
With Martin K. Altman, Herman Bandes, David Kerman, Louis John Latzer, Mitchell Padraic Marcus, Harry Jay Marks, Eve Saxen, Fanny Shack, Jerome Seplow, Harold Smith

WADE IN DE WATER
By Mrs. Jeroline Hemsley
Produced by the New Negro Art Theatre
With Inez Clough and
    Hemsley Winfield

SCENES AND MOODS: AN EVENING
    OF THEATRE AND DANCE
With Catherine Cale and Ruth Parks

1930–35

Produced by Paul and Virginia Gilmore:

THE HAVOC
By H. S. Sheldon
With Lew Dick, Paul Gilmore,
    Virginia Gilmore, Phil Huston

THIS THING CALLED LOVE
Directed by Paul Gilmore
With John Anania, Stuart Blum,
    Charlotte Charlaque, Paul Gilmore,
    Virginia Gilmore, Gail Gregg, Reita
    Hauer, Mable Hill, Kate Jolan,
    Stanley La Butus, Beverly Mae Laska,
    Robert Loynaz, Salvatore Lupo,
    William Monsees, Josephine Palmer,
    Louise Paul, Syd Prevore, Sonya
    Simetsky, Pierre Vekony, Marvin
    Ware, Polly White, Retta D. Wood

GIRLS IN UNIFORM
With Virginia Gilmore

EXPERIENCE

A CHARMING RASCAL
By Clare Kummer

A SUCCESSFUL CALAMITY
By Clare Kummer
Directed by Paul Gilmore
With Harry Forbes, Paul Gilmore,
    Virginia Gilmore, Earle Tuttle

FRIENDLY ENEMIES
By Aaron Hoffman and
    Samuel Shipman

STRICTLY DISHONORABLE
By Preston Sturges

THE DRUNKARD
By W. M. H. Smith
Directed by Ben Cameron

UNDER THE GASLIGHT
By Augustin Daly

SIDEWALKS OF NEW YORK

NO MOTHER TO GUIDE HER
By Anthony Forsythe

ART AND MRS. BOTTLE: OR,
    THE RETURN OF THE PURITAN
By Benn W. Levy

THE BROADWAY PARADE
Book and lyrics by Clinton Lewis
Music by Dixie Brand

1930

THE BIGOT
By Slater LaMaster
Directed by Paul Gilmore
With Rocco Caporaso, Alfred Cooper,
    Harold Kathman, William H. Malone,
    Victoria Montgomery, Doris Ryder,
    Charles Sobel, J. Harrison Taylor,
    Lauriel Wood
Scenic design by Harry Smith

THE SHORT CUT
By Percival Lennon
With Beatrice Nichols, Edward Reese,
    Gordon Westcott

THE PASSION OF JUDAS
By Ivan Sokoloff
Presented by the Dramawrights

CHERRY LANE FOLLIES
With Betty Blanc, Alberta Hunter,
    Evelyne Lee, Stanley Rogers

1932

THE BEAST TAMER
By Leah Medisca
With Ann Allen, Ray Bellows,
    Charles Boehme, Lou Brignoli,
    Sol Burrows, Rose Clayman,
    Guerita Donnelly, Mimosa Fejos,
    Joseph Gallo, Mary Martin McCarthy,
    Neryda Montez, Isabelle Prince,
    Richard Reeves, David Schreiber,
    Mary Shaw, Marie Stark, Francis
    Stone, Harry Wilson

THE BLACK ACE
By C. Gordon Kurtz

1933

HOUSE OF HATE

1934

TROJAN WOMEN
By Euripides

1935–36

PAUL GILMORE'S MYSTERY
    THEATRE

THE PHANTOM
By Dion Boucicault

MURDERED ALIVE
By Wilbur Braun

MAN CRAZY
By Stephen Sanford
With Frances Arnold, Fredric Cali,
    Eloise Ferrier, Evelyn Finkles,
    James Hale, Dolores Leon, Dorothea
    Mallory, Vincent Mallory, Elsia
    Micheal, Thad Sharretts, Sylvia
    Singer, Jack Stern

DOCTOR JEKYLL AND
    MISTER HYDE

BETWEEN OURSELVES

DRACULA
By John L. Balderston and
    Hamilton Deane
Directed by Paul Gilmore
With Stanley Blum, Light Bourne,
    Charlotte Charague, Eleanor Eaton,
    Jerry Gallon, Paul Gilmore, Virginia
    Gilmore, Reita Harowitz, Mable
    Hill, Mary Elizabeth Honaghan,
    Emily Julian, Stanley La Butus,
    Robert Loynaz, Charlotte Luck, Ken
    Michell, Delmar Neutzman, Ann Paul,
    Sydney Prevore, Sonya Simetsky,
    Pierre Vekony, Marvin Ware

1937

THREE MEN ON A HORSE
By John Cecil Holm and George Abbott
Produced by Paul Gilmore

THE BISHOP MISBEHAVES
By Frederick Jackson
Produced by John Golden
With Sidney Cassel, Jean DeBear, Paul
    Gilmore, Virginia Gilmore, Fernand
    Larbaud, Joel Nash, John Regan, Ann
    Rogers, Frank Thune, Charles Willis
Scenic Design by Ann Rogers

1939

RESERVE TWO FOR MURDER
By John Randall

1940

VALESKA GERT
Produced by Mystery Theatre Inc.
Assisted by Sonja Wronkov, singer in six languages

1942

Produced by Savoy Opera Guild:

IOLANTHE
By W. S. Gilbert and Arthur Sullivan

THE GONDOLIERS
By W. S. Gilbert and Arthur Sullivan

THE MIKADO
By W. S. Gilbert and Arthur Sullivan

RUDDIGORE
By W. S. Gilbert and Arthur Sullivan

PATIENCE
By W. S. Gilbert and Arthur Sullivan

THE PIRATES OF PENZANCE and COX AND BOX
By W. S. Gilbert and Arthur Sullivan

H.M.S. PINAFORE
By W. S. Gilbert and Arthur Sullivan

1945

THE EMPEROR JONES
By Eugene O'Neill

ART & MRS. BOTTLE: OR, THE RETURN OF THE PURITAN
By Benn W. Levy

1946

Produced by the Spur Theatre Company:

JUNO AND THE PAYCOCK
By Sean O'Casey
Directed by Carmen Capalbo

AWAKE AND SING!
By Clifford Odets
Directed by Leo Lieberman

DEAR BRUTUS
By Sir James Barrie
Directed by Leo Lieberman

SHADOW AND SUBSTANCE
By Paul Vincent Carroll
Directed by Carmen Capalbo

Produced by On-Stage Theatre Company (founded by Al Hurwitz and Bob Ramsey):

GAS
By Georg Kaiser
Directed by Irv Stiber
With Beatrice Arthur, Ellen Green, Norman Howard, Jean (Gene) Saks, Jerry Stiller
Choreography by Bert Prensky

NO EXIT
By Jean-Paul Sartre

YERMA
By Federico García Lorca
Directed by Alan Harper

1947

THE DOG BENEATH THE SKIN
By W. H. Auden and Christopher Isherwood
With Beatrice Arthur (professional debut), Lynne Rogers, Kim Stanley, Jerry Stiller

LIFE SENTENCE
By Philip Van Dyke
Directed by Marjorie Hildreth
With Earl Booth, Anne Farrell, John Fitzgerald, Barbara Long, Tom Long, Barry Rawlins, Edith West

THE WATCHED POT
By Saki (H. H. Munro)
Directed by Walter Mullen
With Elsie Clauss, Ellen Green, Jan Kindler, Barbara Long, Walter Mullen, Olivia, Jean Saks

HENRY IV
By Luigi Pirandello
Translated by Edward Storer
Directed by Alexis Solomos
Produced by On-Stage
With Louis Criss, Edward Hussey, Victor Jonston, George Joseph, Glenn McCausland, Michael Mear, Henry Proach, Claire Ramsay, Linda Rhodes, Jean Saks, Kchast Sayers, Walter Witcover

THE FAMILY REUNION
By T. S. Eliot

1948

ANGEL STREET
By Patrick Hamilton

THE THIRTEENTH GOD
By Richard Gerson
Directed by Judith Malina
With Judith Malina and Geraldine Page
Scenic design by Julian Beck
This production was a trial run for the Living Theatre at Cherry Lane.

THE ADDING MACHINE
By Elmer Rice
Directed by Robert E. Eley
With Beatrice Arthur, Shelley Collins, Bernard Diamond, Arthur Lewis
Scenic design by Janet Owen
Lighting by Dey Erben

THE OWL AND THE PUSSYCAT
By Stanley Bortner
Directed by Robert T. Eley
Produced by the New York Repertory Group
With Beatrice Arthur, Jimmy McElwain, Christine McKeown, David F. Perkins, Florence Stanley

1949

THIS THING CALLED LOVE
By Edwin J. Burke
Directed by Paul Gilmore

Produced by Off-Broadway Inc., Little Theatre Group (founded by Beatrice Arthur and Gene Saks):

YES IS FOR A VERY YOUNG MAN
By Gertrude Stein
Directed by Lamont Johnson
With Beatrice Arthur, A. L. Dreiblatt, Anthony Franciosa, Michael Vincent Gazzo, Leola Le Sand, Jane Moutrie, Gene Saks, Kim Stanley

TOO MANY THUMBS
By Robert Hivnor
Directed by Curt Conway
Produced by Off-Broadway Inc.
With Sadie Long, Nehemia Persoff,

Dick Robbins, Gene Saks, Kim Stanley

BOURGEOIS GENTLEMAN
By Jean-Baptiste Poquelin de Molière
Directed by Sidney Lumet
With Beatrice Arthur, Frank Corsaro, Eddie Frost, Lynn Hudson, Sadie Long, Ben Malek, Gene Saks
Scenic and costume design by Bertrand Marcotte

ONCE AROUND THE BLOCK
By William Saroyan

1951

Produced by The Living Theatre:[1]

DOCTOR FAUSTUS LIGHTS THE LIGHTS
By Gertrude Stein
With Sudie Bond, Remy Charlip, Patty Dinnell, Tony Grosso, Donald Marye, Constance Mobley, Robert King Moody, Kathe Snyder, Louis Spencer, Larry Swanson, Michael Wright
Choreography by Remy Charlip
Scenic design by Julian Beck
Lighting by Marjorie Spitz
Music by Richard Banks

BEYOND THE MOUNTAIN
By Kenneth Rexroth
With Judith Malina

THE THIRTEENTH GOD
By Richard Gerson

1952

An Evening of Bohemian Theatre:

LADIES VOICES
By Gertrude Stein

SWEENEY AGONISTES
By T. S. Eliot

DESIRE CAUGHT BY THE TAIL
By Pablo Picasso

FAUSTINA
By Paul Goodman
With Julie Bovasso, Walter James, Judith Malina, Paul Smith

MUSIC OF CHANGES
A piece for solo piano
By John Cage
With David Tudor

THE HEROES
A reading by Dylan Thomas
By John Ashbury
Scenic design by Julian Beck

UBU ROI
By Alfred Jarry
Translated by Julian Beck and Judith Malina
Scenic design by Julian Beck

The year 1952 also saw a series of midnight folk music concerts produced by Paddy, Tom, and Liam Clancy. Artists presented included Pete Seeger, Burl Ives, Jean Ritchie, Jack Elliot, Theodore Bikel, and Bob Dylan.

1954–55

Produced by Proscenium Productions:[2]

THE WAY OF THE WORLD
By William Congreve
With Thayer David, Louis Edmonds, Fritz Weaver, Nancy Wickwire
122 performances

MORNING'S AT SEVEN
By Paul Osbourn
Directed by Warren Enters
With Tom Bosley, Richard Bowler, Harrison Dowd, Kate Harrington, Dorrit Kelton, Walter Klavun, Gubi Mann, Martha Morton, June Walker
Scenic design by John Connell
Costume design by Don Crawford
125 performances

DRAGON'S MOUTH
By Jacquetta Hawkes and J. B. Priestley
Directed by Warren Enters
With Lauren Gilbert, Theodore Marcuse, Ruth Matteson, Nancy Sheridan
Scenic design by Robert Merriman
Costume design by Don Crawford
34 performances

THIEVES' CARNIVAL
By Jean Anouilh
With Martin Allen, Marie Andrews, Tom Bosley, Thomas Carlin, Keith Eilliot, Gerry Fleming, Robert Gerringer, Marvin Gordon, Raymond Johnson, William LeMassena, Dolores Mann, Don Redlich, Frances Sternhagen, Jack Tamas, Bernard Tone, Stuart Vaughan
Choreography by Don Redlich
Staging by Warren Enters
Scenic design by Don Crawford

1956

DANDY DICK
By Sir Arthur Wing Pinero
Directed by Warren Enters
With Susan Brown, Felix Deebank, Olive Dunbar, Willard Giles, Walter Klavun, William MacDougall, Skedge Miller, William Moor, Barbara Stanton, George Turner, Dee Victor
Scenic design by Don Crawford
Stage management by Michael Dewell and Ida Redding
14 performances

THE MAN WITH THE GOLDEN ARM
By Jack Kirkland
Directed by Louis MacMillan
Produced by Contemporary Theatre
With Robert Bernard, Maurice Brenner, Dick Campbell, Terry Carter, Maggie Davis, Virginia Downing, Peggy Feury, Vincent Gardenia, Harry Gresham, Lew Guss, Sidney Kay, Robert Loggia, Gene Miller, Frederick O'Neal, Diana Sands, Al Spartic, Dolores Sutton, Bob Weinsko, Metro Welles, Wayne Wilson

---

1. Julian Beck rented Cherry Lane for $900 a month as a space for the Living Theatre after inheriting $6,000 from an uncle who had no children.
2. Proscenium Productions at Cherry Lane became the first off-Broadway company to receive a Special Tony Award for high quality and viewpoint, as shown in *The Way of the World* and *Thieves' Carnival*. The award was presented to Warren Enters, Robert Merriman, and Sybil Trubin in 1955.

Scenic and costume design and lighting
  by Paul Morrison
Stage management by Edward Felton
  and Hal Halvorsen

PURPLE DUST
By Sean O'Casey
Directed by Philip Burton
Produced by Noel Behn and Paul Shyre
With Harry Bannister, Alan Bergmann,
  Stephen Elliot, Alvin Epstein, Peter
  Falk, Robert Gerringer, Stefan
  Gierasch, Bette Henritze, Mike
  Kellin, P. J. Kelly, James Kenny, Sandy
  Kenyon, Kathleen Murray, Paul
  Shyre, Mary Welch; understudies
  included Hugh Palmerston and
  Barbra Streisand[3], understudy and
  assistant stage manager; replacements
  included Roger Evan Boxill, Robert
  Carle, Humphrey Davis, Peter Falk,
  Sandy Kenyon, Liam Lenihan, Scottie
  MacGregor, Hugh Palmerston, Patricia
  Peardon, Roy Poole; understudies
  for replacements included Alan
  Bergmann, Ellen Cobb-Hill, Betsy Holt
Scenic and costume design and lighting
  by Lester Polakov
Stage management by Raymond Frederick,
  Jay Harnick, Richard B. Shull
430 performances, longer than an
  O'Casey play had ever run anywhere

THE ADMIRABLE BASHVILLE
  and THE DARK LADY OF THE
  SONNETS
By George Bernard Shaw
Directed by Charles Olsen
With Thomas Barbour, Leo Bloom
  (replacement), James N. Clark,
  Edward Crowley, J. Robert Dietz,
  Karl Farrar, William Kee, Robert
  Ludlum (replacement), Fran Malis,
  Gerry Matthews, Glen Nielsen,
  Ray Rizzo, Frederick Rolf, Barbara
  Schanz, Ron Soble (replacement),
  Frances Sternhagen
Scenic design by Lester Hackett
Costume design by Jim Oyster
Lighting by Gerald Feil
Stage management by Evelyne Delore,
  John Finkbinder, Jim Oyster
98 performances
1956 Clarence Derwent Award to Frances
  Sternhagen for most promising female
  performance in a supporting role

THREE PREMIERES; ONE-ACT
  PLAYS:

  SIDEWALKS AND THE SOUND
    OF CRYING
  By S. Lee Pogostin

  THIS PROPERTY IS CONDEMNED
  By Tennessee Williams

  ONCE AROUND THE BLOCK
  By William Saroyan

1958

ENDGAME
By Samuel Beckett
Directed by Alan Schneider
Produced by Noel Behn and
  Rooftop Productions
With Alvin Epstein, P. J. Kelly, Lester
  Rawlins, Nydia Westman
Scenic design by David Hays
104 performances

CAMILLE
By Alexandre Dumas
With Colleen Dewhurst

A PARTY WITH BETTY COMDEN
  AND ADOLPH GREEN
By Comden and Green
Music by Leonard Bernstein, Saul
  Chaplin, Roger Edens, Jule Styne,
  André Previn, Jule Styne

THE BOY FRIEND
By Sandy Wilson
Directed by Gus Schirmer
763 performances
This production was considered by many
  to be much truer to the original London
  production than its 1954 Broadway
  predecessor. The orchestra consisted
  of a banjo, drums, and a piano.

1959

DINNY & THE WITCHES: A FROLIC
  ON GRAVE MATTERS
By William Gibson
Directed by Jess Kimmel
Produced by Jess Kimmel and
  Alfred Stern
With Will Albert, Dean Lyman Almquist,
  Julie Bovasso, Kay Doubleday, Ellen
  Bogan Engel, Harry Fritzius, Avril
  Gentles, Bill Heyer, Jesse Jacobs,
  Robert Leland, Bernard Reed, Sylvia
  Shay, E. Francis Simon, Renee Taylor
Choreography by Ted Cappy
Scenic design by John Robert Lloyd
Music by Bobby Scott
Stage management by George Thorn
29 performances

1960

THE PRETENDER
By Lionel Abel
Produced by Frank Perry
With James Earl Jones and
  Roscoe Lee Browne

GAY DIVORCE
Book by Dwight Taylor
Music and lyrics by Cole Porter
Directed by Gus Schirmer Jr.
Produced by Noel Behn and
  New Princess Company
With Frank Aletter, Adele Aron,
  Beatrice Arthur, Tony Aylward,
  Gaylynn Baker, Emory Bass, Kay
  Brower, Charles Davisson, Kathi
  Dean, Mary Jane Doerr, Amy
  Freeman, Judy Johnson, Sigyn
  [Lund], Skedge Miller, Jeanne Rogers
Choreography by Joan Mann
Scenic design by Helen Pond and
  Herbert Senn
Costume design by Ann Roth
Lighting by Charles Levy
Musical direction and arrangements by
  Fred Werner Jr.

THE SUDDEN END OF ANNE
  CINQUEFOIL
By Richard Hepburn

DRUMS UNDER THE WINDOWS
Book by Sean O'Casey
Adapted and directed by Paul Shyre
Produced by the Torquay Company
With George Brenlin, Dana Elcar,
  Pauline Flanagan, Martyn Green,
  James Kenney, Dorothy Patten,
  William Windom
Scenic and costume design by
  Eldon Elder
Lighting by Dean Francis
Musical direction and arrangements by
  Herbert Harris

---

[3] At 15, Barbra Streisand worked at Cherry Lane, "moving sets and painting scenery." She debuted as an understudy in *Purple Dust*.

Stage management by Pierre Epstein
109 performances

ERNEST IN LOVE
Book and lyrics by Anne Croswell
  (based on Oscar Wilde's *The Importance of Being Earnest*)
Music by Lee Pockriss
Directed by Harold Stone
Produced by Noel Behn and
  Robert Kamlot
With John Irving, Lucy Landau,
  Alan Shayne, Kate Wilkinson
Choreography by Frank Derbas

1961

TIGER RAG
Book and lyrics by Seyril Schochen
Music by Kenneth Gaburo
Directed by Ella Gerber
Produced by Lorin Ellington Price
With Nancy Andrews, Carlton Colyer,
  Brennan Moore, Logan Ramsey,
  Patricia Roe
Choreography by Peter Conlow
Lighting by Jules Fisher

SMILING THE BOY FELL DEAD
Book by Ira Wallach
Lyrics by Sheldon Harnick
Music by David Baker
Directed by Theodore Mann
Produced by George Kogel and
  Theodore Mann
With Lucinda Abbey, Russell Bailey,
  Ted Beniades, Claiborne Cary, Gino
  Conforti, Dodo Denney, Charles Goff,
  Justine Johnston, Louise Larabee,
  Phil Leeds, Joseph Macaulay, Danny
  Meehan, Heinz Neumann, Geraine
  Richards, Joseph Schaeffer, Irene
  Siegfried, Warren Wade
Scenic design by Helen Pond and
  Herbert Senn
Costume design by Theoni V. Aldredge
Lighting by David Hays
Musical direction and vocal
  arrangements by Julian Stein
Stage management by Gerald Fell
22 performances

Double Bill
By Edward Albee
Produced by Richard Barr and
  Clinton Wilder
With Rae Allen, John C. Becher,
  Roberts Blossom, Sudie Bond, Helen
  Page Camp, Nancy Cushman, Jane
  Hoffman, John McCurry, Ben Piazza,
  Lee Richardson, Harold Scott
Scenic design by William Ritman:

  THE AMERICAN DREAM

  THE DEATH OF BESSIE SMITH

HAPPY DAYS
World premiere
By Samuel Beckett
Directed by Alan Schneider
With Ruth White and John C. Becher
Scenic design by William Ritman
Stage management by Helen Page Camp
  and Kenneth Geist
28 performances
1962 Obie Awards to Ruth White for
  Distinguished Performance and to
  Samuel Beckett for Best Foreign Play

AND HE MADE HER
By Doric Wilson

POSTCARDS
By James Prideaux
Directed by Richard Barr

LIFE AND DEATH
By Edward Albee

THE LONG CHRISTMAS DINNER
By Thornton Wilder
Directed by Michael Kahn

QUEEN OF FRANCE
By Thornton Wilder
Directed by Michael Kahn

THE HAPPY JOURNEY TO TRENTON
  AND CAMDEN
By Thornton Wilder
Directed by Michael Kahn

1962

Produced by Richard Barr, Clinton
  Wilder, and Edward Albee:[4]

A STAGE AFFAIR
By Paul Crabtree
Directed by Paul Crabtree
Produced by Barry C. Tuttle
With Carleton Carpenter, Maryann
  Gudzin, Richard Higgs, Louise King,
  Tom Pedi
8 performances

ENDGAME
By Samuel Beckett
Directed by Alan Schneider
With John C. Becher, Sudie Bond,
  Vincent Gardenia, Ben Piazza

LITTLE MARY SUNSHINE
Book, music, and lyrics by Rick Besoyan
Directed by Rick Besoyan
With Leonard Frye, Margaret Hall,
  Richard Charles Hoh, Kenneth
  MacMillan, Janice Mars

THIS SIDE OF THE DOOR
By Terrence McNally
With Estelle Parsons and
  William Traylor

EX-MISS COPPER QUEEN ON A SET
  OF PILLS
By Megan Terry

Theatre of the Absurd
Produced by Theater 1962,
  Richard Barr, Clinton Wilder
Directed by Edward Albee, Richard
  Barr, Donald Davis, Alan Schneider,
  George Sherman:

  ENDGAME
  By Samuel Beckett

  DEATHWATCH
  By Jean Genet

  PICNIC ON THE BATTLEFIELD
  By Fernando Arrabal

  GALLOWS HUMOR
  By Jack Richardson

---

[4] Albarwild, a collaboration between producers Richard Barr and Clinton Wilder and playwright Edward Albee, began staging at Cherry Lane. The collaboration was designed to give production opportunities to emerging playwrights.

THE SANDBOX
By Edward Albee

WAITING FOR GODOT
By Samuel Beckett

THE KILLER
By Eugène Ionesco

BERTHA
By Kenneth Koch

THE ZOO STORY
By Edward Albee

A TOY FOR THE CLOWNS
By Gene Feist

CHIT CHAT ON A RAT
By C. Skrivanek Atherton

PROMETHEUS BOUND
By Lawrence Wunderlich

WHISPER INTO MY GOOD EAR
By William Hanley
Directed by Richard Altman
Produced by Theatre 63
With Roberts Blossom and Boris Tumarin
Scenic design by William Ritman
Stage management by John Actman and Tony Musante
48 performances

MRS. DALLY HAS A LOVER
By William Hanley
Directed by Richard Altman
With Estelle Parsons and Robert Drivas
48 performances
1963 Theatre World Awards to Estelle Parsons and Robert Drivas

THE AMERICAN DREAM
By Edward Albee
Directed by Alan Schneider
Produced by Theater 1962
With John C. Becher, Sudie Bond, Alice Drummond, Jane Hoffman, Ben Piazza

THE DEATH OF BESSIE SMITH
By Edward Albee

THE DUMBWAITER
By Harold Pinter
Directed by Alan Schneider
With John C. Becher, Dan Bly (understudy), Dana Elcar, Henderson Forsythe, Gerry Hjert (understudy), Michael Lombard (replacement)
Scenic design by William Ritman
Lighting by Lloyd Burlingame
Stage management by Dan Bly and Robert Moss
578 performances
1963 Obie Award to Alan Schneider for Best Director

THE COLLECTION
By Harold Pinter
Directed by Alan Schneider
With Henderson Forsythe, Eric Parcher (understudy), James Patterson, James Ray, Patricia Roe
Scenic design by William Ritman
Lighting by Lloyd Burlingame
Stage management by Dan Bly and Robert Moss
578 performances
1963 Obie Awards to Alan Schneider for Best Director and to James Patterson for Distinguished Performance

1963

THE AMERICAN DREAM
By Edward Albee

THE ZOO STORY
By Edward Albee

CORRUPTION IN THE PALACE OF JUSTICE
By Ugo Betti
Translated by Henry Reed
Directed by Richard Altman
With C. K. Alexander, Leonardo Cimino, Lance Cunard, Russell Gold, John Hetherington, David Hooks, Wyman Pendleton, Muni Seroff, Sy Travers, Maria Tucci, Dianne Turley
Scenic design by William Ritman
Stage management by Robert Currie
103 performances

1964

THE LOVER
By Harold Pinter
Directed by Alan Schneider
With Hilda Brawner, Charles Kindl, Michael Lipton

Triple Bill
Presented by Edward Albee, Richard Barr, Clinton Wilder, with Rita Fredericks
Scenic design by William Ritman:

PLAY
By Samuel Beckett
Directed by Alan Schneider
With Alice Drummond, Marian Reardon, Ray Stewart

THE TWO EXECUTIONERS
By Fernando Arrabal
Directed by Edward Parone
With George Anderson, Charles Kindl, Ron Mack, Peter Michaels, Marian Reardon, David Spielberg

DUTCHMAN
By LeRoi Jones (Amiri Baraka)
Directed by Edward Parone
With Robert Hooks and Jennifer West

THE GIANTS' DANCE
By Otis Bigelow
Directed by Jack Sydow
Produced by Richard Barr and Clinton Wilder
With Leonard Drum, Alice Drummond, Dillon Evans, Bill Fletcher, Wyman Pendleton, Kelly Jean Peters, Terrence Scammell, Boris Tumarin, Herbert Voland

THE BURIAL COMMITTEE
By Otway Crockett

1965

THE CITY SCENE: PART I

PARADISE GARDENS-EAST
By Frank Gagliano
Directed by Melvin Bernhardt
With John Bakos, Jack K. Harmon, Charlotte Jones, Gustav Sabin, Linda Segal, William Shust, Willy Switkes

Presented by Theater 1965, Playwrights Unit as the Fourteenth Workshop Production of the 1964–65 season:

First Evening of New Playwrights:

UP TO THURSDAY
By Sam Shepard
Directed by Chuck Gnys
With Joyce Aaron and Harvey Keitel
This was Shepard's first professional production.

BALLS
By Paul Foster
With Shirley Stoler

HOME FREE!
By Lanford Wilson
Directed by Marshall W. Mason
With Joanna Miles and Michael
　Warren Powell

Second Evening of New Playwrights:

　PIGEONS
　By Lawrence Osgood
　Directed by Edward Parone
　With Geraldine Fitzgerald,
　　Charlotte Jones, Marian Reardon

　CONERICO WAS HERE TO STAY
　By Frank Gagliano
　Directed by Melvin Gagliano
　With Vicki Blankenship, Jose M.
　　Bonilla, Mark Gordon, Charles
　　Kindl, William Maner, Jaime
　　Sanchez, Linda Segal, Harvey
　　Selsby, Willy Switkes

Third Evening of New Playwrights:

　HUNTING THE JINGO BIRD
　By Kenneth Pressman
　Directed by Chuck Gnys

　LOVEY
　By Joseph Morgenstern
　With James Coco

　DO NOT PASS GO
　By Charles Nolte
　Directed by Alan Schneider
　With Roberts Blossom and
　　Charles Nolte

THAT THING AT THE CHERRY LANE
By Jeff Steve Harris
Additional material by Lesley Davison,
　Michael McWhinney, Jerry Powell,
　Ira Wallach
Directed by Bill Penn
Produced by Richard Barr and
　Theater 1965
With Conard Fowkes, Hugh Hurd,
　Ben Kukoff, Morgan Paull,
　Evelyn Russell, Jo Anne Worley

THE ZOO STORY
By Edward Albee
Directed by Alan Schneider
With George Bartenieff and Ben Piazza
168 performances

KRAPP'S LAST TAPE
By Samuel Beckett
Directed by Alan Schneider
With George Bartenieff
168 performances

HAPPY DAYS
By Samuel Beckett
With Jean-Louis Barrault, Wyman
　Pendleton, Madeleine Renaud

THE DEATH OF BESSIE SMITH
By Edward Albee

A LESSON IN A DEAD LANGUAGE
By Adrienne Kennedy

GOOD DAY
By Emanuel Peluso
Directed by Walt Witcover
With Frank Langella, Nancy Marchand,
　Joel Stewart
1966 Obie Awards to Emanuel Peluso
　for Distinguished Play and to
　Frank Langella for Distinguished
　Performance

THE EXHAUSTION OF OUR SON'S
　LOVE
By Jerome Max
Directed by Walt Witcover
With Clarice Blackburn, Dustin
　Hoffman, Betty Lou Holland, Albert
　M. Ottenheimer, Stephen Strimpell
1966 Obie Awards to Dustin Hoffman
　for Best Actor and to Clarice
　Blackburn for Distinguished
　Performance

THE RAPE OF BUNNY STUNTZ
By A. R. Gurney
Directed by Charles Gnys
Produced by the Playwrights' Unit
　(Edward Albee, Richard Barr,
　Clinton Wilder)
With Rusti Moon, Harry Spillman,
　Helen Westcott

1966

ROOMS: A DOUBLE-BILL
By Stanley Mann
Directed by George Keathley
Produced by Margaret Taylor Barker,
　Gene Persson, Hy Silverman,
　Edwin Wilson
With James Broderick, Irene Dailey,
　Shirley Knight, Dorothy Raymond:

BETTER LUCK NEXT TIME
By Stanley Mann

A WALK IN DARK PLACES
By Stanley Mann
With James Broderick, Irene Dailey,
　Shirley Knight

BIG MAN
By Lawrence Weinberg
With Rue McClanahan and
　Mitchell Mestos

DUET FOR THREE
By Lawrence Weinberg
With Rue McClanahan

POSTCARDS
By James Prideaux
Directed by Richard Barr

LIFE AND DEATH
By Edward Albee

THE LONG CHRISTMAS DINNER
By Thornton Wilder
Directed by Michael Kahn

QUEEN OF FRANCE
By Thornton Wilder
Directed by Michael Kahn

THE HAPPY JOURNEY TO TRENTON
　AND CAMDEN
By Thornton Wilder
Directed by Michael Kahn

THE BUTTER AND EGG MAN
By George S. Kaufman
Directed by Burt Shevelove
With Tyne Daly

NIGHT OF THE DUNCE
By Frank Gagliano
Directed by Joseph Hardy
With Alfred Hinckley, Elaine Hyman,
　Terry Kiser, Salem Ludwig, Tony
　Musante, James Noble, Anne Revere,
　Robert Salvio

1967

THE RIMERS OF ELDRITCH
By Lanford Wilson
Directed by Michael Kahn
With Katherine Bruce, Dena Dietrich,
　Walter Hadler, Betty Henritze,
　Alfred Hinckley, Blanche Lee,

Ruth Manning, Elizabeth Moore, James Noble, Kevin O'Connor, John O'Leary, Richard Orzel, Don Scardino, Helen Stenborg, Amy Taubin, Susan Tyrrell, Kate Wilkinson
Scenic design by William Ritman
32 performances
1967 Obie Award to Betty Henritze for Distinguished Performance

THE PARTY ON GREENWICH AVENUE
By Grandin Conover
Directed by Richard Altman
With Joyce Aaron, Carolyn Coates, Lance Cunard, Edward Easton, James Hall, Michael Heit, Tresa Hughes, Roscoe Orman, Philip Sterling, Clarence Williams III
Scenic design by Rouben Ter-Arutunian
Costume design by Betty Williams
6 performances

Double Bill:

THE BASEMENT
By Murray Schisgal
Directed by Larry Arrick
Produced by Edgar Lansbury and Marc Merson
With James Coco, Sylvia Gassell, Gene Hackman

FRAGMENTS
By Murray Schisgal
Directed by Larry Arick
Produced by Edgar Lansbury and Marc Merson
With Humbert Allen Astredo, James Coco, Gene Hackman, Tresa Hughes

IN CIRCLES
By Gertrude Stein
Directed by Lawrence Kornfeld
Produced by the Judson Poets Theatre
With Theo Barnes, Lee Crespi, Lee Guilliatt, George McGrath
Music by Al Carmines
"This production is for Alice B. Toklas."

1968

NOW
By John Aman, George Hainsoh, and the cast

SAVED
By Edward Bond
Directed by Alan Schneider
With Margaret Braidwood, Kevin Conway, Dorrie Kavanaugh, James Woods

Triple Bill:

I SAW A MONKEY
By Randolph Carter

SAVE IT FOR YOUR DEATHBED
By Randolph Carter

THE LATE LATE SHOW
By Randolph Carter

1969

TO BE YOUNG, GIFTED AND BLACK
Adapted by Robert Nemiroff
Directed by Gene Frankel
Produced by Harry Belafonte/Chiz Schultz and Edgar Lansbury
With Barbara Baxley, John Beal, Rita Gardner, Gertrude Jeanette, Janet League, Stephen Strimpell, Cicely Tyson, Andre Womble
Scenic design by Merrill Sindler
Lighting by Barry Arnold
Sound and production stage management by Gigi Cascio
Musical coordination by William Eaton
Photographic effects by Stuart Bigger

LOVE YOUR CROOKED NEIGHBOR
By Harold J. Chapler

1970

UNFAIR TO GOLIATH
By Ephraim Kishon
Lyrics by Herbert Appleman
Music by Menachem Zur
Produced by Herbert Appleman and Ephraim Kishon With Hugh Alexander, Jim Brochu, Jay Devlin, Corinne Kason, Laura May Lewis
Scenic design and lighting by C. Murawski
Costume design by Pamela Scofield
Musical direction by Menachem Zur
75 performances

THE NUNS
By Eduardo Manet
Adapted by Don Parker and Paul Verdier
Directed by Paul Verdier

With Robert Brink, Maxine Herman, Roy Scheider, Sydney Walker
Scenic design by Peter Harvey
Costume design by Rita Riggs
Lighting by F. Mitchell Dana
Stage management by Elissa Lane

CHILDREN IN THE RAIN
By Dennis McIntyre
Directed by Patrick Donovan (assistant) and Frank R. Giordano
Presented by James Clifford Productions
With Frank R. Giordano, Elizabeth Harrymen, Lane Smith
Scenic design by Patrick Donovan
Stage management by John Van Domlin

THE IMMACULATE MISCONCEPTION
By W. Randolph Galvin
Directed by William E. Kinzer
With Frank Borgman, James Glenn, William Kelsey, Mary McGregor, Gwenn Mitchell, John Swearingen, Tony Thomas
Scenic design by W. Randolph Galvin and William E. Kinzer
Costume design by Mary Lou Harvey
Lighting by Lee Goldman

1971

GODSPELL
Book by John-Michael Tebelak
Music and lyrics by Stephen Schwartz
Directed by John-Michael Tebelak
Produced by Joseph Beruh, Stuart Duncan, Edgar Lansbury
With Lamar Alford, Peggy Gordon, David Haskell, Joanne Jonas, Robin Lamont, Sonia Manzano, Gilmer McCormick, Jeffrey Mylett, Stephen Nathan, Herb Simon
Costume design by Susan Tsu
Lighting by Lowell B. Achziger

GUNPLAY
By Yale M. Udoff
Directed by Gene Frankel
With William Bogert, John Doherty, M'el Dowd, Pat Evans, Arny Freeman, Cheryl Houser, Ralph Maurer, Robert Moberly, Tony Musante, Shane Ousey, Lara Parker, Eugene Troobnick, Jim Weston, Kelly Wood
Scenic design by Ralph Funicello and Marjorie Bradley Kellogg

Costume design by Sara Brook
Lighting by Paul Sullivan
Stage management by Peter M. Mumford
23 performances

UNCLE VANYA
By Anton Chekhov
Adapted and directed by Gene Feist
With Sterling Jensen and Winston May
This Roundabout production was brought to Cherry Lane for an additional week after its scheduled run.

1972

WANTED
Book by David Epstein
Music and lyrics by Al Carmines
79 performances

1973

MYSTERY PLAY
By Jean-Claude van Itallie
Directed by Jacques Levy
Produced by J. Craig Owens
With Tom Brannum, Rod Browning, Shami Chaikin, Nancy Charney, Rick Friesen, Cynthia Harris, Judd Hirsch, Donald Warfield
Scenic design by Philip Gilliam
Costume design by Patricia McGourty
Lighting by Judy Rasmuson
Music by Richard Peaslee
Stage management by Robert J. Bruyr
14 performances

WELCOME TO ANDROMEDA
By Ron Whyte
Directed by Tom Moore
Produced by Sidney Annis, Patricia Gray, Ruth Kalkstein
With David Clennon and Bella Jarrett
Scenic design by Peter Harvey
Costume design by Bruce Harrow
Lighting by Roger Morgan
Stage management by Robert Keegan
24 performances

VARIETY OBIT
By Ron Whyte
Directed by Tom Moore
Produced by Sidney Annis, Patricia Gray, Ruth Kalkstein
With Richard Cox and Andrea Marcovici (singers), David Clennon, Mel Marvin (piano), Gary Mure (drums)
Scenic design by Peter Harvey
Costume design by Bruce Harrow
Lighting by Roger Morgan
Stage management by Robert Keegan
24 performances

L'ÉTÉ
By Romain Weingarten
Translated by Shepperd Strudwick III
Directed by Wendell Phillips
Produced by Margaret Barker
With Michael Higgins, Jerry Mayer, Maureen Mooney, Michael Mullins
Scenic design and lighting by William Strom
Sound by Susan Ain
Stage management by Peter von Mayrhauser
10 performances

NOURISH THE BEAST
By Steve Teisch
Directed by Edwin Sherin
Produced by American Place Theatre, Joseph Beruh, Edgar Lansbury
With R. A. Dow, Olympia Dukakis, Lou Gilbert, James Greene, Randy Kim, Stephen Mendillo, John Randolph, Ken Tigar, Peggy Whitton
Scenic design by Karl Eigsti
Costume design by Whitney Blausen
Lighting by Roger Morgan
Stage management by Gigi Cascio
54 performances

1974

FELIX
By Claude McNeal
Directed by Robert Mandel
With Greg Antonacci, Gerry Black, Sydnee Devitt, Eugene Kallman, Penelope Milford, Dick O'Neill, John Perkins, Ramiro Ray Ramirez, Ed Setrakian, Sloane Shelton, Robert Weil
Scenic design by Robert Mitchell
Costume design by Juliellen Weiss
Lighting by Arden Fingerhut
Stage management by Elizabeth Stearns
6 performances

DEAR NOBODY
By Terry Berlanger and Jane Marla Robbins
With Jane Marla Robbins

1975

BLASTS AND BRAVOS: AN EVENING WITH H. L. MENCKEN
Adapted by Paul Shyre
With Paul Shyre
Scenic design by Eldon Elder
Music by Robert Rines
Stage management by Clint Jakeman
46 performances

HUSTLERS
By A. J. Kronengold

1976

CAN YOU SMELL GAS?
Book by Andrew Davies
Music by Tony Hatch and Rick Jones
With Linda Polan
Scenic design and lighting by Michael Krones
Musical direction by Vel Wade
Production supervision by Ronnie Massin
Stage management by David Levine

Double Bill:

SEXUAL PERVERSITY IN CHICAGO
By David Mamet
Directed by Albert Takazauchas
Produced by Larry Goosen and Jeffrey Wachtel
With F. Murray Abraham, Jane Anderson, Peter Riegert, Gina Rogers
Scenic and costume design by Michael Massee
Lighting by Gary Porto
Music by George Quincy
Stage management by William La Rosa
273 performances
1976 Obie Award to David Mamet for Best New American Play

DUCK VARIATIONS
By David Mamet
Directed by Albert Takazauchas
Produced by Larry Goosen and Jeffrey Wachtel
With F. Murray Abraham, Michael Egan, Michael Kellin, Peter Riegert
Scenic and costume design by Michael Massee
Lighting by Gary Porto
Stage management by William La Rosa
273 performances

1977

I WAS SITTING ON MY PATIO THIS GUY APPEARED I THOUGHT I WAS HALLUCINATING
By Robert Wilson
Directed by Lucina Childs and Robert Wilson
With Lucinda Childs and Robert Wilson
Scenic design by A. Christina Giannini and Robert Wilson
Lighting by Beverly Emmons
Film by Byron Lovelace and Greta Wing Miller
14 performances

PASSION OF DRACULA
By Bob Hall and David Richmond
Directed by Peter Bennett
Produced by Bob Hall, Eric Krebs, David Richmond
With Brian Bell, Christopher Bernau, Michael Burg, Sara Herrnstadt (understudy), Samuel Maupin, K. Lype O'Dell, Giulia Pagano, Elliot Vileen, Alice White, K. C. Wilson
Scenic design by Allen Cornell and Bob Hall
Costume design by Jane Tschetter
Stage management by Andrea Naier

1979

POTHOLES
By Elinor Guggenheimer
Directed by Sue Lawless
With Jill Cook, Brandon Maggart, Carol Morley, Cynthia Parva, Lee Roy Reams, Joe Romagnoli, J. Keith Ryan, Sam Wright
Choreography by Wayne Cliento
Scenic design by Kenneth Foy
Costume design by Ann Emonts
Lighting by Robby Monk
Music by Ted Simons
Musical direction by Steven Olrich
Stage management by Marcia McIntosh
15 performances

WOODY GUTHRIE
By Tom Taylor
Adapted by George Boyd, Michael Diamond, Tom Taylor
Directed by George Boyd
Produced by Michael Diamond and Harold Leventhal
With Tom Taylor
Scenic and costume design by Robert Blackman
Lighting by Daniel Adams
Stage management by Scott Allen
47 performances

1980

AN EVENING WITH W. S. GILBERT
By John Wolfson
Songs, poems, lyrics, and letters by W. S. Gilbert
Music by Osmond Carr, Edward German, Arthur Sullivan
Directed by Richard Smithies
With Lloyd Harris
Scenic design by Douglas McKeown
Costume design by Linda Sampson
Musical direction by Alfred Heller
Stage management by Christine Lawton
33 performances

TO BURY A COUSIN
By Gus Wiell
Directed by Philip Oesterman
With Annie Deutsch Abbott, Robert Bloodworth, Lauren Craig, Virginia Daly, Harry Goz, Harvey Pierce, Reuben Schafer, Diane Tarleton, Walter Williamson
Scenic design by Douglas W. Schmidt
Costume design by Robert Wojewodski
Lighting by David F. Segal
Music by Hayden Wayne
Stage management by Tom Capps
54 performances

ALBUM
By David Rimmer
Directed by Joan Micklin Silver
Produced by Richard S. Bright, John Loesser, Gene Persson, in association with Twentieth Century Fox Productions (and by special arrangement with WPA Theatre)
With Kevin Bacon, Ralph Davies (replacement), Keith Gordon, Jennifer Grey (understudy), Jan Leslie Harding, Bruce MacVittie (understudy), Tracy Pollan (replacement), Sam Robards (replacement), Jenny Wright
Scenic design by David Potts
Costume design by Susan Denison
Lighting by Jeff Davis
Sound by Alex McIntyre
Stage management by Bethe Ward
254 performances

1981

ENTERTAINING MR. SLOANE
By Joe Orton
Directed by John Tillinger
With Barbara Bryne, Maxwell Caulfield, Brad Davis (replacement), Jerome Dempsey (replacement), Richard Eddon (understudy, then replacement), Gwyllum Evans, Richard Lupino (understudy), Joe Maher, Eda Seasongood (understudy)
Scenic design by Mark Haack
Costume design by Bill Walker
Lighting by David N. Weiss
Prop supervision by Leslie Moore
Technical direction by William Camp
Wardrobe by Barbara Perkins
Stage management by Richard Eddon and Kevin Mangan
269 performances
1982 Drama Desk Award for Outstanding Revival

1982

COLORED PEOPLE'S TIME
By Leslie Lee
Directed by Horacena J. Taylor
Produced by the Negro Ensemble Company
With L. Scott Caldwell, Chuck Cooper, Robert Gossett, Jackee Harry, Juanita Mahone, Debbi Morgan, Charles H. Patterson, Charles Weldon, Curt Williams
Scenic design by Felix E. Cochren
Costume design by Myrna Colley-Lee
Lighting by Shirley Prendergast
Sound by Gary Harris
Stage management by Femi Sarah Heggie
32 performances

CAST OF CHARACTERS
By Morton Dauwen Zabel
Adapted by William Bixby Jr., David Kaplan, Patrizia Norcia
Directed by David Kaplan
With Patrizia Norcia
Costume design by Dunya Ramicova
Lighting by Stuart Duke
Music by Steve Lutvak
Stage management by Nora Peck
159 performances

TRUE WEST
By Sam Shepard
Directed by Gary Sinise
Produced by Wayne Adams and

Harold Thau
With Gary Sinise, John Malkovich, Sam Schacht, Margaret Thomson, Joan Kendall (understudy), Bruce Lyons (understudy, then replacement), Wayne Adams (replacement), Jim Belushi (replacement), Jere Berns (replacement), Dan Butler (replacement), Gary Cole (replacement), Mary Copple (replacement), Erik Estrada (replacement), Richmond Hoxie (replacement), Tim Matheson (replacement), Peder Melhouse (replacement), Randy Quaid (replacement), Dennis Quaid (replacement), and Daniel Stern (replacement)
Scenic design by Deb Gohr and Kevin Ringdon
Lighting by Kevin Ringdon
Stage management by Larry Bussard
762 performances
1983 Obie Awards to John Malkovich for Performance and to Gary Sinise for Direction; 1983 Clarence Derwent Award to John Malkovich for most promising male performance in a supporting role; 1983 Theatre World Award for John Malkovich

1985

NUNSENSE
Written and directed by Don Goggin
Produced by Bill Crowder, Joseph Hoesl, the Nunsense Theatrical Company
With Christine Anderson, Vicki Belmonte, Semina DeLaurentis, Marilyn Farina, Susan Gordon-Clark (understudy), Suzi Winson
Scenic design by Barry Axtell
Lighting by Susan A. White
Musical direction by Michael Rice
1986 Outer Critics Circle Awards for Best Off-Broadway Musical, to Semina DeLaurentis for Best Debut Performance, and to Dan Goggin for Best Off-Broadway Book and Music

ALICE AND FRED
By Dan Ellentuck
Directed by Gloria Muzio
Produced by Billy Livingston, Joel Key Rice, Mickey Rolfe, Rolfe Company
With Greg Germann, Laura Innes, Victor Slezak, J. Smith-Cameron, Bruce Tracy
Scenic design and lighting by Dale F. Jordan
Costume design by Lloyd K. Waiwaiole
Music and sound by George Andoniadis
Stage management by Kit Liset
14 performances

1986

SWEETHEARTS
Book by Fred de Gresac and Harry R. Smith
Music by Victor Herbert
Lyrics by Robert B. Smith
Produced by Light Opera of Manhattan
With Tom Boyd, Jon Brothers, George H. Croom, David Green, Mark Henderson, Susan Holmes, Ann J. Kirschner, Mary Setrakian
Musical direction by Todd Ellison

1987

THE NO-FRILLS REVUE
Sketches, music, and lyrics mostly by Michael Abbott, Douglas Bernstein Craig Carnelia, Martin Charnin, David Finkle, Sally Fay, Ronny Graham, Marvin Hamlisch, Brian Lasser, Michael Leeds, Denis Markell, Thomas Meeham, Bill Weeden, Sarah Weeks
Dialogue and segues by Douglas Bernstein, Martin Charnin, Denis Markell
Conceived and originally directed by Martin Charnin
Produced by Beam One Ltd., Del Tenney, David H. Peipers, Anthony J. Stimac (associate)
With Adinah Alexander, Sasha Charnin, Clare Fields, Sarah Knapp, Andre Montgomery, Lynn Paynter, Justin Ross, Bob Stillman
Choreography by Frank Ventura
Scenic design by Evelyn Sakash
Costume design by Perry Ellis
Lighting by Clarke W. Thorton
Musical direction by David Gaines
Orchestrations by Steven M. Alper
Stage management by Robin Gray
207 performances

MONA ROGERS IN PERSON
By Philip-Dimitri Galas
Directed by Lynne Taylor-Corbett
Produced by Hart Entertainment Group, Jane Hotzer (associate), Jon Kane (associate), Pamela Koslow
With Helen Shumaker
Lighting by Mimi Jordan Sherin
Stage management by Lynn Moffat
36 performances

ENO
By Eno Rosenn and Daniel Lappin
Produced by Gene S. Jones and Turner/Ross Productions
With Eno Rosenn
Scenic and costume design by Yael Pardes
Lighting by Zeev Navon
Music by Nir Brandt
Sound by Stan Mark

1988

ENGLISH MINT
By Marguerite Duras
Directed by Paul Verdier
Produced by Stages Trilingual Theatre
With Hal Bokar, Paul Verdier, Grace Zabriskie
Scenic design by Jim Sweeters
Costume design by Emily Payne
Lighting by Kevin Mahn
Production supervision by Judith Alonso (assistant) and Gioras Fischer
Stage management by Sindy Slater
16 performances

THE TAFFETAS
Directed by Steven Harris
Produced by Select Entertainment, James Shellenberger, Adam Sternberg (associate), Arthur Whitehall
With Jody Abrahams, Karen Curlee, Melanie Mitchell, Tia Speros, Jean Tait (understudy)
Choreography by Tina Paul
Scenic design by Evelyn Sakash
Costume design by David Graden
Lighting by Ken Billington
Sound by Raymond D. Schilke
Musical direction by Rick Lewis
Stage management by Allison Somers and Jean Tait
171 performances

1989

S. J. PERELMAN IN PERSON
By Bob Shanks
Directed by Ann Shanks
Presented by Comco Productions Inc.
With Lewis J. Stadlen
Scenic design by Wes Peters
Costume design by Leon I. Brauner
Lighting by Mal Sturchio
46 performances

CLOSER THAN EVER
Music by David Shire
Book by Richard Maltby Jr.
Directed by Richard Maltby Jr. and
 Steven Scott Smith
With Brent Barrett, Claudine Cassan-
 Jellison (understudy), Scott Hayward
 Eck (understudy, then replacement),
 Sally Mayes, Richard Muenz, Jim
 Walton (replacement), Craig Wells
 (replacement), Lynne Wintersteller,
 and bass by Robert D. Renino
Musical staging by Marcia Milgrom
 Dodge
Scenic design by Philipp Young
Costume design by Jess Goldstein
Lighting by Natasha Katz
Musical direction by Patrick S. Brady
Conducted by Patrick S. Brady
312 performances
1990 Outer Critics Circle Award
 nomination to Sally Mayes for Best
 Actress in a Musical; 1990 Outer
 Critics Circle Awards for Best Off-
 Broadway Musical, to David Shire
 for Best Off-Broadway Music, and
 to Richard Maltby Jr. for Best Off-
 Broadway Lyrics

BRILLIANT TRACES
By Cindy Lou Johnson
Directed by Terry Kinney
Produced by the Circle Repertory
 Company
With Kevin Anderson and Joan Cusack
Scenic design by John Lee Beatty
Costume design by Laura Crow
Lighting by Dennis Parichy
Sound by Chuck London and
 Stewart Werner
Stage management by Fred Reinglas

1990

THE SUM OF US
By David Stevens
Directed by Kevin Dowling
With Tony Goldwyn, Richard Venture,
 Neil Maffin, Phyllis Somerville,
 Monica Merrymen (understudy),
 Richard Thomsen (understudy),
 Robert Lansing (replacement),
 Matthew Ryan (replacement), Matt
 Salinger (replacement)
Scenic design by John Lee Beatty
Costume design by Therese A. Bruck
Lighting by Dennis Parichy
Sound by Darron L. West
Stage management by Larry Bussard

335 performances
1991 Outer Critics Circle Award for Best
 Off-Broadway Play; 1991 Obie Award
 to Tony Goldwyn for Performance

1991

BIG NOISE OF '92: DIVERSIONS
 FROM THE NEW DEPRESSION
With Kim McClure and Her All-Girl
 Orchestra, Tom Kosis, Tim Michael,
 Mink Stole, Neilan Tyree
Choreography by Tony Musco
Scenic design by Ann Davis
Costume design by Gregg Barnes
Lighting by Douglas O'Flaherty
Sound by Serge Ossorquine
Musical arrangements by Mario Sprouse

1992

HAUPTMANN
By John Logan
Directed by John Logan
With Gunnar Branson, Dev Kennedy,
 Wendy Lueker, Rod McLachlan,
 Denis O'Hare, Donna Powers,
 Craig Spidle
Choreography by Ann Hartdegen
Scenic design by James Dardenne
Costume design by Claudia Boddy
Lighting by Todd Hensley
Sound by Galen G. Ramsey
Stage management by Kristin Laresen

BUBBE MEISES, BUBBE STORIES
By Ellen Gould and Holly Gewandter
Directed by Gloria Muzio
Produced by Renee Blau, Richard
 Frankel, Paragon Productions
With Ellen Gould
Scenic design by David Jenkins
Costume design by Elsa Ward
Lighting by Peter Kaczorowski
Sound by Raymond D. Schilke
Musical direction and arrangements by
 Bob Goldstone
Stage management by Stacey Fleischer
166 performances

1993

LYPSINKA . . . A DAY IN THE LIFE
By John Epperson
Directed by Michael Leeds
With John Epperson and
 Enrico Kuklafraninalli
Choreography by Michael Leeds
Scenic design by James Schuette

Costume design by Anthony Wong
Lighting by Mark McCullough
Sound by Jim Bay
Puppet design by Randy Carfagno
Stage management by Kate Broderick

TROPHIES
By John J. Wooten
Music by David Brunetti
Directed by John Gulley
With Janet Neil Catt, John Henry Cox,
 R. Ward Duffy, Mark Irish,
 Christen Tassin
Scenic design by Mark Cheney
Costume design by Missy West
Lighting by Mark F. O'Connor
Sound by Scott Stauffer

1994

BLOWN SIDEWAYS THROUGH LIFE
Written and performed by Claudia Shear
Directed by Christopher Ashley
Dance staging by Nafisa Shariff
Music by Richard Peaslee
Scenic design by Loy Arcenas
Costume design by Jess Goldstein
Lighting by Christopher Akerlind
Sound by Aural Fixation
Stage management by Kate Broderick
221 performances

INSIDE OUT
Book by Doug Haverty
Lyrics by Doug Haverty and
 Adryan Russ
Directed by Henry Fonte
Produced by Richard Frankel, Randy
 Kelly, Margot Ross London, Carol
 Ostrow, Marc Routh, Prima K.
 Stephen, George Tunick
With Ann Crumb, Harriett D. Foy,
 Kathleen Mahony-Bennett, Jan
 Maxwell, Cass Morgan, Julie Prosser
Choreography by Gary Slavin
Scenic design by Rob Odorisio
Costume design by Gail Brassard
Lighting by Douglas O'Flaherty
Musical direction by E. Suzan Ott
Orchestrations by Ned Ginsburg
Stage management by Craig Palanker

1995

TROPHIES
By John Wooten
Directed by John Galley
Produced by Steven M. Levy and
 Andrew C. McGibbon

With Janet Nell Catt, John Henry Cox, Ward Duffy, Mark Gush, Mark Irish, Christen Tassin

FORTUNE'S FOOLS
By Frederick Stroppel
Directed by John Rando
Produced by Stewart F. Lane
With Marissa Chibas, Bonnie Comley (understudy), Matthew Edwards (understudy), Dorrie Joiner, Danton Stone, Tuc Watkins
Scenic design by Loren Sherman
Costume design by David Murin
Lighting by Phil Monat
Sound by Jim van Bergen
Projection design by Loren Sherman
Stage management by Christopher De Camillis

1996

Angelina Fiordellisi and Susann Brinkley found the Cherry Lane Theatre Company.

THE NEW BOZENA: WINTER IS THE COLDEST SEASON
Written and performed by David Costabile, Michael Dahlen, Kevin Isola
Directed by Rainn Wilson

1997

The Cherry Lane Alternative is founded by Angelina Fiordellisi, artistic director.

IN-BETWEENS
By Bryan Goluboff
Directed by Dante Albertie
Produced by Joan Firestone, Richard Firestone, Mara Gibbs, Evangeline Morphos, Judith Resnick, Frederick M. Zollo
With Carolyn Baeumler, Tony Cucci, Mark Hutchinson, Andrew Miller

TELL-TALE
By Erik Jackson

1998

BLACK HUMOR: THE COMEDY OF LEWIS BLACK
Directed by Mark Linn-Baker
Produced by Cherry Lane Theatre Company
With Lewis Black

1998 Drama Desk nomination to Lewis Black for Outstanding Solo Performance

1999

BEAUTIFUL THING
By Jonathan Harvey
Directed by Gary Griffin
With Susan Bennett, Kurt Brockner, Daniel Eric Gold, Kirsten Sahs, Matt Stinton

STARS IN YOUR EYES
Book, music, and lyrics by Chip Meyrelles
Directed by Gabriel Barre
With John Braden, David M. Lutkin, Heather MacRae, Christa Moore, Christy Carlson Romano, James Stovall, Barbara Walsh

FULLY COMMITTED
By Becky Mode
Directed by Nicholas Martin
With Roger Bart (replacement), Christopher Fitzgerald (replacement), Mark Setlock

2000

SEVENTY-FIFTH ANNIVERSARY BENEFIT
Directed by Eduardo Machado
With Lewis Black, Tyne Daly, Semina DeLaurentis, Micki Grant, Judith Ivey, Heather MacRae, Richard Maltby Jr., Rue McClanahan, Don Scardino, Mark Setlock, David Shire, Dolores Sutton, Barbara Walshevent

2001

SAINT LUCY'S EYES
By Bridgette Wimberly
Directed by Billie Allen
Produced by Cherry Lane Theatre Company and Angelina Fiordellisi
With Willis Burks II, Ruby Dee, Toks Olagundoye, Sally A. Stewart
Scenic design by Beowulf Boritt
Costume design by Alvin B. Perry
Lighting by Jane Reisman
Music and sound by Michael Wimberly
This production was originally developed in the inaugural season of Cherry Lane's Mentor Project, with Wendy Wasserstein.

HAVANA IS WAITING
By Eduardo Machado
Directed by Michael Garces
Produced by Cherry Lane Theatre Company, Angelina Fiordellisi, Barbara Ligeti, Annette Tapert
With Bruce MacVittie, Ed Vassallo, Felix Solis, and Richard Marquez on percussion
Scenic design by Troy Hourie
Costume design by Elizabeth Hope Clancy
Lighting by Kirk Bookman
Sound by David M. Lawson

2002

21 DOG YEARS: DOING TIME @ AMAZON.COM
Written and performed by Mike Daisey
Directed by Jean-Michelle Gregory
Produced by Peter Cane, David J. Foster, Martian Entertainment
Scenic design by Louisa Thompson
Lighting by Russell H. Champa

HAPPY DAYS
By Samuel Beckett
Directed by Joseph Chaikin
Produced by Cherry Lane Theatre
With Joyce Aaron and Ron Faber
Scenic design by Riccardo Hernandez
Costume design by Katherine Roth
Lighting by Beverly Emmons
This production was revived for Cherry Lane's forty-first anniversary.

2003

THE MYOPIA
Written and performed by David Greenspan
Directed by Brian Mertes
Produced by the Foundry Theatre

IT JUST CATCHES
By Carol Hemingway
Music by Cole Porter
Directed by Ed Hastings
Produced by Cherry Lane Theatre and MODA Entertainment in consultation with Carolyn Rossi Copeland
With David Ackroyd, Ann Crumb, Marsh Hanson, Ryan Shively, Daniel Freedom Stewart, Jessica D. Turner
Scenic design by Riccardo Hernandez
Costume design by David C. Woolard
Lighting by Duane Schuler
Sound by Sten Severson

KIKI & HERB: COUP DE THEATRE
Written and performed by Justin Bond and Kenny Mellman
Directed by Scott Elliott
Produced by Westbeth Entertainment and Steven M. Levy
Scenic design by Derek McLane
Costume design by Marc Happel
Lighting by Jason Lyons
Sound by Ken Travis
2003 Drama League nomination to Justin Bond for Distinguished Performance

WOMEN ON FIRE
By Irene O'Garden
Directed by Mary B. Robinson
Produced by Cherry Lane Theatre
With Judith Ivey
Scenic and costume design by Michael Krass
Lighting by Pat Dignan
Sound by Bart Fasbender
Prop design by Faye Armon
2004 Lucille Lortel nomination for Outstanding Solo Show; 2004 Drama League nomination to Judith Ivey for Distinguished Performance; 2004 Dramatist Guild Fund's Madge Evans and Sidney Kingsley Award to Judith Ivey

2004

OPEN HEART
By Robby Benson
Directed by Matt Williams
Produced by Cherry Lane Theatre
With Robby Benson, Stan Brown, Karla DeVito
Choreography by Luis Perez
Scenic design by Michael Brown
Costume design by Ann Hould-Ward
Lighting by Ken Billington
Sound by Aural Fixation
Musical direction by Kevin Farrell
Media design by Batwin & Robin Productions

MISS JULIE
By August Strindberg
Translated by Truda Stockenström
Directed by Scott Schwartz
Produced by Beowulf Boritt and Jessica Niebanck, and a sponsored project of the Adobe Theatre Company
With Opal Alladin, Michael Aranov, Mimi Bilinski

EVE-OLUTION
By Hilary Illick and Jennifer Krier
Directed by Carolyn Cantor
Produced by Lucy Anda, Mari Nakachi, Meg Staunton
With Carolyn McCormick and Sabrina Le Beauf

2005

SLAG HEAP
World premiere
By Anton Dudley
Directed by Michael Morris
Produced by Cherry Lane Theatre
With Brienan Nequa Bryant, Alexander Flores, Vincent Kartheiser, Polly Lee, Maggie Moore, Janelle Anne Robinson
Scenic design by Michael Brown
Costume design by Michael Krass
Lighting by Jeff Croiter
Sound by Bart Fasbender
Dialect coaching by Stephen Gabis
Fight direction by Rick Sordelet
Stage management by Kate Hefel
Casting by Judy Henderson CSA
Marketing by Walker International Communications Group
Press representation by Keith Sherman & Associates
This production was first developed by Cherry Lane Mentor Project 2003, with Ed Bullins.

RENOVATION: July 2005–April 2006

2006

ON THE LINE
By Joe Roland
With David Prete, Joe Roland, John Zibell
Directed by Peter Sampieri
Produced by Boyett Ostar Productions, Jill Furman, Mike Nichols
Scenic design by Michael McGarty
Costume design by Robin L. McGee
Lighting by Brian J. Lilienthal
Sound by Peter Hurowitz
Technical supervision by Aurora Productions Inc.
Stage management by Jennifer Rogers
General management by 101 Productions Ltd.
Press representation by Pete Sanders Group

BHUTAN
By Daisy Foote
Directed by Evan Yionoulis
Produced by Cherry Lane Theatre in association with New York Stage and Film
With Tasha Lawrence, Sarah Lord, Amy Redford, Jedadiah Schultz
Scenic design by Laura Hyman
Costume design by Rebecca Bernstein
Lighting by Pat Dignan
Sound by Bart Fasbender
2006 Outer Critics Circle Award nomination for the John Gassner Award
Bhutan was originally developed in Cherry Lane's Celebrating Women Playwrights Program in October 2005.

MONDAY NIGHT READINGS
Directed by Pamela Berlin
Produced by No Frills Company:

TOP GIRLS
By Caryl Churchill
With Betsy Aidem, Sue Brady, Patricia Elliott, Wai Ching Ho, Lola Pashalinski, Pamela Payton-Wright, Pippa Pearthree

TWIGS
By George Furth
With Sarah Baker, Sue Brady, Kenneth Boys, William Cain, Cynthia Darlow, John FitzGibbon, Joel Leffert, Matte Osian, Anne Pitoniak

VITA AND VIRGINIA
By Aileen Atkins
With Kathleen Chalfant and Patricia Elliott

2007

DUTCHMAN
By Amiri Baraka (LeRoi Jones)
Directed by Bill Duke
Produced by Cherry Lane Theatre
With Dulé Hill and Jennifer Mudge, with a special appearance by Paul Benjamin
Scenic design by Troy Hourie
Costume design by Rebecca Bernstein
Lighting by Jeff Croiter
Sound by Drew Levy and Tony Smolenski
Video by Aaron Rhyne
Post-performance discussions with Amiri Baraka

Drama Desk nomination to Jennifer Mudge for Outstanding Actress in a Play, Fourth Annual Seldes-Kanin Fellowship to Jennifer Mudge for her performance

Dutchman premiered at Cherry Lane in 1964.

CHERRY LANE THEATRE ARTIST FORUM
With Billie Allen, Amiri Baraka, Paul Benjamin, Michael Bradford, Ed Bullins, Kia Corthron, Bill Duke, Katori Hall, Dulé Hill, Woodie King Jr., Nilaja Sun, Bridgette Wimberly
Filmed by Lincoln Center Library

FUGUE
By Lee Thuna
Directed by Judith Ivey
Produced by Cherry Lane Theatre
With Charlotte Booker, Ari Butler, Lily Corvo, Liam Craig, Deirdre O'Connell, Danielle Skraastad, Rick Stear, Catherine Wolf
Scenic design by Neil Patel
Costume design by Gail Cooper-Hecht
Lighting by Pat Dignan
Sound by Carl Casella and T. Richard Fitzgerald
Music by Stanley Silverman
General management by Roger Alan Gindi

PHALLACY
By Carl Djerassi
With Lisa Harrow, Carrie Heitman, Simon Jones, Vince Nappo
Directed by Elena Araoz
Produced by Redshift Productions

THE NEW YORK INTERNATIONAL FRINGE FESTIVAL
Produced by the Present Company:

THE MERCY SWING
By Lane Bernes

AN AIR BALLOON ACROSS ANTARCTICA
By Darragh Martin

LUCID
By Jordan Smedberg

OUT OF MY MIND
By Marvin Novogrodskit and Doug Vogel

MADONNA AND CHILD AND OTHER DIVAS
By Tom Johnson

LOST! HOW A CERTAIN TV MEGA-HUNK STOLE MY IDENTITY
By Josh Halloway

ASKING FOR IT
By Joanna Rush

Joan of ARPpo
By Gardi Hutter

ROXY FONT
By Liza Lentini

EARTH'S VACATION
By Maura Kelley

CHERRY JUBILEE CELEBRATES MENTOR PROJECT'S TENTH ANNIVERSARY
A gala celebration of Cherry Lane's rich heritage as New York City's oldest continuously running off-Broadway theater and its role in the future of American theater

HOODOO LOVE
By Katori Hall, mentored by Lynn Nottage
Directed by Lucie Tiberghien
Produced by Cherry Lane Theatre
With Keith Davis, Marjorie Johnson, Angela Lewis, Kevin Mambo
Scenic design by Robin Vest
Costume design by Rebecca Bernstein
Lighting by Pat Dignan
Music by Daniel Baker
Fight direction by David Debesse
Casting by Hopkins, Smith & Barden and Pamela Perrell
Marketing by Walker International Communications Group
Press representation by Art Meets Commerce

2008

THE AMERICAN DREAM and THE SANDBOX
Written and directed by Edward Albee
Produced by Cherry Lane Theatre
With Judith Ivey, George Bartenieff, Lois Markle, Kate Mulgrew (replacement), Daniel Shevlin, Harmon Walsh, Jesse Williams
Scenic design by Neil Patel
Costume design by Carrie Robbins
Lighting by Nicole Pearce
Music by William Flanagan
Sound by Arielle Edwards
Marketing by Walker International Communications Group
Advertising by Eliran Murphy Group Ltd.
Press representation by Art Meets Commerce

Cherry Lane wins a 2008 Obie Award in recognition of outstanding achievement in off-Broadway and off-off-Broadway theater during the 2007–8 season, the Ross Wetzsteon Award.

2009

THE AMISH PROJECT
By Jessica Dickey
Directed by Sarah Cameron Sunde
With Jessica Dickey
Scenic and costume design by Lauren Helpern
Lighting by Nicole Pearce
Sound by Jill BC Du Boff

JAILBAIT
By Deirdre O'Connor
Directed by Suzanne Agins
With Kelly AuCoin, Peter O'Connor, Natalia Payne, Wrenn Schmidt
Scenic design by Kina Park
Costume design by Rebecca Bernstein
Lighting by Pat Dignan
Sound by Daniel Kluger and Brandon Wolcott
Stage management by Mei Ling Acevedo (assistant) and Libby Unsworth

THE LADY WITH ALL THE ANSWERS
By David Rambo
Directed by B. J. Jones
With Judith Ivey
Scenic design by Neil Patel
Costume design by Martin Pakledinaz
Lighting by Nicole Pearce
Stage management by Paige van den Burg

2010

NUNSENSE
Twenty-fifth anniversary revival
Written and directed by Dan Goggin
Produced by Cherry Lane Theatre
With Bonnie Lee, Bambi Jones, Maria Montana, Jeanne Tinker,

Stephanie Wahl
Musical staging by Teri Gibson
Scenic design by Barry Axtell
Lighting by Paul Miller
Musical direction by Leo P. Carusone
Stage management by J. P. Elins
2011 Off Broadway Alliance Award nomination for Best Musical Revival
This revival of Nunsense, which was originally produced at Cherry Lane in 1985, was presented as part of Cherry Lane's Heritage Series.

IMAGINING HESCHEL
Staged reading
By Colin Greer
Directed by Noelle Ghoussaini (assistant) and Larry Moss
Presented by the Culture Project
With Richard Dreyfuss and Rinde Eckert
Lighting by Jake Platt
Stage management by Jonathon Goldman and Kathleen E. G. Munroe (assistant)

SOLEDAD BARRIO & NOCHE FLAMENCA
Presented by Martin Santangelo
With Soledad Barrio and guest artists Juan Ogalla and Antonio Jimenez; cantaores Emilio Florido, Manuel Gago, and Miguel Rosendo; guitarristas Salva de Maria and Eugenio Iglesias
Lighting by S. Benjamin Farrar
Technical direction by Christopher Thielking
Production management by Maria de la O Rodriguez Fernandez
Company administration by Michelle Coe

2011

A PERFECT FUTURE
By David Hay
Directed by Wilson Milam
Produced by Whitney Hoagland Edwards, Neal-Rose Creations, Andy Sandberg
With Donna Bullock, Scott Drummond, Daniel Oreskes, Michael T. Weiss
Scenic design by Charles Corcoran
Costume design by Michael McDonald
Lighting by Ben Stanton
Sound by Daniel Kluger
Casting by Pat McCorkle
Stage management by Donald Fried

TEETH OF THE SONS
By Joseph Sousa
Directed by Nicole Haran
With Will Allen, Donald P. Flores, Casandera M. J. Lollar, Shayna Padovano, Joseph Sousa
Scenic design by Josh Iacovelli
Costume design by Victoria Malvagno
Lighting by Niluka Hotaling
Music by Cory Bruce
Sound by Francisco Solorzano

MANIPULATION
By Victoria E. Calderon
Directed by Will Pomerantz
With Robert Bogue, John-Patrick Driscoll, Gabriel Furman, Jeremy Stiles Holm, Brendan McHahon, Elizabeth Norment, Saundra Santiago, Rafi Silver, Marina Squerciati, Michele Vazquez
Scenic design by Bill Stabile
Costume design by Alejo Vietti
Lighting by Kirk Bookman

CRANE STORY
By Jen Silverman
Directed by Katherine Kovner
Presented by Playwrights Realm
With Louis Ozawa Changchien, Susan Hyon, Christine Toy Johnson, Angela Lin, Jake Manabat, Barret O'Brien, David Shih
Scenic design by Michael Locher and Lauren Rockman (assistant)
Costume design by Moria Sine Clinton
Lighting by Ji-youn Chang
Sound by Nathan A. Roberts
Dramaturgy by Christine Scarfuto
Movement design by Musumi Kishimoto and Miki Orihara
Prop design by Layna Fischer
Puppet design by Puppet Kitchen
Stage management by Joanne E. McInerney
Production management by Ryan C. Durham (assistant) and Aaron Verdery

AFTER PARADISE
By Israel Horovitz
Directed by Damien Gray
Presented by Cherry Lane Theatre
With Will Swenson
Music by Peter Lurye

CHARLES WINN SPEAKS
By C. S. Hanson
Directed by Lynn M. Thomson
Presented by Living Image Arts
With Lindsay Gates and Chris Kipiniak
Scenic design by Tijana Bjelak
Costume design by Lisa Loen
Lighting by Heather Smaha
Sound by Geoffrey Roecker

ASUNCION
By Jesse Eisenberg
Directed by Kip Fagan
Presented by Rattlestick Playwrights Theater
With Remy Auberjonois, Justin Bartha, Jesse Eisenberg, Camille Mana
Scenic design by John McDermott
Costume design by Ben Stanton
Sound by Bart Fasbender
Fight direction by Thomas Schall
Technical direction by Katie Takacs
Stage management by Melissa Mae Gragus
Production management by Eugenia Ferneaux

2012

PSYCHO THERAPY
By Frank Strausser
Directed by Michael Bush
Presented by Barbara Ligeti, Mindful Media, Wishing Well Productions
With Alexander Cendese, Jan Leslie Harding, Laurence Lau, Gabrielle Miller
Scenic design by Michael V. Moore
Costume design by Amanda Bujak
Lighting by Jedd Croiter
Sound by Amy Altadonna
Composed by Allison Leyton-Brown

TERESA'S ECSTASY
By Begonya Plaza
Directed by Will Pomerantz
Produced by Jack Sharkey and Jim Weiner
With Shawn Elliott, Linda Larkin, Begonya Plaza
Music by Albert Carbonell

WE PLAY FOR THE GODS
Written, directed, and produced by the 2010–12 Women's Project Lab: Charity Ballard, Alexandra Collier, Elizabeth R. English, Jessi D. Hill, Andrea Kuchlewska, Manda Martin, Dominique Morisseau, Kristen Palmer,

Sarah Rasmussen, Mia Rovegno, Melisa Tien, Nicole A. Watson, Stephanie Ybarra, Stefanie Zadravec
Presented by Women's Project Theater
With Annie Golden, Amber Gray, Alexandra Henrikson, Irene Sofia Lucio, Erika Rolfsrud
Scenic design by Jennifer Moeller
Costume design by Moria Sine Clinton
Lighting by Scott Bolman
Sound by Stowe Nelson

ALL FOR ONE THEATRE FESTIVAL
All For One Theatre Festival's second season featured ten solo shows, including the New York premiere of Emmy winner Leslie Jordan's *Fruit Fly* and shows directed by B. D. Wong, Colman Domingo, and Broadway's Lynne Taylor-Corbett.

WE ARE THEATRE
Speak Out Against Sexism in Theatre!
An evening of monologues, skits, songs, and scenes about sexism in theater. Works by Anonymous, Tiffany Antone, Brooke Berman, Kate Bornstein, Paula Cizmar, Sarah Duncan, Lauren Ferebee, Mila Golubov, Elizabeth Hess, Yvette Heyliger, Velina Hasu Houston, Penny Jackson, Andrea Lepcio, Marianne McDonald, Irina Merkina, Honor Molloy, Sheilah Rae, Theresa Rebeck, Laura Shamas, Caridad Svich, Thelma Virata de Castro, Kathleen Warnock, Shay Youngblood, and Guerrilla Girls On Tour! were read by New York City–based performers.

SPARK
Directed by Scott Schwartz
Produced by Gloria Mann, TECL/Mannatee Films, in collaboration with NoPassport
With Louis Cancelmi, Peter Jay Fernandez, Marin Ireland, Jocelyn Kuritsky, Gloria Mann

A SUMMER DAY
By Jon Fosse
Directed by Sarah Cameron Sunde
Presented by Rattlestick Playwrights Theater
With Carlo Alban, Karen Allen, McCaleb Burnett, Maren Bush, Pamela Shaw, Samantha Soule
Scenic design by John McDermott
Costume design by Deb O
Lighting by Nicole Pearce
Sound by Leah Gelpe
Props by Andrew Diaz

LEGENDARY LIVES: SARAH BERNHARDT, EDNA FERBER, AND HALLIE FLANAGAN
Celebrating the thirtieth anniversary of the League of Professional Women
By Milly Barranger, Julie Gilbert, Ruth Wolff
Produced by Mari Lynn Henry
With Cynthia Enfield and David Spencer
Creative consulting by Shellen Lubin

WOMEN'S WORDS
An evening of women's poetry as expressed by P. J. Gibson, Carol Hall, Anne Hamilton, Harriet Slaughter, Mira J. Spektor, and Gayl Teller
Directed by Cara Reichel
Presented by Harriet Slaughter as part of the League of Professional Theatre Women's thirtieth anniversary 30 Plays Celebrate 30 Years project

ROCKAWAY: A BENEFIT FOR HURRICANE SANDY
Featuring short plays by Lucy Boyle, Andrea Ciannavei, Cusi Cram, Kristoffer Diaz, Jesse Eisenberg, Tyler Fascett, Jason Furlani, Craig "muMs" Grant, Stephen Adly Guirgis, Israel Horovitz, Jonathan Libman, Joe Pintauro, Kristina Poe, Frank Pugliese, Mike Reiss, Michael Reyes, Jose Rivera, Jonathan Marc Sherman, Jennifer Skura, Mark von Sternberg, Dwayne Yancey
Directed by Rose Bonczek, Arthur Kriklivy (assistant), Molly Marinik, Shira-Lee Shalit, Francisco Solorzano
Presented by Barefoot Theatre Company and Francisco Solorzano
With Tala Ashe, Jeremy Brena, Amelia Campbell, Andrea Ciannavei, Sol Crespo, John Doman, Jesse Eisenberg, Danelle Eliav, Angelina Fiordellisi, Caitlin Fitzgerald, John Gazzale, Kevin Geer, Gina Gershon, Craig "muMs" Grant, Arjun Gupta, John Harlacher, Stephanie Janssen, Michael Colby Jones, Margaret Ladd Kessler, Victoria Malvagno, Andrew McLarty, Alfredo Narciso, Jay Nickerson, Cristina Pitter, Will Rogers, Gillian Rougier, Mickey Ryan, Annabella Sciorra, Joseph R. Sicari, Francisco Solorzano, Mickey Sumner, Jennie West
Live music by Ronit Aranoff, Trevor Exter, Aidan Koehler, Mika Nishimura, Daniella Rabbani
Stage management by Michael Denis and Molly Keene (assistant)

2013

THE REVISIONIST
By Jesse Eisenberg
Directed by Kip Fagan
Presented by Rattlestick Playwrights Theater
With Jesse Eisenberg and Vanessa Redgrave
Scenic design by John McDermott
Costume design by Jessica Pabst
Lighting by Matt Fret
Sound by Bart Fasbender
Production management by Eugenia Furneaux

BASILICA
By Mando Alvarado
Directed by Jerry Ruiz
Presented by Rattlestick Playwrights Theater
With Jake Cannavale, Rosal Colon, Bernardo Cubria, Yadira Guevara-Prip, Selenis Leyva, Alfredo Narciso, Felix Solis
Scenic design by Raul Abrego
Costume design by Carisa Kelly
Lighting by Burke Brown
Sound by Jane Shaw
Fight direction by David Anzuelo
Prop design by Andrew Diaz

WAITING . . . A SONG CYCLE
Music and lyrics by Bob Kelly and Kelly Pomeroy
Presented by World's Stage Theatre Company

COLIN QUINN: UNCONSTITUTIONAL
Written and performed by Colin Quinn
Directed by Rebecca A. Trent
Scenic design by James Fauvell
Costume design by Alexis Forte
Lighting by Sarah Lurie

MIKE BIRBIGLIA: WORKING IT OUT
Written and performed by Mike Birbiglia

JOHN SEARLES—HELP FOR THE HAUNTED
A launch event for *Help for the Haunted* by John Searles (William Morrow/HarperCollins)

ASHVILLE
By Lucy Thurber
Directed by Karen Allen
Produced by Cherry Lane Theatre, as part of its Celebrating Women Playwrights program, in association with Rattlestick Playwrights Theater; presented as part of the first annual Theater: Village Festival
With George West Carruth, Aubrey Dollar, Andrew Garman, Tasha Lawrence, James McMenamin, Joe Tippett, Mia Vallet
Scenic design by John McDermott
Costume design by Jessica Pabst
Lighting by Matt Richards
Sound by Bart Fasbender

ONE NIGHT
World premiere
Presented by Angelina Fiordellisi of Cherry Lane Theatre, David van Asselt and Brian Long of Rattlestick Playwrights Theater, Seri Lawrence (associate)
With Grantham Coleman, K. K. Moggie, Matthew Montelongo, Cortez Nance Jr., Rutina Wesley
Scenic design by Clifton Chadick (assistant) and John McDermott
Costume design by Jessica Jahn
Lighting by Nicole Pearce
Sound by Sean O'Halloran
Audio by Paul Piekarz, Ien DeNio, Sam Callahan, Jeffory Barton
Carpentry by Cory Asinofsky, Adam Weppler, Joe Galan
Electricity by Jay Sterkel
Fight direction by UnkleDave's Fight-House
Graphic design by Frank "Fraver" Verizzo
Lighting equipment by the Lighting Syndicate
Lighting programming Alling Langin
Opening night photography by Walter McBride
Production carpentry by Janio Marrero
Production photography by Sandra Coudert Graham
Props by Starlet Jacobs
Pyrotechnics Ted Rathjen
Scenic art by Jessica Orona, Rachael Silverman, Brian Howard
Scenic construction by the Ken Larson Co.
Video by Aaron Gonzales (assistant) and Gil Sperling
Wardrobe by Courtney Irizarry
Casting by Calleri Casting
Stage management by C. Renee Alexander and Kristin Pfeifer (assistant)
Production management by Eugenia Furneaux and Miles Orduna (assistant)
Marketing by Walker International Communications Group/Toni Israel
Press representation by Richard Kornberg & Associates/Don Summa, Sam Rudy
Media relations by Sam Rudy

MENTOR PROJECT 2014 LAUNCH PARTY
An evening of celebration announcing the artists of Mentor Project 2014:

THE HUNTERS
By Jen Silverman, mentored by Lynn Nottage

SONNETS ON TAP
Conceived and directed by Awoye Timpo, mentored by Lisa Peterson

THE RAGGED CLAWS
By Lina Patel, mentored by David Henry Hwang

HOT FUN IN THE WINTERTIME
Presented by the Cherry Lane Theatre's Late Night Series
With Jon Bass, Edmund Donovan, Kaley Ronayne, Fred Williams

2014

MIKE BIRBIGLIA: WORKING IT OUT
Written and performed by Mike Birbiglia
Presented by Bull Journey Productions

ODE TO JOY
Written and directed by Craig Lucas
Presented by Rattlestick Playwrights Theater
With Katheryn Erbe, Roxanna Hope, Arliss Howard
Scenic design by Andrew Boyce
Costume design by Catherine Zuber
Lighting by Paul Whitaker
Sound by Daniel Kluger

A FABLE
By David Van Asselt
Directed by Daniel Talbott
Presented by Piece by Piece Productions and Rising Phoenix Repertory in association with Rattlestick Playwrights Theater
With Edward Carnevale, Liza Fernandez, Dawn-Lyen Gardner, Maxwell Hamilton, Jerry Matz, Hubert Point-Du Jour, Eileen Rivera, Sarah Shaefer, Pamela Shaw, Samantha Soule, Alok Tewari, Sanford Wilson, Gordon Joseph Weiss
Music by Elizabeth Swados
Scenic design by John McDermott
Costume design by Tristan Raines
Lighting by Joel Moritz
Sound by Janie Bullard
Fight direction by UnkleDave's Fight-House
Projection design by Kaitlyn Pietras
Stage management by Andrew Slater
Production management by Dave Nelson

PHOENIX
By Scott Organ
Directed by Jennifer DeLia
Produced by Poverty Row Entertainment, Rattlestick Playwrights Theater, Rian Patrick Durham
Presented by Nicholas Jabbour
With Julia Stiles and James Wirt
Scenic design by Caite Hevner Kemp
Costume design by Amit Gajwani
Lighting by Oona Curley
Sound by Janie Bullard
Scenic art by Burton Machen

TO THE BONE
World premiere
By Lisa Ramirez
Directed by Lisa Peterson
Presented by Cherry Lane Theatre
With Dan Domingues, Liza Fernandez, Annie Henk, Paola Lázaro Muñoz, Lisa Ramirez, Gerardo Rodriguez, Xochitl Romero, Haynes Thigpen
Scenic design by Rachel Hauck and A Ram Kim (assistant)
Costume design by Theresa Squire and Maureen Fitzgerald (assistant)
Lighting by Russell H. Champa and Katy Atwell (assistant)
Sound by Jill BC Du Boff and Beth Lake (assistant)
Dramaturgy by Morgan Jenness

Fight direction by UnkleDave's
  Fight-House and Jesse Geguzis
  (assistant)
Graphic design by Monique Carboni
Prop supervision by Judy Merrick and
  Yudelka Aheyer (assistant)
Stage management by Megan Schwarz
  Dickert and Anne Huston (assistant)
General management by Theresa
  Von Klug
Casting by Kate Murray

THE SAGA OF MARISSA ALEXANDER
Written and performed by
  Sabrina Lamb
Directed by Gretchen Cryer

ME, MY MOUTH AND I
World premiere
Written and performed by Joy Behar
Presented by Cherry Lane Theatre,
  Angelina Fiordellisi, Steve Janowitz

2015

EVERYTHING YOU TOUCH
Presented by Rattlestick Playwrights
  Theater, The Theatre @ Boston
  Court, True Love Productions
With Christian Coulson, Allegra Rose
  Edwards, Chelsea Fryer, Tonya
  Glanz, Lisa Kitchens, Nina Ordman,
  Miriam Silverman, Robbie Tann
Scenic design by Francois-Pierre
  Couture
Costume design by Jenny Foldenauer
Lighting by Jeremy Pivnick
Music and sound by John Zalewski
Props by John Burton
Video by Adam Flemming
Producing stage management by
  Theresa Flanagan and Rachael Gass
  (assistant)

MIKE BIRBIGLIA: WORKING IT OUT
Written and performed by Mike Birbiglia

8 STOPS
Written and performed by Deb Margolin
Directed by Jay Wahl
Presented by All For One Theater

GHOSTLIGHT 9: A MUSICAL GHOST
  STORY
Written and performed by
  Michael Wolk
Directed by Aaron Mark
Presented by All For One Theater

MAJOR TOM
Written, performed, and designed by
  Victoria Melody
Commissioned and produced by
  Farnham Maltings
Presented by All For One Theater

FEAR, LOATHING AND CHAOS:
  TV'S MOST INFLUENTIAL
  SHOWRUNNERS DISCUSS
  BATTLES WON AND LOST IN THE
  TRENCHES OF TELEVISION
With Carmen Finestra, Tom Fontana,
  James Manos, Jr., David McFadzean
Moderated by Matt Williams

THE VAGINA MONOLOGUES
By Eve Ensler
Directed by Jenna Worsham
Presented by V-Day Taconic
With Barbara Barron, Erin Cherry,
  Julissa Contreras, Rhonda Covington,
  Elisia Dones, Brigitte Harris, Miriam
  A. Hyman, Elizabeth Mackintosh,
  Briana Packen, Sharon Richardson,
  Tiffany Rachelle Stewart, Josie
  Whittlesey, Annie Worden Hailed

THE TRAIL TO OREGON
Book by Jeff Blim, Matt Lang,
  Nick Lang
Additional writing by Brian Holden
Music and lyrics by Jeff Blim
Additional music by Drew DeFour
Directed by Nick Lang
Presented by Starkid Productions
With Jaime Lyn Beatty, Jeff Blim, Corey
  Dorris, Lauren Lopez, Joey Richter,
  Rachael Soglin
Choreography by Katie Spelman

CHERRY LANE SCHOOL
Cherry Lane's first ever education
  intensive featuring an array of
  unique and interactive master classes

LAUGH IT UP, STARE IT DOWN
By Alan Hruska
With Jayce Bartok, Katya Campbell,
  Maury Ginsberg, Amy Hargreaves
Scenic design by Kevin Judge
Costume design by Jennifer Caprio
Lighting by Matthew J. Fick
Music and sound by Peter Salett
Casting by Barden/Schnee Casting

CATCH THE BUTCHER
By Adam Seidel
Directed by Valentina Fratti
With Angelina Fiordellisi, Lauren Luna
  Vélez, Jonathan Walker
Scenic design by Lauren Helpern
Costume design by Brooke Cohen and
  Mark Koss (assistant)
Lighting by Graham Kindred
Music and sound by
  Quentin Chiappetta
Fight direction by Ron Piretti
Photography by Carol Rosegg
Prop design by Addison Heeren
Stage management by Sarah Geis
  (assistant) and Alison Hassman

HASAN MINHAJ: HOMECOMING
  KING
Written and performed by
  Hasan Minhaj
Directed by Greg Walloch
Produced by Mike Berkowitz and
  Mike Lavoie
Scenic design by Sara C. Walsh
Costume design by Kristen Buckels
Lighting by Sarah Lurie

COLIN QUINN: THE NEW YORK
  STORY
Written and performed by Colin Quinn
Directed by Jerry Seinfeld

NORA
Adapted from Henrik Ibsen's
  A Doll's House
By Ingmar Bergman
Directed by Austin Pendleton
With Larry Bull, Andrea Cirie,
  Todd Gearhart, Jean Lichty,
  George Morfogen
Scenic design and lighting by
  Harry Feiner
Costume design by Theresa Squire
Sound by Ryan Rumery
Dialect coaching by Patricia Fletcher
Movement consultation by
  Shelley Senter
Stage management by Kelly Ice and
  Denise Wilcox (assistant)

OH, HELLO
Written and performed by Nick Kroll
  and John Mulaney
Scenic design by Connor W. Munion
Costume design by James Fauvell
Lighting by Sarah Lurie

2016

THE ROADS TO HOME
By Horton Foote
Directed by Jonathon K. Musser (associate) and Michael Wilson
Presented by Primary Stages in association with Catherine Adler and Jamie deRoy
With Devon Abner, Dan Bittner, Rebecca Brooksher, Harriet Harris, Hallie Foote, Matt Sullivan
Scenic design by Jeff Cowie
Costume design by David C. Woolard
Lighting by David Lander
Music and sound by John Gromada
Wig design by Paul Huntley
Movement consultation by Hope Clarke
Dialect coaching by Jane Guyer Fujiya
Casting by Stephanie Klapper Casting

OUT OF THE MOUTHS OF BABES
World premiere
By Israel Horovitz
Directed by Barnet Kellman in association with Julie Crosby
Presented by Margarida De Brito, Seri Lawrence (associate), David Youse
With Francesca Choy-Kee, Angelina Fiordellisi, Judith Ivey, Estelle Parsons
Scenic design by Neil Patel
Costume design by Joseph G. Aulisi
Lighting by Paul Miller
Sound by Leon Rothenberg
Action coordination by Rick Sordelet
Prop design by Carrie Mossman
Stage management by Christine Catti and Michael Denis (assistant)
Production management by Janio Marrero
General management by Diane Alianiello
Casting by Kate Murray
Marketing and advertising by Red Rising Marketing
Press representation by Sam Rudy Media Relations

THE VAGINA MONOLOGUES
By Eve Ensler
Directed by Ira Kip
Produced by Mightee Shero Productions with support from V-Day, Cherry Lane Theatre, the King's County Re-Entry Task Force
With Belinda Allyn, Erica Camarano, Rhonda Covington, Julia Crockett, Dana Levinson, Elizabeth Mackintosh, Sharon Richardson, Vanda Seward, Lin Tucci, Tanya Wright

THE BODY OF AN AMERICAN
New York premiere
By Dan O'Brien
Directed by Jo Bonney
Presented by Primary Stages and Rhoda R. Herrick in association with Hartford Stage
With Michael Crane and Michael Cumpsty
Scenic design by Richard Hoover
Costume design by Ilona Somogyi
Lighting by Lap Chi Chu
Sound by Darron L. West
Projection design by Alex Basco Koch
Casting by Binder Casting and Jack Bowdan, CSA

2017

PRIDE AND PREJUDICE
By Kate Hamill
Adapted from the novel by Jane Austen
Directed by Amanda Dehnert and Jamie DeRoy (associate)
Co-presented by Primary Stages and the Hudson Valley Shakespeare Festival
With Mark Bedard, Kimberly Chatterjee, Kate Hamill, Jason O'Connell, Amelia Pedlow, Chris Thorn, John Tufts, Nance Williamson, Laura Baranik (understudy), Michael Broadhurst (understudy), Jeremy Peter Johnson (understudy)
Choreography by Ellenore Scott
Stage management by Andrew Jess Berkey (assistant) and Roxana Khan
Scenic design by John McDermott
Costume design by Tracy Christensen
Lighting by Eric Southern
Sound by Palmer Hefferan
Casting by Stephanie Klapper Casting

INDESTRUCTIBLE
A celebration of the spirit of the people of Puerto Rico and Mexico
In partnership with Barefoot Theater Co., Ensemble Studio Theatre, Harlem Stage, H.O.L.A., InViolet Theater Co., LAByrinth Theater, National Black Theater, Primary Stages, Rattlestick Theater, Rhymes Over Beats, Sol Project, Two River Theater Pregones/Puerto Rican Traveling Theater
Produced by Janio Marrero
With Rosal Colon, Melissa Diaz, Desmar Guevara, Irene Sofia Lucio, Flaco Navaja, Emma Ramos, Ximena Salgado, Elise Santora, David Zayas and more

THE GOSPEL ACCORDING TO THOMAS JEFFERSON, CHARLES DICKENS AND COUNT LEO TOLSTOY: DISCORD
By Scott Carter
Directed by Kimberly Senior
With Duane Boutté, Michael Laurence, Tom Sesma
Scenic design by Wilson Chin
Costume design by David Hyman
Lighting by Jen Schriever
Music and sound by Sunday Jones
Stage management by Christina Baracco (assistant) and Kristi Hess
Casting by Stephen Klapper Casting

THE TRAVELING LADY
Directed by Austin Pendleton
Produced by Cherry Lane Theatre's Second Founders Project and La Femme Theatre Productions
With Larry Bull, Lynn Cohen, Angelina Fiordellisi, Jean Lichty, George Morfogen, Ron Piretti, PJ Sosko, Jill Tanner, Korinne Tetlow, Karen Ziemba
Scenic design and lighting by Harry Feiner
Costume design by Theresa Squire
Music and sound by Ryan Rumery
Dialect design and dramaturgy by Amy Stoller
Wig design by Paul Huntley

LABMEMBERS
Created by David Anzuelo
Episodes written by David Anzuelo, Maggie Bofill, Webb Wilcoxen, and more
Directed by Elizabeth Canavan, Russell G. Jones, Portia, and more
With Erick Bettancourt, Jake Cannavale, Sean Carvajal, Sean Griffin, Yadira Guevara Prip, Paola Lázaro Muñoz, Javana Mundy, Diomargy Nunez, Ron Phippen, Neil Tyrone Pritchard, Rocky Vega, Analisa Velez, Kara Young
Choreography by Jill DeArmon and more
Music by Cristian Amigo

DANIEL'S HUSBAND
New York premiere
By Michael McKeever
Directed by Joe Brancato
Presented by Primary Stages and Ted Snowdon
With Anna Holbrook, Lou Liberatore, Matthew Montelongo, Ryan Spahn, Leland Wheeler
Stage management by Elis Aroyo (assistant) and Michael Palmer
Costume design by Jen Caprio
Lighting by Christina Watanabe
Music and sound by William Neal
Prop supervision by Andrew Diaz
Casting by Stephanie Klapper Casting

NEW GUIDELINES FOR PEACEFUL TIMES: A FABLE
New York premiere
By Bosco Brasil
Translated by Luciana Kezen
Directed by Mary Geerlof
With Emmanuel Mendes-Chumaceiro, Christine Seisler, Hannah Sprung

FADE
New York premiere
By Tanya Saracho
Directed by Jerry Ruiz
With Annie Dow and Eddie Martinez
Scenic design by Maria Sanchez
Costume design by Carisa Kelly
Lighting by Amith Chandrashaker
Sound by M. L. Dogg
Prop supervision by Carrie Mossman
Stage management by Alfred Macias
Casting by Stephanie Klapper Casting

2018

MAX STOSSEL: WORDS THAT MOVE

DOWNSTAIRS
By Theresa Rebeck
Directed by Adrienne Campbell-Holt
Presented by Primary Stages
With Tim Daly, Tyne Daly, John Procaccino
Scenic design by Narelle Sissons
Costume design by Sarah Laux
Lighting by Michael Giannitti
Sound by M. L. Dogg

FINAL FOLLIES
Three one-act plays
By A. R. Gurney
Directed by David Saint
Presented by Primary Stages
With Betsy Aidem, Colin Hanlon, Mark Junek, Piter Marek, Greg Mullavey, Rachel Nicks, Deborah Rush
Scenic design by James Youmans
Costume design by David Murin
Lighting by Cory Pattak
Casting by Stephanie Klapper Casting
Stage management by Pamela Singer
Sound by Scott Killian:

FINAL FOLLIES

THE RAPE OF BUNNY STUNTZ

THE LOVE COURSE

THE NEW ONE
Written and performed by Mike Birbiglia
Additional writing by Jennifer Hope Stein
Directed by Seth Barrish
Produced by Joseph Birbiglia and Mike Lavoie
Scenic design by Beowulf Boritt

FIRST LOVE
By Charles Mee
Directed by Kim Weild
Presented by Cherry Lane Theatre Founders Project
With Angelina Fiordellisi, Taylor Harvey, Michael O'Keefe
Scenic design by Edward Pierce
Costume design by Theresa Squire
Lighting by Paul Miller
Sound by Christian Frederickson
Casting by Stephanie Klapper Casting
Marketing and advertising by Red Rising Marketing
Press representation by Sam Rudy Media Relations

THE GENTLEMAN CALLER
By Philip Dawkins
Directed by Deven Kolluri (assistant) and Tony Speciale
Presented by Abingdon Theatre Company
With Daniel K. Isaac and Juan Francisco Villa
Scenic design by Sara C. Walsh
Costume design by Hunter Kaczorowski
Lighting by Zach Blane
Music and sound by Christian Frederickson
Dialect coaching by Ron Carlos
Fight direction and intimacy consultation by Ryan Bourque
Prop design by Deb Gaouette
Stage management by Lilly Deerwater (assistant) and Lily Perlmutter
Production management by Mary Duffe
Casting by Karrie Koppel

FEEDING THE DRAGON
Written and performed by Sharon Washington
Directed by Maria Mileaf
Presented by Primary Stages in association with Jamie DeRoy and Hartford Stage
Scenic design by Tony Ferrieri
Costume design by Toni-Leslie James
Lighting by Ann G. Wrightson
Music and sound by Lindsay Jones

A WALK WITH MR. HEIFETZ
By James Inverne
Directed by Mêlisa Annis (associate) and Andrew Leynse
Presented by Primary Stages
Featuring performances by Yuval Boim, Adam Green, Erik Lochtefeld, and live music performed by violinist Mariella Haubs
Stage management by Emily Paige Ballou (assistant) and Michal V. Mendelssohn
Scenic design by Wilson Chin
Costume design by Jen Caprio
Lighting by John Froelich
Sound by M. L. Dogg
Dialect coaching by Charise Greene
Casting by Stephanie Klapper Casting

2019

ACTUALLY WE'RE FKED**
By Matt Williams
Directed by John Pasquin
With Mairin Lee, Keren Lugo, Ben Rappaport, Gabriel Sloyer
Scenic design by Robin Vest
Costume design by Theresa Squire
Lighting by Paul Miller
Sound by M. L. Dogg and MuTTT
Projection design by Brad Peterson
Stage management by Christine Catti
Casting by Stephanie Klapper, CSA

LITTLE WOMEN
By Kate Hamill (based on the novel by Louisa May Alcott)
Directed by Sarna Lapine
Produced by Primary Stages in association with Jamie deRoy and Johanna Garfield

With Paola Sanchez Abreu, Michael Crane, Kate Hamill, Ellen Harvey, John Lenartz, Kristolyn Lloyd, Nate Mann, Maria Elena Ramirez, Carmen Zilles
Stage management by Bonnie Mcheffey and Molly Shae (assistant)
Scenic design by Mikiko Suzuki Macadams
Costume design by Valérie Thérèse Bart
Lighting by Paul Whitaker
Sound by Leon Rothenberg
Wig design by David Bova
Composition by Deborah Abramson
Dramaturgy by Kristin Leahey
Casting by Calleri Casting

AMERICAN MOOR
Written and performed by Keith Hamilton Cobb
Directed by Kim Weild
Produced by Elizabeth I. McCann, Evangeline Morphos, Tom Shea, Frederick M. Zollo
Costume design by Dede Ayite
Scenic design by Wilson Chin
Lighting by Alan C. Edwards
Sound by Christian Frederickson

MIKE BIRBIGLIA: WORKING IT OUT
Written and performed by Mike Birbiglia

GET ON YOUR KNEES
Written and performed by Jacqueline Novak
Directed by John Early
Presented by Natasha Lyonne
Produced by Mike Birbiglia

2021

RAMY YOUSSEF LIVE
Written and performed by Ramy Youssef
Produced by Carlee Briglia and Mike Lavoie

UNACCEPTABLE
Written and performed by Neal Brennan
Directed by Derek DelGaudio
Produced by Jake Friedman and Vanessa Lauren
Scenic design by Anna Louizos
Lighting by Adam Blumenthal
Sound by Kevin Heard

2022

WORK IN PROGRESS
Written and performed by Mike Birbiglia

JUST FOR US
By Alex Edelman
Directed by Adam Brace
Produced by Joe Birbiglia, Carlee Briglia, Mike Lavoie
Lighting by Amina Alexander
Sound by Margaret Montagna
Production coordination by Taylor Jo Poer
Company management by Claudia McCoy

COAL COUNTRY
By Jessica Blank and Erik Jensen
Produced by Audible Theater
Directed by Jessica Blank
With Mary Bacon, Amelia Campbell, Ezra Knight, Thomas Kopache, Michael Laurence, Deirdre Madigan
Music by Steve Earle

A SUMMER OF COMEDY: LOOKING FOR PAPA
Written and performed by Annie Hamilton
Directed by Charlotte Benbeniste
Produced by Carlee Briglia and Mike Lavoie

EMMY BLOTNICK AT THE CHERRY LANE THEATRE
Written and performed by Emmy Blotnick

MOLE
Written and performed by Mo Welch

LESS LONELY
Written and performed by Jes Tom
Presented by Elliot Page

OH GOD, A SHOW ABOUT ABORTION
By Alison Leiby
Directed by Lila Neugebauer
Presented by Ilana Glazer
Produced by Bad Robot Live, Carlee Briglia, Chris Burns of AGI Entertainment, Mike Lavoie
Lighting by Amina Alexander
Sound by Margaret Montagna

THIS BEAUTIFUL FUTURE
By Rita Kalnejais
Directed by Jack Serio
With Francesca Carpanini, Angelina Fiordellisi, Austin Pendleton, Uly Schlesinger
Scenic design by Frank J. Oliva
Costume design by Ricky Reynoso
Lighting by Stacey Derosier
Sound by Christopher Darbassie
Musical direction by Emily Erickson
Projection design by Lacey Erb

Citations

COVER
Promotional photo collage for *I Was Sitting on My Patio This Guy Appeared I Thought I Was Hallucinating* by Robert Wilson. Photograph reprinted by permission of Jacob Burckhardt. 1977.

P6
Abbott, Berenice. *Cherry Lane Theatre on Commerce Street*. 1948. Photograph, 8 7/8 x 6 3/4 in. Syracuse University Art Museum, object no. 1981.2176.

P8
Cherry Lane Theatre (New York, NY) photographs, 1956. Performing Arts Research Collections. New York Public Library.

P11
Photograph of gas station at Commerce and Seventh Avenue. Courtesy of Cherry Lane Alternative archives.

P13
Lenox Hill Players and Ensemble Theatre records. Billy Rose Theatre Division. New York Public Library.

P14
Manhattan: Commerce Street—Bedford Street, 1925. Irma and Paul Milstein Division of United States History, Local History and Genealogy. New York Public Library.

P16
Photograph of William S. Rainey, February 17, 1935, reprinted from *Pittsburgh (PA) Press*.

Photograph of Evelyn Vaughn, February 7, 1924, reprinted from *Kansas City (MO) Times*.

Photograph of Reginald Travers, July 14, 1918, reprinted from *Oakland (CA) Tribune*.

P17
McKinney, Kelsey. "In the Galleries: A Map of Greenwich Village from *The Greenwich Village Quill*." *Ransom Center Magazine*, January 5, 2012.

Dumas, Anthony F. *Cherry Lane Playhouse, Grove St. Theatre, and Provincetown Playhouse*. 1926. Pen and ink drawing. Museum of the City of New York, object no. 75.200.8.

P18
"Artists Form New Centre in Greenwich Village." *New York Times*, November 18, 1923.

Lenox Hill Players and Ensemble Theatre records. Billy Rose Theatre Division. New York Public Library.

P19
Bourbon, Diana. "Great Minds on Little Theatres." *New York Times Magazine*, February 10, 1924.

P20
Manhattan: Commerce Street—Barrow Street, 1904. Irma and Paul Milstein Division of United States History, Local History and Genealogy. New York Public Library.

P22
Classified ads. *New York Herald*, April 28, 1874.

P23
Saunders, Hortense. "Actress Is Good Land Dealer, But She Sticks to Her Little Theatre Idea." *Brooklyn Citizen*, November 18, 1923.

P24
Herring farm along Skinner Road, 1795. Manuscripts and Archives Division. New York Public Library.

P25
Manhattan: Commerce Street—Barrow Street. Irma and Paul Milstein Division of United States History, Local History and Genealogy. New York Public Library.

P27
Kingsley, Grace. "Is Tired of Tear Making, Evelyn Vaughn Yearns for Comedy Roles." *Los Angeles Times*, November 17, 1912.

Photograph of sketch background artist Willy Pogany for the Universal film *The Mummy*, 1932. Via ABCDVD Video.

Portrait of Morgan Farley, ca 1930. Reprinted by permission of Everett Collection.

Bushnell Foto. *Reginald Travers, Stage Actor*. 1904. J. Willis Sayre Collection of Theatrical Photographs. University of Washington Libraries, Special Collections.

Van Vechten, Carl. Portrait of Edna St. Vincent Millay. 1933. Photograph.

American poet and lawyer Arthur Davison Ficke (1883–1945). Circa 1920. Photograph by FPG / Getty Images.

Cary Grant oversize photograph signed as "Archie," 1931. Photograph by James Hargis Connelly / RR Auction.

The Theatre Magazine Company, New York. Publicity portrait of Tom Powers for the Broadway stage production *The First Fifty Years* (March–April 1922).

Actor John Barrymore, 1918. J. Willis Sayre Collection of Theatrical Photographs. University of Washington Libraries: Special Collections.

P28
Manhattan: Commerce Street—Bedford Street. Irma and Paul Milstein Division of United States History, Local History and Genealogy. New York Public Library.

P29
Manhattan: Bedford Street—Commerce Street. Irma and Paul Milstein Division of United States History, Local History and Genealogy. New York Public Library.

P30
"Equity Offers *New Englander* as Its Third Bill; Two New Little Theatres to Open Their Doors." *Daily (NY) News*, February 3, 1924.

P31
"Village Theater Is Opened with 'Saturday Night.'" *Daily (NY) News*, February 11, 1924.

"Helps to Build Her Own Theater." *Buffalo Courier*, February 3, 1924.

P33
Photograph from *Opportunity, A Journal of Negro Life*, March, 1927.

P34
"Black and White Love Portrayed at Cherry Lane." *Daily (NY) News*, February 12, 1927.

White, Lucien H. "Brave Playwright Is Daring Ostracism By Miscegenation Drama." *The New York Age*, February 19, 1927.

P35
Atkinson, J. Brooks. "Disturbance in Cherry Lane." *New York Times*, February 11, 1927.

Lewis, Theophilus. "Stigma—An Advance in Acting." *The Messenger*, April, 1927.

P37
Cover art by John Held Jr. for F. Scott Fitzgerald, *The Vegetable, or From President to Postman* (1923).

P38
Fitzgerald, F. Scott. *The Vegetable*. F. Scott Fitzgerald Papers. Manuscripts Division. Department of Special Collections, Princeton University Library.

P39
"Fitzgerald Has a New Play Coming." *Daily (NY) News*, March 10, 1929.

"The Lenox Hill Players Present 'The Vegetable,' by F. Scott Fitzgerald, at the Cherry Lane Theater." *Brooklyn Eagle*, April 11, 1929.

P41
The Bishop Misbehaves playbill. John Golden Papers. Billy Rose Theatre Division. New York Public Library.

P42
A Lady Visiting the Cherry Lane Theater. 1946. Photograph by Jerry Cooke / Getty Images. 1946.

P44
Paul Gilmore collection of clippings. Performing Arts Research Collections—Theatre. New York Public Library.

P45
Paul Gilmore souvenir program courtesy of Cherry Lane Alternative archives.

P46
Manhattan: Commerce Street—Bedford Street. Irma and Paul Milstein Division of United States History, Local History and Genealogy. New York Public Library.

P47
Theatres—US—NY—Cherry Lane. Billy Rose Theatre Division. New York Public Library.

P48–49
All programs courtesy of Cherry Lane Alternative archives.

P51
Photograph of Slater La Master (Completely Kentucky Wiki, CC-BY-SA).

"At Cherry Lane." *Daily (NY) News*, November 8, 1930.

P52–53
Poster and program for *The Bigot* courtesy of Cherry Lane Alternative archives.

P55
"Theatre Notes." *Daily (NY) News*, May 18, 1937.

The Bishop Misbehaves, Los Angeles, 1938. Photograph by Heritage Image Partnership Ltd. / Alamy.

P56–57
The Bishop Misbehaves playbill. John Golden Papers. Billy Rose Theatre Division. New York Public Library.

P59
Gas, 1946. Robert L. Ramsey Papers. The New School Archives.

P60
Photograph of Cherry Lane. Photographer unknown, September, 1949. Courtesy of Cherry Lane Alternative archives.

P62
Photographs, 1946–53. Robert L. Ramsey Papers. The New School Archives.

P63
Gas, 1946. Robert L. Ramsey Papers. The New School Archives.

The Dog Beneath the Skin, 1946. Robert L. Ramsey Papers. The New School Archives.

P64
The Watched Pot, 1947. Robert L. Ramsey Papers. The New School Archives.

No Exit, 1946. Robert L. Ramsey Papers. The New School Archives.

P65
Life Sentence 1947–59. Robert L. Ramsey Papers. The New School Archives.

Yerma, 1946–48. Robert L. Ramsey Papers. The New School Archives.

P66
Life Sentence, 1947–59. Robert L. Ramsey Papers. The New School Archives.

P67
The Watched Pot, 1947. Robert L. Ramsey Papers. The New School Archives.

P68
No Exit, 1946. Robert L. Ramsey Papers. The New School Archives.

The Watched Pot, 1947. Robert L. Ramsey Papers. The New School Archives.

Yerma, 1946–48. Robert L. Ramsey Papers. The New School Archives.

Life Sentence, 1947–59. Robert L. Ramsey Papers. The New School Archives.

P69
On-Stage promotional program. Robert L. Ramsey Papers. The New School Archives and Special Collections.

P70–71
The Watched Pot, 1947. Robert L. Ramsey Papers. The New School Archives.

P72–73
Yerma, 1946–48. Robert L. Ramsey Papers. The New School Archives.

P74–75
No Exit, 1946. Robert L. Ramsey Papers. The New School Archives.

P77
Hirschfeld, Al. *Opening Night for "Pirates of Penzance" at Cherry Lane*. 1942. Reprinted by permission of Al Hirschfeld Estate.

P78
H.M.S. Pinafore; Performed at: Cherry Lane Theatre (New York, NY); Performed by: Savoy Opera Guild, 1942. William Watson Theater Collection Playbills. Rauner Library Archives and Manuscripts, Dartmouth University.

Ruddigore; Performed at: Cherry Lane Theatre (New York, NY); Performed by: Savoy Opera Guild, 1941. William Watson Theater Collection–Playbills. Rauner Library Archives and Manuscripts, Dartmouth University.

The Yeoman of the Guard and *Patience* programs. Performing Arts Research Collections–Music. Billy Rose Theatre Division. New York Public Library.

P79
SOG Saga newsletter courtesy of Cherry Lane Alternative archives.

P80
Photograph from Rudolph Maté, dir. *The Prince Who Was a Thief*. Universal Pictures, 1951. Photograph by Alamy.

P81
Contact print of Tony Curtis and Erwin Piscator with actor. New School Publicity Office Records, Series 7, Dramatic Workshop and Studio Theatre. The New School Archives.

Contact print of Tony Curtis and actors rehearsing. New School Publicity Office Records, Series 7, Dramatic Workshop and Studio Theatre. The New School Archives.

Contact print of Tony Curtis and Harry Belafonte. New School Publicity Office Records, Series 7, Dramatic Workshop and Studio Theatre. The New School Archives.

P83–85
Henry IV, 1946. Robert L. Ramsey Papers. The New School Archives.

P87
Press photo from *Endgame* by Samuel Beckett. Photograph by Gjon Mili for the LIFE Picture Collection / Pond5.

P88
Photograph of woman hanging sign on Cherry Lane awning. Courtesy of Cherry Lane Alternative archives.

P90
Picasso, Pablo. Cover illustration for the Living Theatre playbill. 1951. Courtesy of Cherry Lane Alternative archives.

P91
Photos of *RUR* Living Theatre designs, 1948–67 and undated. Billy Rose Theatre Division. New York Public Library.

P92
Darby, Eileen. *Endgame* rehearsal stills. Performing Arts Research Collections–Theatre. New York Public Library. Courtesy of Eileen Darby Images, Inc.

P93
Both newspaper clippings courtesy of Cherry Lane Alternative archives.

P94–95
Van Vechten, Carl. Photograph of *Ladies Voices*, Living Theatre, 1951. Gertrude Stein Collection. Beinecke Rare Book and Manuscript Library, Yale University.

P96
Living Theatre records, 1951. Series VIII: Productions (1948–83). Billy Rose Theatre Division. New York Public Library.

P97
Van Vechten, Carl. *Faust an opera* or *Dr. Faustus Lights the Lights*, Living Theatre, 1951. Gertrude Stein Collection. Beinecke Rare Book and Manuscript Library, Yale University.

P98–99
Living Theatre designs, 1948–67 and undated. *Ubu the King*. Billy Rose Theatre Division. New York Public Library. Reprinted by permission of Garrick Beck.

P100
Paradise Now, complete box of notes, scripts, files. Living Theatre Records. Beinecke Rare Book and Manuscript Library, Yale University.

P101
Production stills from *Paradise Now*, 1968–69. Living Theatre Records. Beinecke Rare Book and Manuscript Library, Yale University.

P102
Photo by Roy Schatt, © James Dean, Inc. JAMES DEAN ™ IS A TRADEMARK OF JAMES DEAN, INC.

P103
Dean, James. Doodles on the back of the *Women of Trachis* flyer. Courtesy of James Dean Estate, James Dean, Inc.

P104
Women of Trachis by Sophocles, translated by Ezra Pound (staged reading, double bill with *Electra*, Cherry Lane Theatre, New School of Social Research, February 1954). Anne Jackson and Eli Wallach Papers. Harry Ransom Center. University of Texas.

P105
Photo by Roy Schatt, © James Dean, Inc. JAMES DEAN ™ IS A TRADEMARK OF JAMES DEAN, INC.

P106
Gypsy Rose Lee as a child. Billy Rose Theatre Division. New York Public Library.

P107
Gypsy Rose Lee on the road with Rolls Royce with showgirls. Billy Rose Theatre Division. New York Public Library.

Striptease certificate for Gypsy Rose Lee issued by Minsky's Theatre. Billy Rose Theatre Division. New York Public Library.

P108
Gypsy Rose Lee and chorus in the stage production *Star and Garter*. Billy Rose Theatre Division. New York Public Library.

P109
Gypsy Rose Lee signing an autograph outside of theater hosting her show *A Curious Evening with Gypsy Rose Lee*. Billy Rose Theatre Division. New York Public Library.

Jerome Robbins, Stephen Sondheim, Gypsy Rose Lee (who confessed that she felt "like a ghost at a banquet"), Arthur Laurents, and Jule Styne during rehearsals for the stage production *Gypsy*. Billy Rose Theatre Division. New York Public Library.

P111–12
Press photo from *Endgame* by Samuel Beckett. Photograph by Gjon Mili for the LIFE Picture Collection / Pond5.

P113
Endgame: photographs. Photograph by Alix Jeffry. Billy Rose Theatre Division. New York Public Library.

P115
Up to Thursday, 1964. Papers. Lee Kissman Alternative Theater Collections. Special Collections, Washington University.

P116
Publicity photograph of Harold Pinter in front of Cherry Lane Theatre. Billy Rose Theatre Division. New York Public Library.

P118
Showcard. *Zoo Story*. Edward Albee. Cherry Lane, Village South, 1963–65. Alix Jeffry photographs. Houghton Library, Harvard University.

P119
Portrait of Sam Shepard, Paul Foster, and Lanford Wilson outside Cherry Lane. *Dutchman*. Prints, 1964. Jeffry, Alix. Alix Jeffry additional papers, 1935–94. 1935. Houghton Library, Harvard University.

Dutchman. Prints, 1964. Jeffry, Alix. Alix Jeffry additional papers, 1935–94. 1935. Houghton Library, Harvard University.

P120
Gene Hackman and James Coco in the stage production *The Basement*. Billy Rose Theatre Division. New York Public Library.

P121
Illustration by William Auerbach-Levy of James Earl Jones as Jesse Prince and Royce Wallace as Marianne Prince in *The Pretender*. 1960. Museum of the City of New York.

P122
Photograph from "Wrote First Play During a Vacation." *The Daily News*. March 11, 1962. Courtesy of Cherry Lane Alternative archives.

Newspaper ad courtesy of Cherry Lane Alternative archives.

Krapp's Last Tape newspaper clipping. Zoo Story. Edward Albee. Cherry Lane, Village South, 1963–65. Alix Jeffry photographs. Houghton Library, Harvard University.

P123
Sand Box. Edward Albee. Cherry Lane, 1962. Alix Jeffry photographs. Houghton Library, Harvard University.

P124
Albarwild photo Alix Jeffry photographs. Houghton Library, Harvard University. 1968.

P127
George Grizzard, Uta Hagen, and Arthur Hill in the stage production *Who's Afraid of Virginia Woolf?* Billy Rose Theatre Division. New York Public Library.

Leslie Rivers as the Mother, Ellen Holly as the Duchess of Hapsburg, Cynthia Belgrave as Queen Victoria, and Norman Bush as Jesus in *Funnyhouse of a Negro*: photograph, 1964. Alix Jeffry photographs. Houghton Library, Harvard University.

P128
Up to Thursday, 1964. Papers. Lee Kissman Alternative Theater Collections. Special Collections, Washington University.

Zoo Story. Edward Albee. Cherry Lane, Village South, 1963–65. Alix Jeffry photographs. Houghton Library, Harvard University.

P129
Series 5, Sub-series 2: Clippings. Papers. Lee Kissman Alternative Theater Collections. Special Collections, Washington University.

PG130
Three one-act plays. Thornton Wilder. Cherry Lane, 1966. Alix Jeffry photographs. Houghton Library, Harvard University.

PG131
Three one-act plays. Thornton Wilder. Cherry Lane, 1966. Alix Jeffry photographs. Houghton Library, Harvard University.

P132–33
Posters and prints, 1964–1990. Wyman Pendleton Papers. Billy Rose Theatre Division. New York Public Library.

P135
Playwright Edward Albee and Ben Piazza in publicity photo for the 1961 off-Broadway production of *The American Dream*. Billy Rose Theatre Division. New York Public Library.

P136
Sudie Bond, Nancy Cushman, Ben Piazza, Jane Hoffman, and John C. Becher in the 1961 off-Broadway production of *The American Dream*. Billy Rose Theatre Division. New York Public Library.

P137
Jane Hoffman and Sudie Bond in the 1961 off-Broadway production of *The American Dream*. Billy Rose Theatre Division. New York Public Library.

P139
Robert Hooks as Clay and Jennifer West as Lula in *Dutchman* at Cherry Lane Theatre: photograph, 1964. Alix Jeffry photographs. Houghton Library, Harvard University.

P140
Harvey Selsby, Sue Carol Davis, and Richard Mansfield as passengers in *Dutchman* at Cherry Lane Theatre: photograph, 1964. Alix Jeffry photographs. Houghton Library, Harvard University.

P141
Robert Hooks as Clay and Jennifer West as Lula in *Dutchman* at Cherry Lane Theatre: photograph, 1964. Alix Jeffry photographs. Houghton Library, Harvard University.

P142
Singing in small group with Lorraine Hansberry and Nina Simone, 1963. Music Division. New York Public Library.

P143
Swope, Martha. Publicity photograph for the stage production *To Be Young, Gifted and Black*. 1968–69. Billy Rose Theatre Division. New York Public Library.

P144
Photographs from booklet accompanying Lorraine Hansberry, *To Be Young, Gifted and Black*. Originally released in 1971. Caedmon Records TRS 342. 3 LPs.

P145
Cicely Tyson, James Baldwin, guest, and singer Harry Belafonte attend *To Be Young, Gifted and Black* gala on January 2, 1969 at Cherry Lane Theatre in New York City. Photograph by Ron Galella, Ltd. / Ron Galella Collection / Getty Images.

P147
Swope, Martha. Photograph of actors (L–R) Jeffrey Mylett, Herb Simon, Robin Lamont, Lamar Alford, Joanne Jonas, Sonia Manzano, Peggy Gordon, and Gilmer McCormick (front) in a scene from the off-Broadway musical *Godspell* (New York), 1971. Billy Rose Theatre Division. New York Public Library.

P148
Photograph by Michael Mauney for John Camposa and Ron Alexander, "The New Shape of Tradition." *New York Times Magazine*, September 19, 1976. Reprinted by permission of Michael Mauney.

P150
Photographs from "David Mamet: The Solace of a Playwright's Ideals." *After Dark*, August 1976.

P151
Playbill from David Mamet's double bill courtesy of Cherry Lane Alternative archives.

P152
Godspell poster, circa 1976. Performing Arts Research Collections—Theatre. Billy Rose Theatre Division. New York Public Library.

P153
Sonia Manzano, Lamar Alford (kneeling), Stephen Nathan, David Haskell, Herb Braha, and Robin Lamont in *Godspell*, 1971 June. Billy Rose Theatre Division. New York Public Library.

P155
Swope, Martha. Photograph of actors (front L–R) David Haskell and Stephen Nathan with cast in a scene from the off-Broadway musical *Godspell* (New York), 1971. Billy Rose Theatre Division. New York Public Library.

P156
Swope, Martha. Photograph of actresses (L–R) Peggy Gordon, Sonia Manzano, Joanne Jonas, Gilmer McCormick (top), and Robin Lamont in a scene from the off-Broadway musical *Godspell* (New York), 1971. Billy Rose Theatre Division. New York Public Library.

P157
Swope, Martha. Photograph of actors (top–bottom) David Haskell and Stephen Nathan in a scene from the off-Broadway musical *Godspell* (New York), 1971. Billy Rose Theatre Division. New York Public Library.

P159–60
Photographs by Shaun Considine / Burke Photos.

P161
Poster for David Mamet's *Sexual Perversity in Chicago* and *Duck Variations*. Courtesy of Cherry Lane Alternative archives.

P163 and 165
Gotfryd, Bernard. Photographs of *Passion of Dracula*, 1977.

P164
Passion of Dracula; Performed at: Cherry Lane Theatre (New York, NY); Performed by: Dracula Theatrical Company; With: Burg, Michael, 1978. William Watson Theater Collection Playbills. Rauner Library Archives and Manuscripts, Dartmouth University.

P167
Swope, Martha. Photograph of (R–L) Actors Gary Sinise and John Malkovich in a scene from the off-Broadway revival of the play *True West* (New York), 1982. Billy Rose Theatre Division. New York Public Library.

P168
Property tax photo of 38 Commerce Street. Reprinted by permission of New York City Municipal Archives.

P170
Both playbills courtesy of Cherry Lane Alternative archives.

P171
Marshak, Bob. *Brilliant Traces* production still. Performing Arts Research Collections—Theatre. New York Public Library. Courtesy of Amy and Hila Parks.

Keith Gordon as Boo and Kevin Bacon as Billy in *Album*. Museum of the City of New York.

P172
Swope, Martha. Photograph of actors (L–R) Alice Drummond, James Greene, Alvin Epstein, and Peter Evans in a scene from the off-Broadway revival of the play *Endgame* (New York), 1984. Billy Rose Theatre Division. New York Public Library.

P173
Poster for *Endgame*. Courtesy of Cherry Lane Alternative archives.

P174
Poster for *True West*. Courtesy of Cherry Lane Alternative archives.

P175
Photograph of theater exterior. Courtesy of Cherry Lane Alternative archives.

P176–77
Swope, Martha. Photograph of (R–L) actors Gary Sinise and John Malkovich in a scene from the off-Broadway revival of the play *True West* (New York), 1982. Billy Rose Theatre Division. New York Public Library.

Swope, Martha. Photograph of (R–L) actors Gary Cole and Jim Belushi in a scene from the off-Broadway revival of the play *True West* (New York), 1982. Billy Rose Theatre Division. New York Public Library.

Swope, Martha. Photograph of (L–R) actors/brothers Dennis and Randy Quaid in a scene from the off-Broadway revival of the play *True West* (New York), 1982. Billy Rose Theatre Division. New York Public Library.

Swope, Martha. Photograph of (L–R) actors Daniel Stern and Tim Matheson in a scene from the off-Broadway revival of the play *True West* (New York), 1982. Billy Rose Theatre Division. New York Public Library.

P179
Swope, Martha. Photograph of (L–R) actors Gary Sinise and John Malkovich in a scene from the off-Broadway revival of the play *True West* (New York), 1982. Billy Rose Theatre Division. New York Public Library.

P180
Swope, Martha. Photograph of (L–R) actors Gary Sinise and John Malkovich in a scene from the off-Broadway revival of the play *True West* (New York), 1982. Billy Rose Theatre Division. New York Public Library.

P181
Swope, Martha. Photograph of actors Gary Sinise, John Malkovich, and Mary Rausch in a scene from the off-Broadway revival of the play *True West* (New York), 1982. Billy Rose Theatre Division. New York Public Library.

P183
Newman, Adam. *Nunsense* production still. Billy Rose Theatre Division. New York Public Library. In copyright.

P184
Production still from *Nunsense*. Courtesy of Cherry Lane Alternative archives.

P185
Playbill from *Nunsense*. Courtesy of Cherry Lane Alternative archives.

P187
Rosegg, Carol for Martha Swope. *Sum of Us* contact sheet of production photos. Billy Rose Theatre Division. New York Public Library. Reprinted by permission of Carol Rosegg. 1990.

P188–89
Poster and playbill from *Sum of Us*. Courtesy of Cherry Lane Alternative archives.

P191
Production still from *99 Histories*. Courtesy of Cherry Lane Alternative archives.

P192
Photograph from the opening night of *This Beautiful Future* by Rita Kalnejais. Courtesy of Emilio Madrid. 2022.

P194
Photograph by Gabe Evans of *American Dream* courtesy of Cherry Lane Alternative archives. 2008.

P195
All posters courtesy of Cherry Lane Alternative archives.

P196
Photograph by Gabe Evans for Ginia Bellafante, "'60s Prejudice and Capitalism as a Big Blond Metaphor." *New York Times*, January 24, 2007.

P197
Kleiman, Dennis. Production still from *Happy Days*, 2002.

P198
Photograph of Susann Brinkley and Angelina Fiordellisi. Courtesy of Cherry Lane Alternative archives.

P201
Staff photo outside Cherry Lane courtesy of Cherry Lane Alternative archives. 2003.

P202
Production still from *Nollywood Dreams* by Jocelyn Bioh by Russ Rowland. Courtesy of Russ Rowland Photo. 2017.

Production still from *Peerless* by Jiehae Park, mentored by Kwame Kwei-Armah. 2015. Reprinted by permission of Chasi Annexy.

P205
All posters courtesy of Cherry Lane Alternative archives.

P206–207
Production stills from the Mentor Project courtesy of Cherry Lane Alternative archives.

P208
Strong, Rob. Production stills, 2017. Courtesy of JAG Productions.

P213–15
Rosegg, Carol. Production stills. 1999.

P217
Crockett, Jaisen. Production stills. 2007.

P218
Portrait of Katori Hall by Nicole Bengiveno for Stuart Miller, "Playwright Who's Got the Memphis Blues." *New York Times*, October 14, 2007.

Cast and crew of *Hoodoo Love* courtesy of Cherry Lane Alternative archives. Photographer unknown. 2007.

P219
Poster for *Hoodoo Love*. Courtesy of Cherry Lane Alternative archives.

P221
Production still from *First Love* by Charles Mee. Courtesy of Monique Carboni. 2018.

P222
Coudert, Sandra. Production still from *The Revisionist* by Jesse Eisenberg. 2013.

P224
Martin, Charles. Illustrated cover of *The New Yorker*. Reprinted by permission of Condé Nast. May 14, 1960.

The Birthplace of Off Broadway:
100 Years of Cherry Lane Theatre

A24 Films LLC
New York, NY
a24films.com

HEAD OF PUBLISHING
Perrin Drumm

PUBLISHING MANAGER
Shayan Saalabi

EDITOR
LinYee Yuan

CONTRIBUTING EDITOR
Natka Bianchini

COPY EDITOR
Lauren Hooker

PROOFREADER
Danielle Carter

BOOK DESIGN
Bryan Cipolla

TYPOGRAPHY
Bureau Grotesque, Columba

PAPER
Munken Lynx

PRINTER
Printing House KOPA

COVER IMAGE
Promotional image for *I Was Sitting on My Patio This Guy Appeared I Thought I Was Hallucinating* by Robert Wilson. The photographic collage for the Cherry Lane production plays with scale and features Lucinda Childs (woman with her back to the audience) and Robert Wilson (man seated) on a side table that was used as a stage prop. Photograph by Jacob Burckhardt, 1977.

SPECIAL THANKS
Andrea Felder, Noah Gillard, Mary Haegert, Liam Hamell, David Jacobson, Jeremy Megraw, Nicolette Norton, Heather N. Paxton, Greg Ramsey, Katia Read, Jenny Swadosh, Matthew Warwick

©2025 A24 Publishing LLC & A24 Commerce St LLC

All rights reserved; no part of this publication may be reproduced, stored in a retrieval system, or transmitted in any form or by any means, electronic, mechanical, photocopying, recording, or otherwise, without prior written consent of the publisher.

The publisher apologizes for any errors. Please send any corrections for future reprints or editions of this book to publishing@a24films.com.

ISBN 978-1-960078-35-3

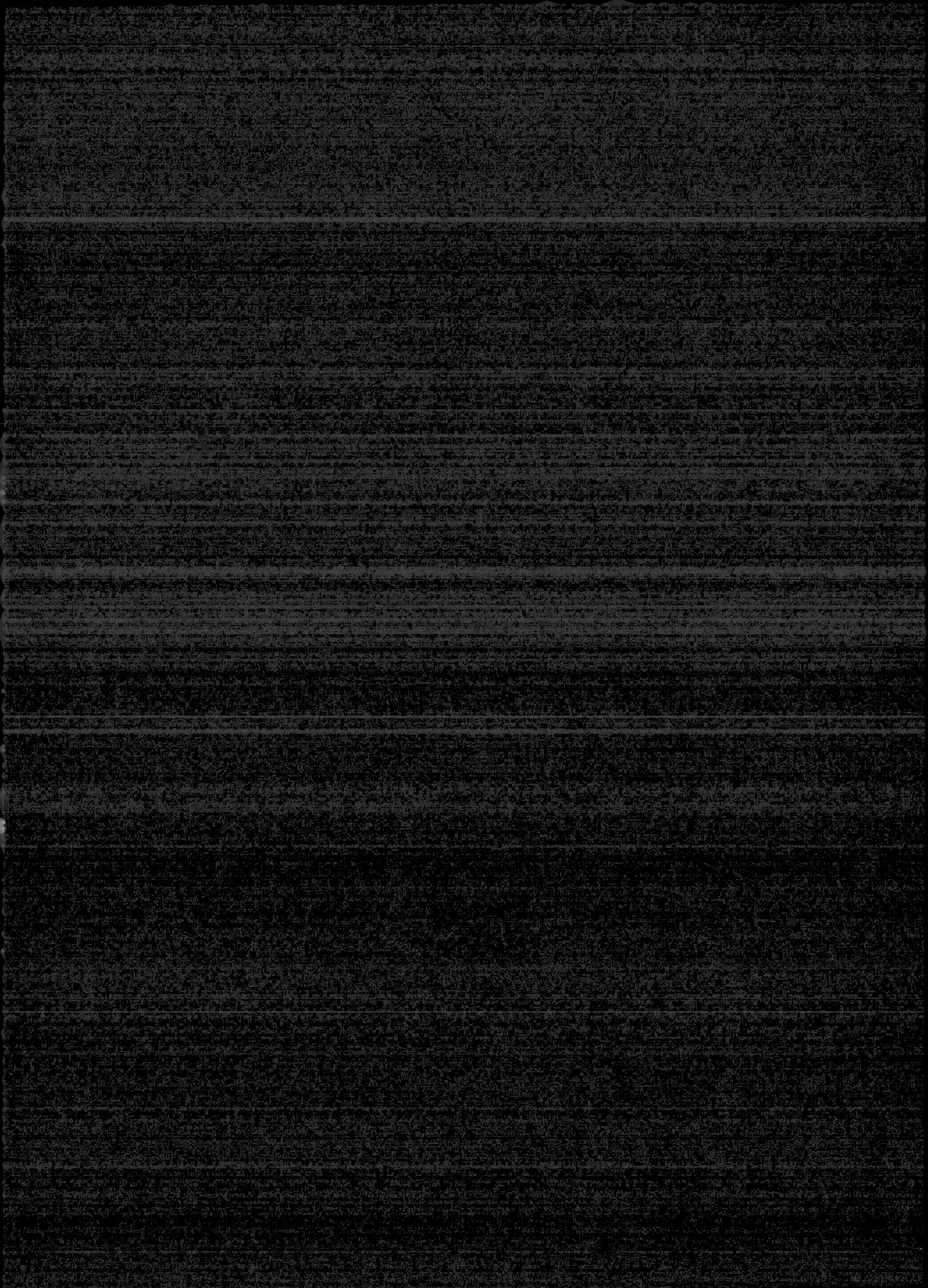